Native American Rights

Other Books in the Current Controversies Series:

Date Due

DEC 1 8 2002		
JAN 1 9 2016		

Native American Rights

David Bender, *Publisher*
Bruno Leone, *Executive Editor*

Brenda Stalcup, *Managing Editor*
Scott Barbour, *Senior Editor*

Tamara L. Roleff, *Book Editor*

CURRENT CONTROVERSIES

Cover Photo: Nina Berman/SIPA Press

Library of Congress Cataloging-in-Publication Data

Native American rights / Tamara L. Roleff, book editor.
    p. cm. — (Current controversies)
    Includes bibliographical references and index.
    ISBN 1-56510-685-7 (lib. bdg.: alk. paper). — ISBN 1-56510-684-9 (pbk. : alk. paper)
    1. Indians of North America—Government relations. 2. Indians of North America—Civil rights. 3. Indians of North America—Legal status, laws, etc. I. Roleff, Tamara L., 1959–   .
    E93.N288   1998
    323.1'197—dc21   97-37078
                                                 CIP

Contents

Chapter 1: Is Native American Culture Threatened?

Yes: Native American Culture Is Threatened

and choose among Indian beliefs threaten the integrity of Native American spirituality. Only Indians can legitimately participate in Indian ceremonies.

No: Native American Culture Is Not Threatened

Chapter 2: Is Indian Gaming Beneficial to Native Americans?

ing the tribes' government financial aid. Since Native Americans will likely lose their competitive advantage in the gaming industry, tribes that do not develop alternative sources of revenue may one day find themselves back in poverty and in need of federal assistance that is no longer available.

Yes: Indian Gaming Is Beneficial to Native Americans

No: Indian Gaming Is Not Beneficial to Native Americans

Chapter 3: How Should Tribal Resources Be Used?

Chapter 4: Should Indian Sovereignty Be Restricted?

Yes: Indian Sovereignty Should Be Restricted

No: Indian Sovereignty Should Not Be Restricted

Foreword

By definition, controversies are "discussions of questions in which opposing opinions clash" (Webster's Twentieth Century Dictionary Unabridged). Few would deny that controversies are a pervasive part of the human condition and exist on virtually every level of human enterprise. Controversies transpire between individuals and among groups, within nations and between nations. Controversies supply the grist necessary for progress by providing challenges and challengers to the status quo. They also create atmospheres where strife and warfare can flourish. A world without controversies would be a peaceful world; but it also would be, by and large, static and prosaic.

The Series' Purpose

The purpose of the Current Controversies series is to explore many of the social, political, and economic controversies dominating the national and international scenes today. Titles selected for inclusion in the series are highly focused and specific. For example, from the larger category of criminal justice, Current Controversies deals with specific topics such as police brutality, gun control, white collar crime, and others. The debates in Current Controversies also are presented in a useful, timeless fashion. Articles and book excerpts included in each title are selected if they contribute valuable, long-range ideas to the overall debate. And wherever possible, current information is enhanced with historical documents and other relevant materials. Thus, while individual titles are current in focus, every effort is made to ensure that they will not become quickly outdated. Books in the Current Controversies series will remain important resources for librarians, teachers, and students for many years.

In addition to keeping the titles focused and specific, great care is taken in the editorial format of each book in the series. Book introductions and chapter prefaces are offered to provide background material for readers. Chapters are organized around several key questions that are answered with diverse opinions representing all points on the political spectrum. Materials in each chapter include opinions in which authors clearly disagree as well as alternative opinions in which authors may agree on a broader issue but disagree on the possible solutions. In this way, the content of each volume in Current Controversies mirrors the mosaic of opinions encountered in society. Readers will quickly realize that there are many viable answers to these complex issues. By questioning each author's conclusions, students and casual readers can begin to develop the critical thinking skills so important to evaluating opinionated material.

Current Controversies is also ideal for controlled research. Each anthology in the series is composed of primary sources taken from a wide gamut of informational categories including periodicals, newspapers, books, United States and foreign government documents, and the publications of private and public organizations. Readers will find factual support for reports, debates, and research papers covering all areas of important issues. In addition, an annotated table of contents, an index, a book and periodical bibliography, and a list of organizations to contact are included in each book to expedite further research.

Perhaps more than ever before in history, people are confronted with diverse and contradictory information. During the Persian Gulf War, for example, the public was not only treated to minute-to-minute coverage of the war, it was also inundated with critiques of the coverage and countless analyses of the factors motivating U.S. involvement. Being able to sort through the plethora of opinions accompanying today's major issues, and to draw one's own conclusions, can be a complicated and frustrating struggle. It is the editors' hope that Current Controversies will help readers with this struggle.

Greenhaven Press anthologies primarily consist of previously published material taken from a variety of sources, including periodicals, books, scholarly journals, newspapers, government documents, and position papers from private and public organizations. These original sources are often edited for length and to ensure their accessibility for a young adult audience. The anthology editors also change the original titles of these works in order to clearly present the main thesis of each viewpoint and to explicitly indicate the opinion presented in the viewpoint. These alterations are made in consideration of both the reading and comprehension levels of a young adult audience. Every effort is made to ensure that Greenhaven Press accurately reflects the original intent of the authors included in this anthology.

"The rights of Native Americans have been expanded and curtailed at various times throughout the nation's history."

Introduction

The history of federal policy toward Native Americans has reflected changing ideas about whether Indians should be assimilated into white society or whether tribes should retain their sovereignty—their right to be independent and self-governing entities. Native Americans have always maintained that each individual tribe is a sovereign nation and should therefore be authorized to govern itself without outside influence. Official recognition of Native American sovereignty has fluctuated according to the beliefs of presidents, Congress, and the U.S. Supreme Court. Consequently, the rights of Native Americans have been expanded and curtailed at various times throughout the nation's history.

When Europeans first colonized North America, each settlement recognized its neighboring Indian tribes as self-governing, independent entities. The settlers negotiated treaties with Indians to secure peace and regulate trade and the expansion of white settlements. After the Revolutionary War, the U.S. Constitution gave Congress "plenary" power over all tribes; Congress continued to recognize Indian tribes as foreign nations and negotiated treaties with them as equal governments.

Federal policy toward America's native residents changed, however, when Andrew Jackson—renowned for his military campaigns against the Indians—became president in 1829. The Indian Removal Act of 1830 required most of the eastern tribes to give up their lands and move west of the Mississippi River, despite any guarantees of permanent residence in their existing treaties with the government. When the Cherokees sued the state of Georgia in 1831 to prevent the enforcement of the act, the U.S. Supreme Court ruled in favor of the state, declaring that Indian tribes were "domestic dependent nations" that had lost their status as independent, foreign nations. Forty years later, Congress enacted legislation that changed the status of tribes forever; the new law (known as Section 71) eliminated the need for treaties with the Indian nations altogether by allowing Congress to use legislation—which did not require the Indians' consent—to govern the tribes.

The Dawes Act of 1887 further changed the lives of Indians. The act, also known as the General Allotment Act, attempted to force the assimilation of Indians into white culture by mandating the education of Indian children in specially built schools, forbidding Native American ceremonies, and dismantling the reservations. Individual Indians were given plots of reservation land to farm; the remaining land was sold to white farmers. Congress hoped that surrounding the Indians with white culture would encourage them to adopt white

13

beliefs and practices, but this policy failed abysmally because most Indians did not want to give up their culture.

During the Great Depression, Congress passed legislation intended to restore some sovereignty to Indian tribes: the Indian Reorganization Act (IRA) of 1934. The purpose of the new law was to "rehabilitate the Indian's economic life and to give him a chance to develop the initiative destroyed by a century of oppression and paternalism." The IRA prohibited the further breakdown of reservations, added land to existing reservations, and encouraged tribes to adopt their own constitutions and become self-governing.

Federal Indian policy shifted course again in 1953 under a congressional resolution known as "termination." The new policy was an attempt to assimilate Native Americans into white society and to encourage self-sufficiency by terminating federal benefits to the tribes and by abolishing the reservations. Under this policy, federal benefits for more than one hundred tribes were eliminated. Many reservations were broken up, tribal assets were distributed among the tribes' members, and tribal governments were dissolved. Moreover, for the first time Congress gave some state governments full jurisdiction over criminal offenses and partial jurisdiction over civil matters that occurred on the reservations. Up until then, the states had never had any jurisdiction over Native Americans, their land, or their property.

From the 1960s through the 1980s, several laws were enacted that were designed to secure Native American rights and encourage development on Indian reservations. One new law sought to promote self-determination and economic development by forbidding states to acquire any more authority over tribes without the tribe's express approval (1968). Other legislation established loan programs to develop Native American businesses and resources (1968); allowed tribes to administer federal programs themselves (1975); granted tribes many of the tax benefits enjoyed by state governments (1982); and permitted tribes to sponsor high-stakes bingo and gambling in states that permitted any other form of gambling (1988).

The Indian Gaming Regulatory Act (IGRA) of 1988 has been the cause of much debate in recent years. The law requires tribes to negotiate agreements, or "compacts," with state governments about the types of gambling that will be allowed on their reservations. The act also ensures that Indian casinos are wholly owned by the tribe so that the tribe collects the profits. Neither the states nor the tribes are entirely happy with IGRA; the states maintain that the act forces them to accept forms of gambling that they may not want, while the tribes contend that the act limits their sovereignty by forcing them to negotiate with the states.

Another disagreement between the tribes and the states concerns the revenues from Indian casino gambling and other tribal businesses. In 1996, profits from Indian gaming in over 230 high-stakes bingo parlors and gambling casinos in 29 states were about $6 billion. Under IGRA, tribes are required to use their gaming revenues to pay for tribal government operations and services, to improve the welfare of their citizens, to support economic development, and to make charitable donations. The tribes maintain that gaming proceeds have given them the money they long have needed to pull themselves out of poverty, become self-sufficient, preserve their heritage, and take charge of their future. "The tribes don't have any money unless we do gaming, because we don't have a tax base," asserts Rick Hill, a Wisconsin Oneida Indian and chairman of the National Indian Gaming Association. "We have lived in Third World poverty conditions, but gaming has proven to be mutually beneficial to state and tribal governments." While the states are unable to tax tribal revenues, Hill explains, Indian gaming is beneficial to states because state governments can tax the non-Indian businesses—such as hotels and restaurants and their suppliers—that spring up around the casinos. Native Americans adamantly insist that tribal enterprises remain untaxed by state governments. Ada Deer, assistant secretary of Indian Affairs, asserts that Indian tribes are sovereign governments and, as such, are immune from taxation by the state:

> It is a fundamental principle of law that governments do not tax other governments. The logic is that government revenues should be used to support the governmental services, functions, and activities of each respective government.

While the tribes may believe that gaming income benefits both Indians and non-Indians, others think differently. According to some state and local government officials, Indian gaming revenues should be subject to the same taxes as non-Indian casinos. They argue that the high numbers of customers at the reservations' casinos put a strain on the local roads and police and fire departments. Critics complain that the casinos receive the benefits of improved roads and fire and police protection, yet they do not pay their fair share to support these services. Such a drain on the limited tax revenues is unfair, they maintain.

Furthermore, according to some critics of Indian gaming, the proceeds from casinos and other tribal enterprises put non-Indian businesses at a distinct disadvantage. Indian-owned reservation businesses—such as casinos, hotels, restaurants, gas stations, and stores—do not have to pay business, property, or sales taxes. Non-Indian companies, on the other hand, are required to pay such taxes and must pass on the cost to the consumer in the form of higher prices. Critics contend that the higher prices charged by non-Indian businesses encourage many consumers to make their purchases on the reservation, thus threatening the survival of non-Indian businesses.

The debate over taxation reflects the broader question of sovereignty—that is, whether or not Indian tribes should be considered independent, self-governing entities. Sovereignty is at the heart of the issues considered in *Native American Rights: Current Controversies*. Throughout this anthology, authors discuss the rights of Native Americans regarding Indian culture, religion, gaming, and control over natural resources.

Chapter 1

Is Native American Culture Threatened?

Chapter Preface

The medicine man, or shaman, plays an important role in Native American culture. The shaman intercedes with the spiritual world on behalf of the tribe, asking for victory in war, for good weather, for bountiful hunting and harvests, or for help with other problems. The medicine man also tends to the sick, cares for sacred objects of the tribe, and is responsible for teaching native lore and history to tribal members.

Some shamans share their knowledge and traditional ceremonies with non-Indians as well, in the belief that all races can benefit from native spirituality. Sharing Indian lore supports native culture, they believe, and permits people of all backgrounds to demonstrate their reverence and respect for the earth. Hyemeyohsts Storm, an author, lecturer, and medicine man who leads native ceremonies for non-Indians, maintains that allowing non-Indians to partake in Indian ceremonies strengthens native beliefs and heritage. "The whole idea is to bring [people] together," Storm asserts. "If love and balance, harmony and caring dilute the Indian tradition, then the Indian tradition is in trouble, because that's what I teach." Jonathan Altman, who runs a sweat lodge at a New Age retreat in Dulzura, California, agrees. "We're not trying to diminish [native culture]," Altman declares. "If anything, we're trying to support it."

On the other hand, many Native Americans feel that their beliefs are distorted and trivialized when they are sold to non-Indians who want to take part in traditional Indian ceremonies. Some critics call these non-Indian spiritual leaders "opportunists," "profit prophets," "culture vultures," and "plastic medicine men." Suzan Shown Harjo, director of the native-rights Morning Star Institute, contends, "Cultural appropriation is cultural theft. We don't need another generation of people . . . doing the modern version of the land grab." Other critics and spiritual leaders argue that the "traditional" Native American ceremonies offered by these false Indian leaders are actually a hodgepodge of different native cultures and traditions detrimental to both non-Indians and Native Americans. "[White people] pay this money and they get fooled into it and think they are conducting themselves like the Cheyenne, but they're not," maintains Jeanette Costo, a Native American elder. Others complain that sacred Native American sites are being desecrated by non-Indians who practice their faux or non-native beliefs there.

Whether American Indians have the right to practice their religion freely and without interference from both well-meaning admirers or hostile or indifferent observers is a controversial issue. In the following chapter, the authors examine this and other concerns that affect Native American culture.

Using Indian Names for Sports Teams Harms Native Americans

by Ward Churchill

About the author: *Ward Churchill, a Native American activist, is the author of numerous books and articles on Native Americans.*

Since the early 1990s, there has been an increasing wave of controversy regarding the names of professional sports teams like the Atlanta "Braves," Cleveland "Indians," Washington "Redskins," and Kansas City "Chiefs." The issue extends to the names of college teams like Florida State University "Seminoles," University of Illinois "Fighting Illini," and so on, right on down to high school outfits like the Lamar (Colorado) "Savages." Also involved have been team adoption of "mascots," replete with feathers, buckskins, beads, spears, and "warpaint" (some fans have opted to adorn themselves in the same fashion), and nifty little "pep" gestures like the "Indian Chant" and "Tomahawk Chop."

A Racist Practice

A substantial number of American Indians have protested that use of native names, images and symbols as sports team mascots and the like is, by definition, a virulently racist practice. Given the historical relationship between Indians and non-Indians during what has been called the "Conquest of America," American Indian Movement leader (and American Indian Anti-Defamation Council founder) Russell Means has compared the practice to contemporary Germans naming their soccer teams the "Jews," "Hebrews," and "Yids," while adorning their uniforms with grotesque caricatures of Jewish faces taken from the Nazis' anti-Semitic propaganda of the 1930s. Numerous demonstrations have occurred in conjunction with games—most notably during the November 15, 1992 match-up between the Chiefs and Redskins in Kansas City—by angry Indians and their supporters.

Excerpted from Ward Churchill, "Crimes Against Humanity," *Z Magazine*, March 1993. Reprinted by permission of the author.

In response, a number of players—especially African Americans and other minority athletes—have been trotted out by professional team owners like Ted Turner, as well as university and public school officials, to announce that they mean not to insult but to honor native people. They have been joined by the television networks and most major newspapers, all of which have editorialized that Indian discomfort with the situation is "no big deal," insisting that the whole thing is just "good, clean fun." The country needs more such fun, they've argued, and "a few disgruntled Native Americans" have no right to undermine the nation's enjoyment of its leisure time by complaining. This is especially the case, some have argued, "in hard times like these." It has even been contended that Indian outrage at being systematically degraded—rather than the degradation itself—creates "a serious barrier to the sort of intergroup communication so necessary in a multicultural society such as ours."

Okay, let's communicate. We are frankly dubious that those advancing such positions really believe their own rhetoric, but, just for the sake of argument, let's accept the premise that they are sincere. If what they say is true, then isn't it time we spread such "inoffensiveness" and "good cheer" around among *all* groups so that *everybody* can participate *equally* in fostering the round of national laughs they call for? Sure it is—the country can't have too much fun or "intergroup involvement"—so the more, the merrier. Simple consistency demands that anyone who thinks the Tomahawk Chop is a swell pastime must be just as hearty in their endorsement of the following ideas that—by the logic used to defend the defamation of American Indians—should help us all really start yukking it up.

First, as a counterpart to the Redskins, we need an NFL team called "Niggers" to honor Afro-Americans. Half-time festivities for fans might include a simulated stewing of the opposing coach in a large pot while players and cheerleaders dance around it, garbed in leopard skins and wearing fake bones in their noses. This concept obviously goes along with the kind of gaiety attending the Chop, but also with the actions of the Kansas City Chiefs, whose team members—prominently including black team members—lately appeared on a poster looking "fierce" and "savage" by way of wearing Indian regalia. Just a bit of harmless "morale boosting," says the Chiefs' front office. You bet.

> *"Use of native names, images and symbols as sports team mascots and the like is, by definition, a virulently racist practice."*

So that the newly formed Niggers sports club won't end up too out of sync while expressing the "spirit" and "identity" of Afro-Americans in the above fashion, a baseball franchise—let's call this one the "Sambos"—should be formed. How about a basketball team called the "Spearchuckers?" A hockey team called the "Jungle Bunnies?" Maybe the "essence" of these teams could be depicted by images of tiny black faces adorned with huge pairs of lips. The players could appear on TV every week or so gnawing on chicken legs and spitting watermelon seeds at one another. Catchy, eh? Well, there's "nothing to be upset about," according to those who love wearing "war bonnets" to the Super Bowl or having "Chief Illiniwik" dance around the sports arenas of Urbana, Illinois.

Other Groups to Include

And why stop there? There are plenty of other groups to include. "Hispanics?" They can be "represented" by the Galveston "Greasers" and San Diego "Spics," at least until the Wisconsin "Wetbacks" and Baltimore "Beaners" get off the ground. Asian Americans? How about the "Slopes," "Dinks," "Gooks," and "Zipperheads?" Owners of the latter teams might get their logo ideas from editorial page cartoons printed in the nation's newspapers during World War II: slant-eyes, buck teeth, big glasses, but nothing racially insulting or derogatory, according to the editors and artists involved at the time. Indeed, this Second World War vintage stuff can be seen as just another barrel of laughs, at least by what current editors say are their "local standards" concerning American Indians.

Let's see. Who's been left out? Teams like the Kansas City "Kikes," Hanover "Honkies," San Leandro "Shylocks," Daytona "Dagos," and Pittsburgh "Polacks" will fill a certain social void among white folk. Have a religious belief? Let's all go for the gusto and gear up the Milwaukee "Mackerel Snappers" and Hollywood "Holy Rollers." The Fighting Irish of Notre Dame can be rechristened the "Drunken Irish" or "Papist Pigs." Issues of gender and sexual preference can be addressed through creation of teams like the St. Louis "Sluts," Boston "Bimbos," Detroit "Dykes," and the Fresno "Fags." How about the Gainesville "Gimps" and Richmond "Retards," so the physically and mentally impaired won't be excluded from our fun and games?

> *"Indians are (falsely) perceived as being too few, and therefore too weak, to defend themselves effectively against racist and otherwise offensive behavior."*

Now, don't go getting "overly sensitive" out there. None of this is demeaning or insulting, at least not when it's being done to Indians. Just ask the folks who are doing it, or their apologists like Andy Rooney in the national media. They'll tell you—as in fact they *have* been telling you—that there's been no harm done, regardless of what their victims think, feel, or say. The situation is exactly the same as when those with precisely the same mentality used to insist that Step 'n' Fetchit was okay, or Rochester on the Jack Benny Show, or Amos and Andy, Charlie Chan, the Frito Bandito, or any of the other cutsey symbols making up the lexicon of American racism. Have we communicated yet?

Let's get just a little bit real here. The notion of "fun" embodied in rituals like the Tomahawk Chop must be understood for what it is. There's not a single non-Indian example used above which can be considered socially acceptable in even the most marginal sense. The reasons are obvious enough. So why is it different where American Indians are concerned? One can only conclude that, in contrast to the other groups at issue, Indians are (falsely) perceived as being too few, and therefore too weak, to defend themselves effectively against racist and otherwise offensive behavior.

> *"A concerted, sustained, and in some ways accelerating effort has gone into making Indians unreal."*

Fortunately, there are some glimmers of hope. A few teams and their fans have gotten the message and have responded appropriately. Stanford University, which opted to drop the name "Indians" from Stanford, has experienced no resulting drop off in attendance. Meanwhile, the local newspaper in Portland, Oregon decided its long-standing editorial policy prohibiting use of racial epithets should include derogatory team names. The Redskins, for instance, are now referred to as "the Washington team," and will continue to be described in this way until the franchise adopts an inoffensive moniker (newspaper sales in Portland have suffered no decline as a result).

Such examples are to be applauded and encouraged. They stand as figurative beacons in the night, proving beyond all doubt that it is quite possible to indulge in the pleasure of athletics without accepting blatant racism into the bargain.

Nuremberg Precedents

On October 16, 1946, a man named Julius Streicher mounted the steps of a gallows. Moments later he was dead, the sentence of an international tribunal composed of representatives of the United States, France, Great Britain, and the Soviet Union having been imposed. Streicher's body was then cremated, and—so horrendous were his crimes thought to have been—his ashes dumped into an unspecified German river so that "no one should ever know a particular place to go for reasons of mourning his memory."

Julius Streicher had been convicted at Nuremberg, Germany of what were termed "Crimes Against Humanity." The lead prosecutor in his case—Justice Robert Jackson of the United States Supreme Court—had not argued that the defendant had killed anyone, nor that he had personally committed any especially violent act. Nor was it contended that Streicher had held any particularly important position in the German government during the period in which the so-called Third Reich had exterminated some 6,000,000 Jews, as well as several million Gypsies, Poles, Slavs, homosexuals, and other untermenschen (subhumans).

The sole offense for which the accused was ordered put to death was in having served as publisher/editor of a Bavarian tabloid entitled *Der Sturmer* during the early-to-mid 1930s, years before the Nazi genocide actually began. In this capacity, he had penned a long series of virulently anti-Semitic editorials and "news" stories, usually accompanied by cartoons and other images graphically depicting Jews in extraordinarily derogatory fashion. This, the prosecution asserted, had done much to "dehumanize" the targets of his distortion in the mind of the German public. In turn, such dehumanization had made it possible—or at least easier—for average Germans to later indulge in the outright liquidation of Jewish "vermin." The tribunal agreed, holding that Streicher was therefore complicit in genocide and deserving of death by hanging.

During his remarks to the Nuremberg tribunal, Justice Jackson observed that, in implementing its sentences, the participating powers were morally and legally binding themselves to adhere forever after to the same standards of conduct that were being applied to Streicher and the other Nazi leaders. In the alternative, he said, the victorious allies would have committed "pure murder" at Nuremberg—no different in substance from that carried out by those they presumed to judge—rather than establishing the "permanent benchmark for justice" which was intended.

American Indian Genocide

Yet in the United States of Robert Jackson, the indigenous American Indian population had already been reduced, in a process which is ongoing to this day from perhaps 12.5 million in the year 1500 to fewer than 250,000 by the beginning of the 20th century. This was accomplished, according to official sources, "largely through the cruelty of [EuroAmerican] settlers," and an informal but clear governmental policy which had made it an articulated goal to "exterminate these red vermin," or at least whole segments of them.

Bounties had been placed on the scalps of Indians—any Indians—in places as diverse as Georgia, Kentucky, Texas, the Dakotas, Oregon, and California, and had been maintained until resident Indian populations were decimated or disappeared altogether. Entire peoples such as the Cherokee had been reduced to half their size through a policy of forced removal from their homelands east of the Mississippi River to what were then considered less preferable areas in the West.

Others, such as the Navajo, suffered the same fate while under military guard for years on end. The United States Army had also perpetrated a long series of wholesale massacres of Indians at places like Horseshoe Bend, Bear River, Sand Creek, the Washita River, the Marias River, Camp Robinson, and Wounded Knee.

Through it all, hundreds of popular novels—each competing with the next to make Indians appear more grotesque, menacing, and inhuman— were sold in the tens of millions of copies in the U.S. Plainly, the Eu-

> *"The treatment of Indians in American popular culture is not 'cute' or 'amusing' or just 'good, clean fun.'. . . It causes real pain . . . to real people."*

roAmerican public was being conditioned to see Indians in such a way as to allow their eradication to continue. And continue it did until the Manifest Destiny of the U.S.—a direct precursor to what Hitler would subsequently call Lebensraumpolitik (the politics of living space)—was consummated.

By 1900, the national project of "clearing" Native Americans from their land and replacing them with "superior" Anglo-American settlers was complete; the indigenous population had been reduced by as much as 98 percent while approximately 97.5 percent of their original territory had "passed" to the invaders. The survivors had been concentrated, out of sight and mind of the public, on scattered "reservations," all of them under the self-assigned "plenary" (full) power of the federal government. There was, of course, no Nuremberg-style tribunal passing judgment on those who had fostered such circumstances in North America. No U.S. official or private citizen was ever imprisoned—never mind hanged—for implementing or propagandizing what had been done. Nor had the process of genocide afflicting Indians been completed. Instead, it merely changed form.

Between the 1880s and the 1980s, nearly half of all Native American children were coercively transferred from their own families, communities, and cultures to those of the conquering society. This was done through compulsory attendance at remote boarding schools, often hundreds of miles from their homes, where native children were kept for years on end while being systematically "deculturated" (indoctrinated to think and act in the manner of EuroAmericans rather than as Indians). It was also accomplished through a pervasive foster home and adoption program—including "blind" adoptions, where children would be permanently denied information as to who they were/are and where they'd come from placing native youths in non-Indian homes.

The Genocide Convention

The express purpose of all this was to facilitate a U.S. governmental policy to bring about the "assimilation" (dissolution) of indigenous societies. In other words, Indian cultures as such were to be caused to disappear. Such policy objectives are directly contrary to the United Nations 1948 Convention on Punishment and Prevention of the Crime of Genocide, an element of international law arising from the Nuremberg proceedings. The forced "transfer of the children" of a targeted "racial, ethnical, or religious group" is explicitly prohibited as a genocidal activity under the Convention's second article.

Article II of the Genocide Convention also expressly prohibits involuntary sterilization as a means of "preventing births among" a targeted population. Yet, in 1975, it was conceded by the U.S. government that its Indian Health Service (IHS) then a subpart of the Bureau of Indian Affairs (BIA), was even then conducting a secret program of involuntary sterilization that had affected approximately 40 percent of all Indian women. The program was allegedly discontinued, and the IHS was transferred to the Public Health Service, but no one was punished. In 1990, it came out that the IHS was inoculating Inuit children in Alaska with Hepatitis-B vaccine. The vaccine had already been banned by the World Health Organization as having a demonstrated correlation with the HIV-

Syndrome which is itself correlated to AIDS. As this is written, a "field test" of Hepatitis-A vaccine, also HIV-correlated, is being conducted on Indian reservations in the northern plains region.

The Genocide Convention makes it a "crime against humanity" to create conditions leading to the destruction of an identifiable human group, as such. Yet the BIA has utilized the government's plenary prerogatives to negotiate mineral leases "on behalf of" Indian peoples paying a fraction of standard royalty rates. The result has been "super profits" for a number of preferred U.S. corporations. Meanwhile, Indians, whose reservations ironically turned out to be in some of the most mineral-rich areas of North America, which makes us the nominally wealthiest segment of the continent's population, live in dire poverty.

By the government's own data in the mid-1980s, Indians received the lowest annual and lifetime per capita incomes of any aggregate population group in the United States. Concomitantly, we suffer the highest rate of infant mortality, death by exposure and malnutrition, disease, and the like. Under such circumstances, alcoholism and other escapist forms of substance abuse are endemic in the Indian community, a situation which leads both to a general physical debilitation of the population and a catastrophic accident rate. Teen suicide among Indians is several times the national average.

The average life expectancy of a reservation-based Native American man is barely 45 years; women can expect to live less than three years longer.

Such itemizations could be continued at great length, including matters like the radioactive contamination of large portions of contemporary Indian Country, the forced relocation of traditional Navajos, and so on. But the point should be made: Genocide, as defined in international law, is a continuing fact of day-to-day life (and death) for North America's native peoples. Yet there has been— and is—only the barest flicker of public concern about, or even consciousness of, this reality. Absent any serious expression of public outrage, no one is punished and the process continues.

A salient reason for public acquiescence before the ongoing holocaust in Native North America has been a continuation of the popular legacy, often through more effective media. Since 1925, Hollywood has released more than 2,000 films, many of them rerun frequently on television, portraying Indians as strange, perverted, ridiculous, and often dangerous things of the past. Moreover, we are habitually presented to mass audiences one-dimensionally, devoid of recognizable human motivations and emotions; Indians thus serve as props, little more. We have thus been thoroughly and systematically dehumanized.

Making Indians Unreal

Nor is this the extent of it. Everywhere, we are used as logos, as mascots, as jokes: "Big Chief" writing tablets, "Red Man" chewing tobacco, "Winnebago" campers, "Navajo" and "Cherokee" and "Pontiac" and "Cadillac" pickups and automobiles. There are the Cleveland "Indians," the Kansas City "Chiefs," the

Atlanta "Braves," and the Washington "Redskins" professional sports teams—not to mention those in thousands of colleges, high schools, and elementary schools across the country—each with their own degrading caricatures and parodies of Indians and/or things Indian. Pop fiction continues in the same vein, including an unending stream of New Age manuals purporting to expose the inner works of indigenous spirituality in everything from pseudo-philosophical to do-it-yourself styles. Blond yuppies from Beverly Hills amble about the country claiming to be reincarnated 17th century Cheyenne Ushamans ready to perform previously secret ceremonies.

In effect, a concerted, sustained, and in some ways accelerating effort has gone into making Indians unreal. It is thus of obvious importance that the American public begin to think about the implications of such things the next time they witness a gaggle of face-painted and warbonneted buffoons doing the "Tomahawk Chop" at a baseball or football game. It is necessary that they think about the implications of the grade-school teacher adorning their child in turkey feathers to commemorate Thanksgiving. Think about the significance of John Wayne or Charleton Heston killing a dozen "savages" with a single bullet the next time a western comes on TV. Think about why Land-o-Lakes finds it appropriate to market its butter with the stereotyped image of an "Indian princess" on the wrapper. Think about what it means when non-Indian academics profess—as they often do—to "know more about Indians than Indians do themselves." Think about the significance of charlatans like Carlos Castaneda and Jamake Highwater and Mary Summer Rain and Lynn Andrews churning out "Indian" bestsellers, one after the other, while Indians typically can't get into print.

Think about the real situation of American Indians. Think about Julius Streicher. Remember Justice Jackson's admonition. Understand that the treatment of Indians in American popular culture is not "cute" or "amusing" or just "good, clean fun."

Know that it causes real pain and real suffering to real people. Know that it threatens our very survival. And know that this is just as much a crime against humanity as anything the Nazis ever did. It is likely that the indigenous people of the United States will never demand that those guilty of such criminal activity be punished for their deeds. But the least we have the right to expect—indeed, to demand—is that such practices finally be brought to a halt.

Studying Indian Remains Violates Native Americans' Beliefs

by Devon A. Mihesuah

About the author: *Devon A. Mihesuah is an associate professor of American Indian history at Northern Arizona University in Flagstaff.*

Among the many problems American Indians have to contend with today is the removal of their ancestors' remains along with sacred tribal items from burial grounds for the purpose of scientific study and museum display, or for sale through the underground market and at auctions. The argument between Indians who want Indian skeletal remains and funerary objects repatriated (or "matriated," as one Indian puts it) and anthropologists who do not, is a volatile one, taking on emotional, spiritual, intellectual, and monetary elements. For black-market grave robbers, the issue appears to be purely monetary.

Throughout the years, I have heard or read the same statements at committee meetings, conferences, and in the scholarly literature:

> *"Indians are too ignorant to know what's good for them."*
> *"The only good Indian is a dead, unreburied one."*
> *"How would you like it if your grandparents were dug up?"*
> *"I wouldn't mind if my ancestors were studied since only the spirit goes to heaven, not the entire body."*
> *"Archaeologists and anthropologists are the only ones who benefit from studying Indian remains."*
> *"How has the study of Indian skeletal remains helped to alleviate the problems Indians face today?"*
> *"Since we all emerged from the same place—Africa—then why should anyone mind if remains are studied; my past is your past."*

The comments go on, of course, but this short list does illustrate the complexity of the problem.

The desecration problem appears to be everywhere. Since becoming involved in the repatriation issue about ten years ago, I have learned that not all peoples possess the same religious, moral, or philosophical values when it comes to disinterment of the deceased and funerary items. While a graduate student at Texas Christian University in Fort Worth, I was a member of the Texas Indian Commission's and the Texas Historical Commission's Committee for the Protection and Preservation of Skeletal Remains and Cultural Objects—a committee comprised of anthropologists, museologists, tribal leaders, Indian activists, educators, lawyers, and concerned citizens, both Indian and non-Indian. All members learned a great deal through the activities and dialogues of this very active committee.

Insensitivity

I had the opportunity to visit many museums, and to view Indian bones displayed in almost every one, the strangest presentation being hand bones on the window sill of the ladies' room in a small east Texas museum. I walked through archives of universities that held thousands of Indian skeletal remains in dust-covered boxes and watched as customers haggled over the price of skulls and medicine bundles at Texas gun shows. I read newspaper articles that chronicled the adventures of would-be Texas Indiana Joneses (i.e., "amateur archaeologists") and saw burial sites that had been bulldozed and ransacked by grave robbers looking for skulls and burial items to sell. Still in my activist graduate student mode, I argued with anthropologists (such as D. Gentry Steele and Robert J. Mallouf, fellow committee members) over what I perceived to be their insensitivity to Indians' concerns, protested to hobbyists about their seemingly innocent excavations that in reality destroy sites, and argued with some staunch advocates of reburial over their desire to speak for all tribes, and indeed, their need for attention. I worked intensively on this issue for years, writing articles, speaking to reporters, and in conference sessions.

Although I am presently an associate professor of history, I also have taught high school biology and physics and can appreciate the theory that studying human skeletal remains can yield data that will benefit mankind. As an American Indian, however, I am all too aware of the severe physical, political, and economic problems among Indians. Where is the information anthropologists are supposed to be acquiring that can help present-day tribes? If studies of tribes in the United States are supposed to be important, how are investigations by archaeologists

> *"Where is the information anthropologists are supposed to be acquiring that can help present-day tribes?"*

and physical anthropologists serving the needs of Indians today? In dialogues with social scientists, Indians plead for convincing evidence that having the remains of their ancestors scrutinized, then stored for decades in basements and vaults of universities and museums, in addition to being separated from the grave goods with which they were buried, contributes to the well-being of Indian people.

No Benefits to Indians Found

It is quite possible that at one time the study of old Indian bones did play a role in the development of medicine, proper diet, and prevention of bone disease. With the sophistication of science, however, doctors have developed the ability to perform organ transplants, limb reattachments, sex changes, and growth stimulation. It would therefore appear that further excavation and examination of Indian people is no longer necessary. Dr. Emery Johnson, former Assistant Surgeon General, has even commented, "I am not aware of any current medical diagnostic or treatment procedure that has been derived from research on Indian remains. Nor am I aware of any during the thirty-four years that I have been involved in American Indian health."

If the Society for American Archaeology ever gives a suitable answer as to the benefits of studying Indian skeletons, some tribes might be receptive to scholars who study remains. But to date, the garnered scientific information has not been used to decrease alcoholism or suicide rates, nor has it influenced legislative bodies to return tribal lands, or to recognize the sad fact that Indians are still stereotyped, ridiculed, and looked upon as novelties. Indeed, mannequins dressed as Indians stand outside tourist shops, Hollywood still

"Further excavation and examination of Indian people is no longer necessary."

portrays Indians incorrectly, and sports teams, automobiles, and clothing lines all use stereotypes of Indians to sell products. What do Indian skulls that are displayed alongside pottery in museums tell visitors? Is this a message that Indians are inferior beings, items for display, just like animals? Since other Americans are not on view like Indians are, there is without question a double standard at work: non-Indian burials are left alone and those accidentally uncovered are immediately reburied, but archaeologists and pothunters deem it good and necessary to dig up Indians and display their remains and funerary items.

This is also a monetary issue. American Indian remains, their cultural objects, in addition to their images serve as the focal points of many anthropologists' careers. The fact that Indians exist allows these people—as well as historians—to secure jobs, tenure, promotion, merit increases, fellowships, notoriety, and scholarly identity—all without giving anything back to Indian communities. Millions of dollars, hundreds of jobs, and numerous journals would be at stake if anthropologists could no longer study Indian remains and their burial items.

Not All Studies Are Worthless

Indians are curious about their histories, and they do not believe that all scientific and social scientific studies are worthless. Indians are often treated as if they have no comprehension of science or are too ignorant to understand the need for continuing research. On the contrary, Indians are aware that gaps in tribal histories have been filled by the investigations of anthropologists, archaeologists, and historians. The conflict arises because many archaeologists assume that they are the caretakers and owners of the past, not respecting the fact that Indians have oral traditions. Among traditional Indians, it is the responsibility of the present generation to remember stories for future generations. Despite what archaeologists think, Indians do not believe that tribal histories are created by archaeologists' findings. An attractive proposition for many Indians is that Indians and archaeologists work together to help each other form a more complete picture of the past, but the problem is that most archaeologists view oral histories as "fantasy" and "embellished" and refuse to consult with Indian informants. More likely, they do not want to enter into dialogue with tribes because it invites the risk of having their research project taken away from them.

> *"The garnered scientific information has not been used to decrease alcoholism or suicide rates, nor has it influenced legislative bodies to return tribal lands."*

Anthropologists and museum directors often offer their opinions about the intelligence of Indians, many believe that Indians will not know how to take care of items that are returned to them. In response, Raymond Apodaca, chairman of the Human Rights Committee for the National Congress of American Indians says, "What are they talking about? These things belong to us, were created by us, and are highly respected by us." Pemina Yellow Bird, a Hidatsa/Arikara repatriation activist, agrees: "How do you think these ancient things got in their possession if Native people didn't know how to take care of them? And who are they to tell us how to take care of our own sacred objects?"

Religious Beliefs

To scientists, skeletal remains and funerary items are "tools of education," and any skeleton or grave more than one hundred years old is viewed as an artifact that is fair game. Scientists believe that the cradle of civilization is in Africa; therefore, because we all have common ancestors, they claim the right to study all human remains. To Indians, however, the remains represent either direct ancestors or families they consider to be their "cultural ancestors."

Many Indians do not believe that they crossed the Siberian land bridge to North America. They believe they emerged from sacred sites on the North American continent. Why should ancient bones be considered "fair game" for study? Is it because archaeologists feel it is safer to assert that there is no one alive who can claim relation to the old bones? After all, archaeologists have to study something. Lynne Goldstein and Keith Kintigh tell us in their 1990 essay, "Ethics and the Reburial Controversy," that "To claim that archaeologists have no right to excavate or examine an entire class of information is to deny our background and training." ("Who asked them to become archaeologists and study Indians anyway?" respond Indians and non-Indians who have discussed their essay.)

Scientists and pothunters also like to hold up the Christian belief that the body and soul separate after death, so why be concerned about physical remains if the soul is (it is hoped) on his or her way to heaven? But that is not how many Indians see it. Generally speaking, because all tribes have differences in religion, unearthing of skeletal remains and funerary objects is disruptive. Among some tribes, if the bones are uncovered, and especially if they are separated from the burial relics, the spirit may not be at peace. Hence the importance of keeping remains and funerary objects buried.

Indians and some social scientists have come to some agreement over how remains should be handled and studied, if at all. Like historians, there are many archaeologists who wish Indians would stay out of it, or even better, were all dead so they would not have to deal with the descendants of the people they study. A former member of the executive committee for the Society of American Archaeology has commented, "the only good Indian is a dead, unreburied one." Indeed, I have heard numerous times from anthropologists that Indians are "uneducated" and "cannot understand what we do." Despite my four university degrees and numerous academic awards, I have been told I am "ignorant" and "cannot possibly know" what I am talking about. Because of such racism, Indians often place scientists in the same category as grave robbers. To them the only difference between an illegal ransacking of a burial ground and a scientific one is the time element, sun screen, little whisk brooms, and the neatness of the area when finished. Indians perceive many social scientists and all pothunters as adept at exploiting them for profit and see both groups as disrespectful of the individuals resting in the ground. Indians remain perplexed by the attitude of some anthropologists who assert that their work is more important than the religious beliefs and dignity of the descendants of those Indians they study.

> *"Since other Americans are not on view like Indians are, there is without question a double standard at work: non-Indian burials are left alone."*

Academics and Economics Versus the Indians

Because pothunters, archaeologists, physical anthropologists, and paleopathologists spend a good portion of their time in graveyards and laboratories handling human remains and sacred tribal objects, this is undoubtedly a religious issue. When addressing the repatriation issue, some Indians speak from a religious standpoint, while scholars who study remains and sacred objects speak a different scientific language. Scholars cry "academic freedom," but Indians are concerned about "religious freedom," resulting in miscommunication, conflicts, and assumptions. Indians have taken refuge in the First Amendment to protect their religious beliefs, but this strategy is rarely effective, as tribal lawyers have discovered. At least anthropologists and archaeologists will speak to Indians; black-market grave robbers and pothunters rarely will. Nor will they speak to archaeologists except perhaps to argue, as Arizona grave robber Peter Hester does:

> Archaeology is a dead science. Archaeology is a dead end. Business is business; there are thousands of sites, and thousands of useless pots. The information has already been gained from most sites. How many pots of the same type do you need to figure something out? The only difference between what I do and the professional archaeologists do is that I sell what I find.

The collecting of Native American art in the form of baskets, paintings, pottery, jewelry, beadwork, and rugs has been a hobby and business among non Indians for decades. Almost everywhere whites are seen wearing turquoise rings or squash blossoms; in their homes are Navajo rugs and Pueblo pottery. Most of these common items are obtained legally from an art gallery, pow wow, or reservation tourist shop. An old problem, and one that appears to be developing, is the illegal removal of sacred tribal items and the remains of the tribal people themselves from Indian burial grounds to be sold through underground markets, either to people ignorant of the origin of these items or to disreputable collectors fully aware of what they are buying. Despite the Texas committee's differences of opinion over academia's return of Indian skeletal remains and funerary objects to tribes, one thing the committee agreed on was that the looting of Indian burial sites must be stopped (the problem in Texas is particularly serious), and that Texas museums should not display Indian skeletal remains and sacred objects. Indians and archaeologists usually can agree that burial sites should be "protected" from pothunters, and that the latter should be fully prosecuted when possible. But the term "protection" has two meanings. To many Indians, it means no burial-ground disturbances whatsoever. To archaeologists and physical anthropologists it means "hands off" any newly discovered site until they arrive to conduct their research. Museum directors want protection of their "collections" even if these "tools of education" are kept in archives and never seen again.

Exploiting Graveyards for Profit

Most grave robbers appear to be of a different mind-set altogether and use any excuse that comes to mind as to why they should be able to exploit graveyards for profit. An experience in 1985 led me to believe that sensitizing grave robbers to the concerns of many American Indians and sympathetic academics would be nearly impossible. The incident occurred when I and several representatives of the American Indian Movement, American Indians Against Desecration, and the aforementioned Texas committee attended a closed-door auction at the Texas Ranger Hall of Fame in Waco, Texas. The auction hall was filled with the requisite and costly Texas paraphernalia such as saddles, blankets, and antiques but, to our dismay, there also were tables laden with jewelry, pipebags, and medicine bundles with price tags informing potential buyers that they were acquired from Indian burials.

The most shocking item for sale, at least to me, was an exquisitely carved, glass-topped coffee table with a full skeleton inside that had been christened "Ernest"—probably a Mescalero Apache. After explaining to the auction officials who we were and our concerns, we were led outside by the auction guards—replete with sidearms—to a picnic table to discuss the issue. The auctioneer promised to pull the funerary items and Ernest from sale, but to our disappointment we later found out that they were auctioned by telephone to bidders in Germany and Japan. The Corps of Engineers in Fort Worth told us that this particular auctioneer made a living from selling the contents of burials from a variety of Texas and Southwest tribes.

> *"Despite cultural differences, . . . [Indians] share the desire to keep their ancestors resting in peace (not in pieces)."*

After graduate school I moved to Arizona where, in the midst of twenty reservations (and their countless sacred sites, shrines, and burial grounds), I encountered a whole new world of desecration. Museums and archives are packed with skeletal remains and cultural objects, and wealthy grave robbers make their livings by purchasing land they know contain burials and then unearthing the remains and artifacts to sell. When finished plundering, they then they sell the land and buy more. Vandalism of prehistoric sites (i.e., petroglyphs, ruins, middens, and shrines) has reached such epidemic proportions in the Southwest that cartographers are considering leaving their locales off of new maps and out of guide books.

The issue also hits me close to home. My husband, a Comanche, has numerous relatives, including a sister, buried in the Ishiti cemetery outside of Duncan, Oklahoma. Over the past twenty years, the cemetery has been vandalized and desecrated by looters looking for funerary objects the Comanches buried with their dead, such as saddles, jewelry, and medicine bundles. In response, some of the graves have been covered with cement by concerned relatives. But the looting of these burials puts us in a quandary for where can the next generations be interred, if not in a large city cemetery? Many other Indians also have seen the desecration of their families' burials; and no doubt they wonder the same thing.

No Quick Solution

Regardless of the differences in their cultures, American Indians are becoming increasingly concerned about taking proper care of unearthed remains of their ancestors and of sacred objects in or out of the ground. Despite cultural differences and the personal enmities Indians may have for one another, they share the desire to keep their ancestors resting in peace (not in pieces) as well as the desire to reinter those remains that have been disturbed. Many scientists have indeed become more sensitive to Indians' concerns but, in the meantime, grave-robbing, high-priced auctions, gun shows, private and amateur archaeology, and seemingly innocent arrowhead-hunting continue to provide excuses for collecting. The problem is complicated, but is one that needs to be addressed with more sensitivity. Until the various parties involved in unearthing the deceased and sacred objects take a long hard look at all the factors—including the human one—the problem will stay with us.

Native Americans' Free Exercise of Religion Is Threatened by Prisons

by Iron Thunderhorse

About the author: *Iron Thunderhorse, a Native American artist and shaman, is the author of* Return of the Thunder Beings, *in which he writes of his incarceration in a Texas prison.*

Try to imagine what it would be like to be in a prisoner-of-war camp where only a small handful of people are Christians and the prisoners who are Christians are further separated from each other because your captors don't want any of you to congregate.

Every day you are subjected to ridicule. Your crucifix is confiscated and kept locked away. Your Bible is kept always out of reach. If you denounce your Christian traditions you can have anything you want. Religious leaders from all other religions are allowed to come into the POW camp regularly. You are under constant pressure to give up being Christian in order to enjoy the simple privileges that the "others" are allowed.

Let this feeling sink down deep into your bones, your heart and your gut. Each time you try to break the cycle of harassment and oppression the retaliation gets worse. Your oppressors rough you up and spread rumors against you.

If you could begin to imagine how this would feel, day and night, for 17 long years, then you have an idea of how it has been for me.

Physical Abuse

In 1978, after spending a year in county jails going through several criminal trials, I petitioned the District Court of Grayson County, Texas, for an injunction to keep the Texas Department of Corrections (TDC) from cutting my hair because it had been a part of my religious practice for many years. Judge William Ralph Elliott issued a Temporary Restraining Order (TRO) to prevent

From Iron Thunderhorse, "Religious Freedom: A Myth for Native American Prisoners," *Witness*, January/February 1995. Reprinted with permission.

TDC from cutting my hair.

I was taken to the TDC Diagnostic Unit on September 12, 1978. The reception area had been cleared. Along with Assistant Warden Billy Ware there were over a dozen ranking officers and inmates called "building tenders" (inmates who worked as guards), all carrying ax handles and bats. I was told to get in the barber chair. When I tried to produce the TRO, I was told, "You're in Texas now, Ol' Thang, we run this prison. Get your hair cut or get your head busted." I was beaten almost to unconsciousness.

> *"[The Texas Department of Corrections] want[s] to decide who can practice our religion and who cannot."*

While at the Diagnostic Unit I was asked what my race was. I said, "Native American," and they laughed, saying there are only three racial categories, black, white, and hispanic. They asked my religion and I said, "Native American shamanism," and they laughed again, saying, "There ain't no such religion."

I was assigned to the Ellis 1 Unit where I was interviewed by a major who told me that he hated Indians and jailhouse lawyers. "If you don't get your heart right, my boys will know how to handle it," he said.

A 17-Year Holy War

Thus began a 17-year war, a holy war between the Texas prison system and Native American religious freedom. The first thing I did was prepare an appeal in the civil case which issued the TRO, but the court never received it. At the time, TDC was being sued by inmates for serious mail tampering.

In retaliation for my legal work the building tenders organized hit-squads and made several assassination attempts on my life. There were other inmates who rallied behind me and a series of confrontations developed. I was labeled a trouble maker and placed on death row, even though I wasn't sentenced to death.

Judge William Wayne Justice eventually abolished the use of building tenders and forced TDC to clean up its act, but TDC resisted. For the first six or seven years I would be given a haircut by force every few months until Judge Justice ruled that TDC could no longer use force against me. However, I was denied all visitation, commissary privileges, recreation privileges, etc. My typewriter was confiscated on several occasions because several of us organized to challenge TDC in the courts and in the media.

I was eventually placed in administrative segregation where I was kept out of sight and out of mind. I have spent 85 percent of my time in TDC locked away from others.

For a while TDC allowed me to have my medicine bag, ceremonial pipe, eagle feathers, etc. and in 1991 we formed a Native American Cultural and Religious Council. I was released into the Wynne Unit population with braids down to my waist. I was paroled in June of 1991.

My parole was violated in 1992 because I left a hospital without permission. I was charged with escape (although I was on parole and no warrant had been served on me) and given 20 more years.

I am now back in segregation after a year of solitary confinement and confrontations. As soon as I arrived back in TDC, officers of rank began harassing me, calling me "Thunderbolt," "Thunderturd." I was denied meals (unless I cut my hair) on several occasions. When these tactics failed, officers tried using force.

In 1994, after the Religious Freedom Restoration Act was passed by Congress, TDC revised its religious policy. On its face it appears to give all inmates equal access to religion. The section on Native Americans allows inmates to have a sacred pipe, medicine bag, stone, shell, herbs, feathers, bandannas, etc. I made arrangements to have all these items sent to my unit so that we could practice our religion. The items were stored in the chapel. Soon after they arrived and I requested use of them, I was placed in segregated status and told I could not use them until I was released into population, which means that when I cut my hair, then I can have my religious freedom. The policy says nothing about being denied access to spiritual items for people in administrative segregation. Although it was the chaplain who advised me of this restriction, it was authorized by the warden. So much for separation of church and state.

> *"Our ancient traditions are not a form of devil-worship."*

In my culture (Algonquian) I hold the tradition of being a *powwau* which means "dream-power," alluding to the dream fasts we practice in ceremony to obtain divine revelations. I have been a spiritual leader of my people for over 30 years, and in our traditions only certain people who are trained after receiving a traditional calling are authorized to conduct our ceremonies. Numerous inmates have signed requests for TDC to allow me to work with prisoners leading the ceremonies, but TDC refuses. TDC does not know the fundamentals of Native American religions. They want to decide who can practice our religion and who cannot.

No Recognition for Native American Religion

TDC spends a sizable budget each year for Christian inmates. Regular Christian revivals are the only events allowed. (TDC has to entice many inmates with football stars, magicians, and free soap and shampoo in order to get inmates to attend.) The TDC administration hasn't spent a penny on acquiring ceremonial items for Native American prisoners. I've had to do this on my own.

I have yet to see a multi-cultural revival in prison in TDC. In other penitentiaries this is a common thing and each ethnic religion is allowed a special day of celebration.

I do not think or act like white people because I was raised differently. I feel like an alien who has lived on another planet for the past 17 years—cut off from my culture and traditions. Instead of taking advantage of my status as a spiritual leader and allowing me to conduct ceremonials for other Indian inmates, TDC has tried its best to break my spirit and force me to worship their way.

End the Injustice

Change can only take place if and when the Christian people themselves take action. I ask that all true Christians make good on their promise to end the wrongs and injustices done to Native Americans in the past 500 years.

Christians can contact the ministries which come into prison on a regular basis such as: Chuck Colson Ministries, Bill Glass Ministries, Texans Do Care, etc. and request that multi-cultural revivals be provided. Many Native Americans have accepted a hybrid form of Christian worship in their spirituality. It can be done by Christians as well.

Christians could also visit Indian communities, get to know them and invite the elders to these multi-cultural revivals at the prisons so that they can visit the Indian prisoners, especially those in segregation who cannot attend the revivals. Since these elders have no transportation they should be helped so transportation is provided and they are welcomed.

By observing and participating in this way, Christians and the prison administration will see that our ancient traditions are not a form of devil-worship. People call the Great Spirit by different names and we each use our own symbols and instruments to honor the Great Mystery. But we are all saying similar things through traditions that have been handed down since the beginning of time.

The Public Interferes with Native American Religious Activities on Public Lands

by Charles Levendosky

About the author: *Charles Levendosky is the editorial page editor of the Casper (WY) Star-Tribune. He has won numerous awards for his commentary on First Amendment issues.*

When the National Park Service shows some sensitivity to the religious needs of Native Americans, stomp it.

And be sure to grind a heel into American Indian religious liberty.

That's the way Mountain States Legal Foundation in Denver apparently views it. The foundation filed a lawsuit against the Park Service's cultural sensitivity in March 1996.

Devils Tower, located in northeast Wyoming, has been a sacred site for many northern Plains Indian tribes for centuries.

It was designated as America's first national monument by President Teddy Roosevelt in 1906 and is administered by the National Park Service.

Park Service officials at Devils Tower recognize that it is a significant landmark in tribal narratives and for traditional tribal ceremonies. It is now attempting to accommodate those beliefs—in real terms.

But Devils Tower is also one of the premiere crack climbing sites in the United States. Thousands of climbers arrive at the monument each year to test themselves against the vertical columns of the volcanic monolith. They represent a little more than 1 percent of the annual half-a-million visitors to the site each year.

Clashing Cultures

There's the clash: a climbers' culture vs. Native American cultures.

Think of someone hammering climbing bolts into one of the towers of St.

From Charles Levendosky, "Face Off at Devils Tower: Climbers vs. Religion," *Casper (Wyo.) Star-Tribune*, March 24, 1996.

Patrick's Cathedral on Easter Sunday, and yelling to another climber while you try to pray down in the pews. That's the clash—in real Christian terms.

In 1995, the Park Service superintendent at Devils Tower implemented a climbing management plan to better serve the religious concerns of the Lakota, Crow, Arapaho, Cheyenne, Kiowa, and Shoshone tribes.

The plan was the creation of a working group comprised of climbers, tribal leaders, environmentalists, a county commissioner, and members of the Park Service.

Their plan asks climbers to accept a voluntary ban on climbing Devils Tower during the month of June so that tribes can celebrate religious rites undisturbed at the monument. Although most climbing occurs during the months of May through September, on average, more climbers come to the tower in June.

> *"The tower was a holy place long before it became a national monument or a climbers' paradise."*

The plan also forbids placing new bolts or fixed pitons in the tower, but does allow replacing worn bolts or pitons—as a compromise with Native Americans who consider the bolts desecrating a holy site.

June is the month of the summer solstice when many tribes celebrate their religions on the land surrounding Devils Tower with a Sun Dance, prayer offerings, sweatlodge ceremonies, and vision quests.

The plan is meant to show respect for Native American religions and for the monument itself.

During June of 1995, only 193 people climbed the tower; during the previous June that number was 1,293. The voluntary ban was dramatically successful in its first year.

Meanwhile the Park Service has attempted to inform the general public and climbers about the cultural and religious resource that Devils Tower represents. The ban promised to be adopted by even more climbers in June 1996.

Then came Mountain States Legal Foundation.

The Lawsuit

In response to the voluntary climbing ban, the foundation filed a lawsuit against the superintendent of the Devils Tower National Monument, the National Park Service, and Secretary of Interior Bruce Babbitt. The suit claims that the Park Service has violated the "Establishment Clause" of the First Amendment by creating the June climbing ban for "religious purposes."

In this suit, the foundation is representing a multiple use association, a climbing guide, and four climbers—all from Wyoming.

The foundation requests that the Wyoming federal district court end the climbing ban permanently. Even though the ban is voluntary. [In June 1996 a ban on the issuance of permits to climbing guides during the month of June was declared unconstitutional.]

If Native American religions were truly recognized as "equal before the law" with mainstream religions, this would be no more than a frivolous lawsuit. It would be summarily dismissed.

Unfortunately, American Indian religions seldom win in the courts because they are considered suspect, second class, even.

When Native Americans tried to preserve sacred sites like the Rainbow Natural Bridge (Utah), Bear Butte (S.D.), and portions of the San Francisco Peaks (Ariz.) for religious ceremony, they lost in the courts—tourism and skiing were deemed more important.

In 1987, the U.S. Supreme Court allowed logging roads through the Chimney Rock area of the Six Rivers National Forest in northern California. Chimney Rock is a spiritual site.

This time, however, the attack comes not from government, but from private individuals.

A Sacred Site

It is clear from history that Devils Tower is a sacred site for a number of Native American tribal beliefs. The area around the tower was also used as a burial grounds for northern Plains tribes.

Think of the tower as a cathedral in nature.

The tower was a holy place long before it became a national monument or a climbers' paradise. Once that fact is accepted, then one must acknowledge that this ban is not a violation of the Establishment Clause, but an accommodation of a spiritual nature that already exists.

That raises the question about interfering with Native Americans' right of free exercise of religion. Climbers do interfere with religious ceremonies at the base of the tower, as they would rappelling from the vaulted ceiling of your church during mass.

Interfering with spiritual activities at recognized holy sites should be a violation of the First Amendment's protections of religious liberty.

The National Park Service has a mandate to protect and preserve the cultural resources under its authority, as well as the constitutional rights of Native Americans who want to use their historic resources. The Park Service does not have a multiple use mandate; it is there to preserve designated cultural and natural resources.

> *"Climbers do interfere with religious ceremonies at the base of the tower, as they would rappelling from the vaulted ceiling of your church during mass."*

If the people who are suing would think for a moment they might realize that nothing has been lost by this voluntary ban and something important has been gained—acceptance of and respect for another's religion.

Serious climbers who do not climb in June will climb some other month of the year.

For climbing guides the June ban is mandatory—after all, their permit to make money in the national park is a privilege, not a constitutional right. But they won't lose business; it will average out in the other months.

And the park has preserved a multiple use of its resources, only the multiple use isn't simultaneous. Multiple use seldom is. Generally, people don't water ski and cross-country ski on the same day.

Unfortunately, this ill-conceived lawsuit will have long-lasting, damaging repercussions if the Park Service loses. No sacred site will be protected. And that will shame us all.

In an interview with CNN, broadcast in October 1995, Elaine Quiver, a Lakota from the Pine Ridge Reservation in South Dakota, put it this way: "As long as we have a misunderstanding that my culture is better than yours, we'll never succeed. We'll always be fighting at the base of the Tower and the Tower will be standing forever."

New Age Practitioners Threaten Indian Spirituality

by Rick Romancito

About the author: *Rick Romancito, a Taos and Zuni Indian, is the arts and entertainment editor for the weekly* Taos News *in Taos, New Mexico.*

The quest for spiritual enlightenment and knowledge is a worthy pursuit and should be encouraged. But something is happening within the New Age movement that has many American Indian people very concerned. It has to do with a misconception that their native religions are openly accessible to non-Indians.

No Single Religion

To begin, the beliefs held by the widely varied group of indigenous tribes throughout North America are not part of a single religion. The concept of spiritual entities called *Kachinas* is not part of the same religion as the belief in a spirit road as pursued by followers of the Native American Church, nor is the Plains Indian Sun Dance ritual part of the cycle of ceremonies related to the deer, buffalo, and turtle dances as practiced by the Tiwa Indians of Taos Pueblo.

Each tribe, through centuries of change and often independent of one another, developed different beliefs to try to understand their place in the universe. Some may have grown out of reaction to their environments, or as the result of significant incidents, or as a way to protect their tribes from becoming dissolved into the social and cultural network of surrounding peoples—just like most of the world's religions. But each has always been in a state of active evolution.

The native religion seen in the fifteenth century by Fray Marcos de Niza at Hawikuh, one of the Zuni villages in New Mexico, was likely not the same as he would have seen had he visited some 200 years before. Today the differences are even more significant. Then there is the peyote religion, which spread from Mexico and was adopted among some Plains Indian tribes during the nineteenth century. It, too, has undergone a wide variety of changes and was subject to a number of influences from native and non-Indian sources during its nearly 200

From Rick Romancito, "American Indians and the New Age: Subtle Racism at Work," *Skeptical Inquirer*, Fall 1993. Reprinted with permission.

years of existence among the Plains and even older life among the Huichol and others in Mexico.

Yet these differences and their state of evolution never appear to be part of advertisements for "Native American ceremonialism" workshops or seminars. To the uninitiated, it would seem as though the same belief is shared by all Indians, but to Indians, the distinctions are all-important.

When so-called New Age practitioners begin selectively picking and choosing spiritual concepts from several different Indian religions, as if they're products for sale in a cosmic supermarket, the integrity of native beliefs is threatened. On a more subversive level, they exhibit contempt by assigning Indians to a racist stereotype.

A False Image

The image of Indians as the repositories of "indigenous spiritual knowledge" should share the same garbage heap as that of the drunken Indian and the romantic "end of the trail" warrior. However, it is this image so many New Age non-Indian believers possess about Indians that does more damage to the people they celebrate than they'll ever know.

For example, native religion among Pueblo Indians is closely guarded for a reason. It was practiced for centuries before being forced underground by Christian missionaries accompanying Spanish colonists who began arriving here [in New Mexico] in the seventeenth century. It exists today as totally nonproselytizing: Pueblo Indian religion seeks no converts. Tribal membership is the only way in and requires a lifelong commitment to the

> "The image of Indians as the repositories of 'indigenous spiritual knowledge' should share the same garbage heap as that of the drunken Indian."

annual performance of rituals that maintain harmony in the spiritual and physical worlds. Each part is important to the whole and cannot be separated without losing its meaning.

This belief system and their native languages are some of the few intangible aspects of native culture that clearly define the identity of tribal members. Despite whatever physical appearance of assimilation, these invisible elements held within their hearts are their pillars of strength.

But, because New Age seekers fail to recognize insurmountable barriers, the unwanted interest in ferreting out "the secrets of Indian religion" continues, and the real concerns of Indian people are overlooked and trivialized as a result.

High unemployment, HIV-AIDS, substandard education, the violation of First Amendment rights to practice native religion, and persistent discrimination and prejudices, all apparently are a little too inconvenient to deal with when a seeker is filled with the fantasy of meeting a "real Native American shaman."

It's time for New Age seekers to get real:

- Those who are genuinely pursuing their native religions don't let non-Indians in on it for pay.
- The authentic practitioners of native religion only deal with Indians.
- You cannot learn anything about Indian religion from a workshop or a seminar.
- The only way to participate in an Indian ceremony is to *be Indian.*

The quest for enlightenment should be encouraged, but not at the expense of robbing a culture because of some fantasy about how Indians worship. Instead, maybe seekers ought to look to their own culture to find those things that are truer to their own natures.

The Supreme Court Threatens Native Americans' Religious Use of Peyote

by Walter Echo-Hawk

About the author: *Walter Echo-Hawk is a Native American activist and the senior staff attorney with the Native American Rights Fund in Boulder, Colorado.*

> *The Indian plays much the same role in our American society that the Jews played in Germany. Like the miner's canary, the Indian marks the shift from fresh air to poison gas in our political atmosphere; and our treatment of Indians, even more than our treatment of other minorities, marks the rise and fall of our democratic faith.*
>
> *—Felix Cohen, the "Father of Federal Indian Law"*

[The] Supreme Court [has] created a crisis in religious liberty for Native Americans. [It] held that the First Amendment does not protect tribal religious practices and referred the task of protecting Native worship to Congress. Stripped of any constitutional or statutory protections under American law, Indian religion has become the "miner's canary." In excluding traditional Indian worship from the First Amendment, the court has so narrowed the scope, meaning and protections of the Free Exercise Clause that it has seriously weakened religious liberty for all Americans.

This viewpoint examines the impact of the new Supreme Court doctrine—which has been described by constitutional law scholars as "the rise and fall of the Free Exercise Clause"—on Native religious freedom. Felix Cohen's words are prophetic when one views the resurgence of racism, censorship, intolerance, and the growing trend toward restricting other civil liberties during a time when American Indian worship has been excluded from constitutional protection. If our legal system cannot protect basic freedoms of even the weakest among us,

Excerpted from Walter Echo-Hawk, "Loopholes in Religious Liberty," *Cultural Survival Quarterly*, Winter 1994. Reprinted with permission.

does it lack sufficient vitality to protect the rest of society? As Native Americans ask Congress to protect the "miner's canary," this may test the nation's "democratic faith" and commitment to underlying values of the Bill of Rights.

Government Policy

Since Columbus' arrival 500 years ago, a basic feature of society's relationship with American Indians has been government insensitivity to Native religious beliefs and practices. At times government insensitivity included formal policies to suppress tribal religion and culture in order to "civilize" Indians. Even though the Pilgrims and other immigrants came to America in search of religious freedom which has been enshrined in the First Amendment by

> *"The [Supreme] court . . .has seriously weakened religious liberty for all Americans."*

the Founding Fathers, those values were disregarded in the federal government's treatment of American Indians. That history provides a backdrop for understanding the present crisis in Native religious freedom.

In 1979, the Secretary of the Interior submitted a report to Congress that recounts the historic treatment of Native religion by the federal government. One cornerstone of federal Indian policy was to convert the "savage" Indians into Christian citizens and separate them from their traditional ways of life. President Andrew Jackson's Indian removal policy was justified in the name of converting and civilizing the Indians. Christian missionaries, hired as government Indian agents, were an integral part of the federal Indian policy for over one hundred years. The government placed entire reservations and Indian Nations under the administrative control of church denominations. Indian lands were conveyed to missionary groups in order to convert the Indians and separate them from their traditions.

Separation of church and state was disregarded in the government's treatment of Indians. The Secretary's report to Congress found as follows:

> That Christianity and federal interests were often identical became an article of faith in every branch of the government and this pervasive attitude initiated the contemporary period of religious persecution of the Indian religions. It was not, to be certain, a direct attack on Indian tribal religions because of their conflict with Christianity, but an oblique attack on the Indian way of life that had as its by-product the transformation of Indians into American citizens. Had a Christian denomination or sect, or the Jewish community been subjected to the same requirements prior to receiving affirmation of their legal and political rights, the outcry would have been tremendous.

Criminalizing Religious Practices

By the 1890's, after tribes were placed on reservations, government treatment of their religions took a darker turn. In that decade, U.S. troops were called in to stamp out the Ghost Dance religion of the tribes who were confined on reservations. In 1890, Sioux Ghost Dance worshippers were slaughtered at Wounded Knee. In 1892, Pawnee Ghost Dance leaders were arrested in Oklahoma. And soon that religion ceased to exist as it was suppressed among other tribes. In 1892, the BIA [Bureau of Indian Affairs] outlawed the Sun Dance religion and banned other ceremonies which were declared "Indian offenses" and made punishable by withholding of rations or 30 days' imprisonment.

Formal government rules prohibiting tribal religions continued into the 1930's. In 1904, BIA Court of Indian Offenses regulations stated in very stark terms:

> Fourth. The "sun dance" and all other similar dances and so-called religious ceremonies, shall be considered "Indian offenses," and any Indian found guilty of being a participant in any one or more of these offenses shall . . . be punished by with holding from him his rations for a period of not exceeding ten days; and if found guilty of any subsequent offense under this rule, shall be punished by withholding his rations for a period not less than fifteen days nor more than thirty days, or by incarceration in the agency prison for a period not exceeding thirty days. . . .

> Sixth. The usual practices of so-called "medicine men" shall be considered "Indian offenses". . . [punishable by confinement] in the agency guardhouse for a term not less than ten days, or until such time as he shall produce evidence satisfactory to the court, and approved by the agent, that he will forever abandon all practices styled Indian offense under this rule.

Though Indians were not granted citizenship until 1924, this does not justify the outright government ban on their right to worship which was in effect until 1934.

An Attempt to Remedy the Persecution

Serious problems in Native religious freedom persisted into the 1970's, with numerous arrests of traditional Indians for possession of tribal sacred objects such as eagle feathers, criminal prosecutions for the religious use of peyote, denial of access to sacred sites located on federal lands and interference with religious ceremonies at sacred sites. After hearings held in 1978, Congress recognized the need to protect Indian religious freedom, including worship at sacred sites and the use and possession of sacred objects. The hearings revealed that much of the problem resulted from a simple government lack of knowledge about traditional religious practices.

> *"Congress recognized the need to protect Indian religious freedom, including worship at sacred sites and the use and possession of sacred objects."*

To remedy the problem, Congress enacted the American Indian Religious Freedom Act of 1978 (AIRFA). AIRFA established a federal policy to protect and preserve the traditional religions of native people, including worship at sacred sites. Though AIRFA was considered a landmark breakthrough at the time, in the intervening 13 years, tribes found that its policy has no teeth and has meant nothing to federal agencies.

The treatment of Native Worship by the Supreme Court in *Employment Division v. Smith,* analyzed below, is especially troubling when considered in the context of the above history. It is a testament to the vitality of tribal religion that it has persisted, despite a long history of government suppression that is unprecedented for any other religion in this country. But whether these unique religions can survive without any American legal protection is highly doubtful. . . .

The *Smith* Case

In 1990, the Supreme Court denied constitutional protection of an entire Indian religion of pre-Colombian antiquity which involves sacramental use of a cactus plant named peyote against state criminal prohibition of peyote use. For Indians who lost constitutional protection for worship in the name of the "Drug War," *Smith* was devastating. For the rest of society, *Smith* caused an outcry because it dramatically departs from First Amendment law, weakens the Free Exercise Clause and religious liberty, and makes it easier for government to intrude upon freedom of worship.

> *"Peyotism is a spiritually profound religion and way of life that ranks among the oldest, largest and most continuously practiced tribal religions."*

Peyote is a cactus plant that grows in parts of the Rio Grande River valley of Northern Mexico and Southern Texas. Native religious use of peyote predates the founding of the United States. Peyotism is a spiritually profound religion and way of life that ranks among the oldest, largest and most continuously practiced tribal religions of the Western Hemisphere. It is also interwoven with Native culture that contemporary tribal culture cannot be completely understood without knowledge of the long history of peyote worship.

Though harmless, peyotism is controversial because the cactus has psychedelic qualities and its ingestion is unlawful in most states. Although some states prosecuted Indian religious use earlier in this century, today the federal government and 28 states exempt the religious use of peyote by American Indians from drug laws. Many have done so for almost 30 years without experiencing any associated law enforcement or other problems. Nor has a single health problem among Indians ever been documented throughout centuries of sacramental use. In upholding the First Amendment right of Indians to practice this age-old religion, one court noted:

> [T]he right to free religious expression embodies a precious heritage of our history. In a mass society which presses at every party toward conformity, the protection of a self-expression, however unique, of the individual and group becomes ever more important. The varying currents of the subcultures that flow into the mainstream of our national life give it depth and beauty. We pre-

serve a greater value than an ancient tradition when we protect the rights of the Indians who honestly practiced an old religion in using peyote one night at a meeting in a desert hogan near Needles, California.

In *Smith,* the high court was asked to protect the First Amendment rights of members of the Native American Church who were fired from their jobs for off-duty religious use of peyote. Oregon asserted the First Amendment should not protect this

> *"Peyotism is far removed from the nation's drug problem."*

form of worship because state law made peyote use illegal and contained no exemption for Native religious use.

The Court's Decision

Prompted by "Drug War" fear and speculation promoted by Oregon, the court went to great lengths to deny protection for the Indian Peyote Religion, even though peyotism is far removed from the nation's drug problem. First, the court threw out the traditional "compelling state interest" test [the state must show a compelling reason why it must infringe on religious freedoms]; then it exempted an entire body of law—criminal law—from First Amendment limitation altogether; and finally it suggested that free exercise rights may not be entitled to protection unless some other constitutional right is also impaired by government action.

The court discarded the First Amendment test which had been applied for decades in religious cases, because it believed that the test too strictly protected religious liberty. Stating that America's religious diversity is a "luxury" that our pluralistic society "cannot afford," the court left religious accommodation up to the legislative political process instead of the courts and the Bill of Rights, despite an admitted hardship upon unpopular or minority faiths: "Leaving accommodation to the political process will place at a relative disadvantage those religious practices that are not widely engaged in; but that unavoidable consequence of democratic government must be preferred."

Justice Sandra Day O'Connor joined in the result and, as such, was not concerned about impacts of the decision upon Native religion. However, for the rest of society she expressed deep concern: "In my view, today's holding dramatically departs from well settled First Amendment jurisprudence, appears unnecessary to resolve the question presented, and is incompatible with our Nation's commitment to individual religious liberty."

She decried the inherent danger of making individual freedoms dependent upon politics, quoting *West Virginia State Board of Education v. Barnette.*

> The very purpose of the Bill of Rights was to withdraw certain subjects from the vicissitudes of political controversy. . . . One's right to life, liberty, and property, to free speech, a free press, freedom of worship and assembly, and other fundamental rights may not be submitted to vote; they depend on the outcome of no elections.

Mourning the declining role of the Bill of Rights in protecting religious freedom, Justice O'Connor warned about hard times ahead in the political arena, where Native citizens now find themselves:

> The First Amendment was enacted precisely to protect the rights of those whose religious practices are not shared by the majority and may be viewed with hostility. The history of our free exercise doctrine amply demonstrates the harsh impact majoritarian rule has had on unpopular or emerging religious groups.

Today, in the wake of *Smith* other religious groups are being treated like Indians by the courts. The Eighth Circuit observed that *Smith* "does not alter the rights of prisoners; it simply brings the free exercise rights of private citizens closer to those of prisoners." While some courts have expanded the *Smith* doctrine into the civil area, others reluctantly apply it with "deep" or "profound regret."

Entire segments of the population are experiencing adverse effects of the new doctrine: "Smith cut back, possibly to minute dimensions, the doctrine that requires government to accommodate, at some cost, minority religious preferences: the doctrine on which all the prison religion cases are founded."

Indian religion is the "miner's canary." Its shameful treatment signals danger to American religious life.

A Trust Responsibility

Since 1831, the United States has maintained a trust responsibility for Indian tribes that has been continuously recognized by the Supreme Court and Congress. That federal trust duty includes a duty to preserve Native communities "as distinct cultural entities." It is time for Congress to "fulfill its constitutional role as protector of tribal Native Americans" and legislate to protect religions that are crucial to the cultural survival of the tribes. Congress has ample constitutional authority for such legislation under the Indian trust doctrine.

> *"It is time for Congress to . . . legislate to protect religions that are crucial to the survival of the tribes."*

There is a need for our legal system to protect . . . the endangered religions of Native people. We can only regret the enormous loss of our nation's heritage caused by a long history of government suppression of tribal religions. It is not enough, however, for our generation to mourn that loss. Rather, our challenge is to safeguard what little remains. After 500 years since the arrival of Columbus, the time is long overdue for his descendants to come to terms with those who were here first. Such is the nature of America's "Unfinished Business" as our maturing society observes its approaching quincentennial.

Using Indian Names for Sports Teams Does Not Harm Native Americans

by Andy Rooney

About the author: *Andy Rooney is a syndicated columnist and commentator for the weekly television news show* 60 Minutes.

Is there anything wrong with a team calling itself "The Redskins"?

I never thought much about it until a group of American Indians complained about the name "Atlanta Braves" during the 1991 World Series and demonstrated against the "Washington Redskins" at the 1992 Super Bowl game.

Going into the stadium in Minneapolis for the Super Bowl, I was asked by a reporter what I thought about the demonstration.

"I think it's silly," I said. "American Indians have more important problems than to worry about sports teams calling themselves by Indian nicknames."

Ever since, I've been getting angry letters from Indians and friends of the Indians, of whom there are a great many.

No Racial Bias Against Indians

It's interesting that for all the problems they've had with white Americans, American Indians were never subjected to the same kind of racial bias that blacks were. They were never forced to sit in the back of the bus. In spite of the fact that they surrounded the wagon trains and shot flaming arrows into the stagecoach carrying the new schoolmarm, Indians were always considered to be brave, strong, stoic, resourceful, true to their word and unconquerable. Anyone with a touch of Indian blood in their ancestry is proud of it.

There have been many efforts to assimilate the Indians into our society but, for the most part, Indians don't want any part of it. To some extent it's happening whether they want it or not. People who are part white and part Indian are having more children than people who are 100 percent Indian.

The real problem is, we took the country away from the Indians, they want it back and we're not going to give it to them. We feel guilty and we'll do what we can for them within reason, but they can't have their country back. Next question.

Little Cultural Impact

While American Indians have a grand past, the impact of their culture on the world has been slight. There are no great Indian novels, no poetry. There's no memorable Indian music. Their totem poles do not rank with the statuary of Greece and there's no Indian art, except for some good craft work in wool, pottery and silver. Their genius was for living free in a wild state . . . without damaging the ozone layer.

The best thing about Indians is their fierce independence and this virtue has made life tough for them. The colonists tried to make slaves of Indians but it didn't work.

The two million American Indians alive today are reluctant to concede that it's no longer practical to maintain a lifestyle that is an anachronism. The time for the way Indians lived is gone and it's doubly sad because they refuse to accept it.

They hang onto remnants of their religion and superstitions that may have been useful to savages 500 years ago but which are meaningless in the present.

"American Indians have more important problems than to worry about sports teams calling themselves by Indian nicknames."

No one would force another religion on them but what if an Indian belief, involving ritualistic dances with strong sexual overtones, is demeaning to Indian women and degrading to Indian children?

Should they, on Indian land within the United States, be encouraged, with government money, to continue that? Should Indians be preserved on reservations like the redwoods and the American eagle, or should they join the mainstream?

Unemployment as high as 50 percent and alcoholism among Indians are more serious problems than whether a team uses an Indian name or symbol.

Illiteracy is widespread among Indians. Indians and whites blame whites for what's wrong and, historically, that may be true, but it is the Indians who are doing the drinking. The phenomenon of Indian alcohol addiction has existed since the 1600s.

If Indians are truly offended by these names and symbols we use for fun, we'll drop them, but someone should tell the Indians living on reservations that the United States isn't a bad country to be part of.

Studying Indian Remains Provides Useful Information

by Patricia M. Landau and D. Gentry Steele

About the authors: *Patricia M. Landau is a former graduate student in the department of anthropology at Texas A&M University. D. Gentry Steele is a professor of anthropology at Texas A&M University and the author of several articles on prehistoric anthropology.*

One of the most controversial kinds of studies anthropologists undertake is that of the biological remains of Native Americans. The motivations of physical anthropologists to study human remains often seem unfathomable to some members of Native American communities, and our methods seem also to be misunderstood. We recognize the differences between the values and spiritual beliefs of Native Americans and those of other Americans, and we respect the right of all people to maintain their personal belief and ethical systems. We want to explain the reasons why some physical anthropologists value the study of human biology and history, and why we place so much importance on the study of human remains. We also want to explain what kinds of information can be gained from such studies, the methods used in them, and the impact of these on the remains being studied.

The Native American Graves Protection and Repatriation Act (NAGPRA, P.L. 101-601) calls for the repatriation of Native American remains whose cultural affiliation can be determined by a preponderance of evidence. Physical anthropologists are willing to comply with NAGPRA's terms, but the need remains for long-term study of some skeletal collections before repatriation.

An Innate Need to Know

Why do physical anthropologists study the biological remains of the deceased? An innate need to know is universally characteristic of humans, even though the subjects of our inquiry may vary from culture to culture. Physical anthropologists have an interest in learning just who humans are—their origins and their heritage. Although no simple statement can explain all the reasons why some physical anthropologists study human remains, one very fundamental reason is that human remains offer direct, tangible evidence of our history, how we have become biologically suited to the many environments in which we live, and how we behave.

Other people have similar interests in origins and heritage, but the means used to answer these questions vary

> *"An innate need to know is universally characteristic of humans."*

widely. How we come to know ourselves varies from individual to individual as well as from society to society. Some societies rely on personal revelation, on the advice of spiritual leaders, or on oral traditions. Physical anthropologists, like other scientists, adhere to methods that have their roots in the ancient societies of the Mediterranean and North Atlantic. Explanations or hypotheses are proposed to explain relationships between facts or conditions of the physical world. These explanations are then tested by observation of additional measurable facts or physical conditions; if an explanation is supported by these additional observations, it can be accepted as valid or true. The results of the tests of hypotheses or explanations must be repeatable: if an explanation is tested a second or third time the results must be the same as the results of the first test, and if the explanation is tested using the same method on other material, the results of that test must also be the same or very similar. Further, observers should be interchangeable; any trained individual performing the test must get the same or very similar results. If any of these conditions are not met, the explanation is speculative at best, or must be rejected.

This method of acquiring knowledge and understanding is based on a belief system that relies on empirical data gathered from the observation of the material world. Knowledge, for those who share this belief system, is gained through the accumulation of many interrelated insights about the issue being studied.

In examining our heritage, physical anthropologists seek to understand the biological history and origins of all humans in all geographical areas. Our focus is on all humankind. While each human society has its own history, all human societies can be linked by migration and intermarriage through time to be categorized as a single species, *Homo sapiens,* humankind. Each society's biological history is an integral part of the complete and continuing story of all humankind.

Why is the information we get from skeletal remains unique, and why can't it be acquired from living peoples? There are three ways in which data is gathered about past populations: 1) by the study of the artifacts left behind, 2) by the study of the living, and 3) by the study of biological remains. Each of these ways of studying our past has advantages and disadvantages, but the study of the remains themselves has the unique advantage of providing direct information about our ancestors.

Our Ancestors' Health

Consider questions regarding the health of our ancestors. Did they suffer from the same diseases as we do? Did their particular lifeways or habits subject them to specific diseases and hardships? Were they subjected to new diseases or biological disorders when their lifestyles changed or they came into contact with new peoples migrating into their area? A study of the plant and animal debris discarded in prehistoric living areas gives some evidence of what they ate, and certainly this provides valuable indirect evidence of their health. The study of coprolites, preserved human feces, may reveal more directly what they ate. Further, this line of evidence can give unique information about some of the parasites that may have affected their health. Even the examination of artifacts, such as figurines depicting people who lived in the community, or tools such as lice scratchers or bloodletters, can provide evidence of the health of past peoples. However, each of these lines of evidence is indirect.

A clear example of a health study that documents the singular contribution of studies of human remains is the question of the origin of treponemal disease. Treponemae, a type of spirochetal organism, causes syphilis, pinta, and yaws. Although these diseases are all caused by treponemae, their distribution and mode of transmission is different. Yaws thrives in hot, humid tropical environments worldwide, while pinta is found in the tropical New World. Endemic syphilis is found in subtropical North Africa and the Near East and temperate zones of Asia. None of these conditions require sexual contact for transmission. In contrast, venereal syphilis has a worldwide distribution and is spread through sexual contact. It is unclear whether these diseases are all caused by different treponemal organisms. One hypothesis is that all treponemal organisms are descended from an early Old World organism that was not exclusively sexually transmitted; another view suggests that yaws, pinta, endemic syphilis, and venereal syphilis are caused by the same organism and that the physical expression of the disease depends on climatic and social factors like urbanization, sanitation, and population density.

Studies of living populations in which the disease is present and of historical records of the spread of the disease could not determine its origin or how it reacted when encountering new populations. In Europe, a particularly virulent epidemic seemed to spread shortly after the discovery of the Americas. In the New World, syphilis spread rapidly and tragically among Native American pop-

> *"The study of the [human] remains themselves has the unique advantage of providing direct information about our ancestors."*

ulations as they came into contact with Europeans. The examination of prehistoric skeletal remains in the New World, however, has documented the presence of the disease in the Americas before the arrival of Columbus. Ample evidence also exists for the presence of syphilis or other treponemal diseases in Europe prior to Columbus' return to the New World. Knowing this, it has become evident that the disease, probably in the form of a new and virulent strain, reinfected historic Native American populations with tragic results. The study of syphilis, with the use of prehistoric human remains as evidence, has provided humankind with one of the best documented records of the complex origin, spread, and reinfestation of a population by a contagious and deadly disease. Our understanding of our relationship to all contagious diseases has been dramatically improved by our unraveling of the history of treponemal diseases.

Study Provides Unique Data

A brief examination of the history of cranial modification in the Americas provides another example of how the study of the biological remains of past peoples furnishes unique and valuable evidence. The basic shape of the human head is roughly globular, but this shape can be modified by placing uneven pressures on the head of a growing child. This uneven pressure can be brought about unintentionally by placing a baby in the same resting position time after time, such as in a cradle board or crib. Intentional alteration of cranial shape also has been practiced on a worldwide basis. Although intentional cranial modification is usually not practiced in North America today, many early Native American groups deliberately altered skull shapes by compressing the heads of infants with bands or flat surfaces. Ninety-two percent of all individuals in a prehistoric Adena population displayed evidence of the intentional modification of cranial shape, and an early study of an Ohio population revealed that 77 percent of all crania exhibited evidence of intentional modification. By historic times, however, these societies had changed and cranial shape alteration became much less widely practiced. Without the information provided by the study of biological prehistoric remains, the widespread nature of this practice in the Mississippi valley would not be known.

A 1993 study of the biological remains of a Mimbres population in the American Southwest by D.H.Y. Holliday has added an interesting twist to the story of cranial shape modification in the Americas. Her work has

> *"The examination of prehistoric skeletal remains in the New World . . . has documented the presence of [syphilis] in the Americas before the arrival of Columbus."*

documented that, not uncommonly, infections developed in the bone at the point of contact at which pressure was applied. In some cases this infection was serious enough to endanger the life of the child by directly exposing the underlying brain to infection. Again, the analysis of human remains has provided singular evidence of common health threats in past populations.

Many aspects of prehistoric life would be unknown without the analysis of human remains, and these aspects are not restricted to health, daily activities, and other behaviors. Crow Creek Village, a large fourteenth century settlement encompassing nearly eighteen acres, was the home to at least 800 people. The analysis of skeletal remains excavated from this site reveals that a minimum of 486 men, women, and children were killed in a massive siege of the village. Roughly 90 percent of the dead showed evidence of scalping, and indications of decapitation were seen in about 25 percent of the victims. Equally important, the presence of healed and healing wounds suggestive of scalping in some individuals indicates that this form of violence was not a unique happening. The occurrence of this prehistoric massacre would not have been known without the recovery of data from human remains.

> *"Many aspects of prehistoric life would be unknown without the analysis of human remains."*

Corroboration of Historic Accounts

The study of human remains also provides useful corroboration of ethnographic accounts of historical events. The analysis of skeletal material from the King site, a Georgia site occupied between A.D. 1535–1570, may support accounts of atrocities perpetrated by the Spanish during the early years after European contact. This study indicates that King site residents enjoyed uncharacteristically good health with relatively low levels of nutritional and environmental stress. Paradoxically, an unusually high death rate was documented. More than 20 percent of the individuals who died displayed cuts and punctures on their bones. The form, angle, and position of the wounds indicated the victims were struck from above with a metal blade at least 60 cm long while facing their assailants. A significant number of these individuals were interred in common graves rather than the single interments seen in the majority of the burials at this site, a burial pattern characteristic of mass disasters in small communities. The victims were predominantly young adult females and people of both genders over 40. Ethnographic and historical data indicate that Native American groups in this time period and area customarily killed young adult males while taking females captive. Thus, if these people were victims of a conflict with another Native American group, we would expect to find mostly young adult males in the common graves and very few females. Therefore, because young adult males appear to have been selectively excluded from the conflict, it appears that these individuals do not represent victims of conflict between Native American groups. Historical and ethnographic sources record that the Hernando de Soto expedition sometimes captured older individuals and young females for slave labor and forced prostitution. The type of wounds, the demographic identities of the wounded, and ethnographic and historical data indicate that these individuals represent casualties of a Native American/Spanish conflict, most probably an attack by the Spanish on a carefully selected portion of a Native American community, perhaps as part of an attempt to capture slaves.

One of the most amazing aspects of humanity's biological heritage that has been elucidated by the study of human biological remains is cannibalism. Ethnographic and archaeological evidence supporting the rare occurrence of cannibalism in modern humans and our ancestral species of *Homo* is a matter of some debate, but direct evidence from the study of human remains clearly indicates that cannibalism, a practice recorded in many other parts of the world, occurred under rare circumstances in the American Southwest as well.

These examples illustrate that information gathered during the analysis of human remains is unique because it provides direct data that can come from no other source. Other anthropological disciplines and ethnographic data can supplement, but not replace, information gathered during the study of human remains. The information gathered from the study of human remains is valuable to physical anthropologists and other scientists because it provides unique direct data and because it allows us to answer questions about prehistoric human life in great depth from many different perspectives.

Ancestral Origins

What can we learn about our ancestral origins from the study of human remains? The colonization of the Americas is one of the largest and most recent events in the spread of humanity throughout the world, which is why it is of such enormous interest to physical anthropologists. Many lines of evidence have been presented to explain the peopling of the Americas, including the study of human biological remains. Christy G. Turner, relying on the study of teeth, has substantiated the other lines of evidence that have indicated that the ancestors of Native Americans came from northern Asia near the end of the Pleistocene. Using the evidence gathered from examination of early Native American teeth, Turner has proposed that the peopling of the Americas occurred in three migrations. The first, representing the ancestors of most Native Americans, arrived near the end of the Pleistocene, passing through an ice-free corridor in Canada, and rapidly spreading throughout North and South America. Peoples of the second migration were the Na-Dene, ancestors of the Athabascan-speaking peoples, most of whom settled along the Northwest Coast of North America. Some of these peoples, however, penetrated into the American Southwest within the last few thousand years. The final migration Turner proposes was the spread of the Eskimo-Aleut peoples, a population that came to inhabit the

> *"The study of human remains also provides useful corroboration of ethnographic accounts of historical events."*

northern fringes of North America.

While Turner's explanation for the peopling of the Americas is well-documented, there are other studies that provide modifications of his explanation. C. Loring Brace and David Philip Tracer have proposed that, instead of a single migration before that of the Athabascan-speaking peoples, there were at least two populations present in the Americas prior to the Athabascans. D. Gentry Steele and J.F. Powell have provided information that early North American populations differed in appearance from living Native Americans and northern Asians by having a relatively longer and narrower braincase and a narrower face. These studies, and those of Brace and Tracer, suggest that the earliest northern Asian peoples in the New World arrived before the broader features of living northern Asians and Native Americans had developed.

> *"Information gathered during the analysis of human remains is unique because it provides direct data that can come from no other source."*

Study Reveals Behavior

What information about the behavior of past peoples can be acquired from the study of human remains? The examination of human remains also yields information about an area that is frequently difficult or impossible to explore the mundane daily activities of peoples of the past. A proven relationship exists between the shape of an individual's body and the activities in which the individual engaged; habitual or prolonged activities often cause skeletal and dental tissues to assume unusual shapes and forms. Therefore, we often can infer some activities of past populations from irregularities in altered skeletal and dental morphology. Many indications of activity patterns are related to the consumption of particularly abrasive foods or grinding the teeth in an abnormal pattern, as evidenced by the abnormal anterior tooth loss seen in some prehistoric Sadlermiut females who softened skins with their teeth. Evidence of the use of teeth as a tool also is seen in unusual grooves related to cordage production on the anterior dentition of Native Americans at the Stone Lake site in California.

Other signature indications of daily activities found on human skeletal material include enlarged, roughened attachment sites for massive muscles and signs of stress in the related joints. An example of this is seen in the overdeveloped attachment site of the muscle in the lower arm and arthritis in the elbow joint that is related to spear throwing and slinging and pitching. Further examples of indications of daily activities are seen in the changes in articular surfaces of bones of the leg and ankle detected in people who spend a good deal of time in squatting positions. Some habitual activities may cause stress fractures like those seen in the vertebrae of individuals who carry heavy loads on the tops of their heads; other types of more generalized stress may be indicated by bone degeneration and bone spurs in the lower portion of the vertebral column associated with generalized stress and lateral bending and flexion.

Although daily activities like these might be inferred to occur in past populations, skeletal and dental markers offer direct, empirical proof of their common occurrence. These reconstructions of mundane daily behaviors of past peoples are important because they provide indications of everyday activities that were important, and in some cases necessary in the lives of our ancestors. . . .

Archeological Studies Benefit the Living

How does the study of human remains, particularly the study of Native American remains, benefit living people? The study of treponemal disease in past populations and its ancient distribution has provided valuable information on how epidemics spread among populations. Other studies of medical disorders affecting past populations have had measurable impact on modern health and treatment of disease as well.

The study of rheumatoid diseases like arthritis is such an example. Human remains offer unique opportunities for the study of rheumatoid diseases because an entire bony joint can be examined three-dimensionally, an option not available in the study of living individuals. This is important because diagnosis by visual assessment of bony changes has proven to be much more sensitive than assessment by x-ray of the impaired joint. In a recent study, rheumatoid anomalies were readily detected by visual examination in sixteen of twenty-four skeletal specimens, while the analysis of x-rays of the same material revealed abnormalities in only two of the same twenty-four individuals. It is possible to gather detailed information about changes in bony joints during the early stages of rheumatoid disorders using visual inspection that might escape detection. Therefore, the study of prehistoric and historic skeletal samples has aided in our understanding of the patterns of early development of this disorder and this knowledge in turn may be used eventually in the early diagnosis and treatment of living peoples suffering from rheumatoid arthritis.

Information gathered from the reconstruction of ancient diets, accomplished in part through the chemical analysis of human remains, is helpful in tackling modern health problems. The causes of chronic kidney failure, or end-stage renal disease in children are not fully understood, but information gathered from the study of the diets of past populations is giving new insight into its causes and, most importantly, its treatment. Data indicates that prolonged hyperfiltration, excessive filtering of liquid in the kidneys, plays an important role in the development of this condition. Hyperfiltration occurs in healthy kidneys as a response to a sudden rise in the amount of urea, a sub-

"The examination of human remains also yields information about . . . the mundane daily activities of peoples of the past."

stance produced during protein digestion, and other waste products that must be flushed from the body. Ethnographic evidence indicates hunter/gatherer populations had an intermittent, feast-or-famine dietary pattern that may have resulted in the evolution of many physiological mechanisms to accommodate fluctuations in nutrient intake. Analyses of human skeletal remains can provide corroborative evidence for feast-or-famine patterns among early peoples through the identification of indications of periodic episodes of dietary stress. Because feast-or-famine patterns were characteristic of early human groups, hyperfiltration may have developed as an appropriate response to the sudden rise of digestive waste products, especially those from protein digestion. As humans began to consume relatively less animal protein, this physiological response became less critical for survival but lingered on in our genetic makeup. The traditional medical approach to chronic kidney disease associated with hyperfiltration included an elevated protein intake. Recent studies, though, suggest that dietary protein restrictions are beneficial.

Studies of human remains also corroborate ethnographic accounts of our history. Ethnographic accounts are important evidence, especially when they offer information about the early days of European contact and colonization of North America. Ethnographic accounts do not necessarily require corroboration by other data, but they are strengthened when they are confirmed by physical evidence. As an example, physical evidence of European atrocities committed during the exploration and colonization of the New World may be provided by study of remains from sites like the King site in Georgia.

And how can knowledge of the prehistoric Crow Creek massacre or the practice of scalping be viewed as helpful to people of today? The answer can only be that our total history is who we are. The good and the violent. The noble and the ignoble. That is all of our history. Certainly, violence and scalping were not behaviors found only in the New World. They are part of human history in the Old World as well. We can only hope that by acknowledging that history can we keep it from being a part of our future.

A Goal Worth Pursuing

In this viewpoint, we have explained why we want to study the past, why we want to study human skeletal remains, and why these studies are important. Many of these views have been expressed by other physical anthropologists. We recognize that our beliefs may not be appreciated or accepted by all, but we believe our views are as valuable and supportable as are alternative, Native American views. Just as Native Americans experience a heart-felt sense of responsibility toward the skeletal remains of ancestral peoples, physical anthropologists feel an equally profound, personal sense of responsibility toward the remains of peoples of the past. Like Native Americans, we believe that ancestry is not always limited to the closest of kin; in a broad sense, all ancient peoples are the ancestors of modern peoples. We revere all ancestors by preserving their memories and by unraveling mysteries, mundane and extraordinary, about their lives. We wish to recover lost information about ancient peoples; to accomplish this, we gather tiny threads of information from whatever source we can, constantly revising our picture of the past.

Balancing these beliefs against other spiritual and emotional needs is a difficult task, but it is a goal worth pursuing, and effective communication of ideas will help us to attain it.

Prison Regulations Do Not Violate Native Americans' Free Exercise of Religion

by C. Arlen Beam and David R. Hansen

About the authors: *C. Arlen Beam and David R. Hansen are appellate judges for the Eighth Circuit Court of Appeals in St. Louis, Missouri.*

Editor's note: The following viewpoint is excerpted from a 1996 court decision from the District Court for the Western District of Missouri Court of Appeals. Mark Juan Hamilton had previously filed suit against the Missouri prison officials at Potosi Correctional Center, charging that prison policies that required him to cut his hair and denied him access to a sweat lodge violated his right to free exercise of religion. The district court ruled in his favor, but the prison officials appealed, and the appeals court reversed the lower court's decision and ruled in favor of the prison policy.

Mark Juan Hamilton, an American Indian, initiated the present action under the Civil Rights Act of 1871, [section 1983], alleging that Missouri prison officials violated his First Amendment right to free exercise of religion by requiring him to cut his hair and by denying him access to a sweat lodge. Applying the Religious Freedom Restoration Act (RFRA), the United States District Court for the Western District of Missouri enjoined prison officials from enforcing a hair length regulation and ordered them to provide a weekly sweat lodge ceremony. Prison officials appealed. Because the prison regulation and policy at issue do not violate Hamilton's right to free exercise of religion as protected by the First Amendment and RFRA, we reverse [the district court's decision].

Hamilton is incarcerated at the maximum security Potosi Correctional Center (Potosi). The facility provides cross-denominational religious facilities inside prison buildings. American Indian inmates at Potosi are allowed to pray, to gather together for regularly scheduled services, to meet with outside spiritual

Excerpted from the C. Arlen Beam and David R. Hansen's contribution to the decision in the appeal of *Mark Juan Hamilton v. Dora Schriro, Paul Delo, Jody Jackson, Bill Armontrout*, no. 94-3845, January 12, 1996, St. Louis, Missouri.

leaders, and to obtain religious reading material from the library. American Indians are also allowed to carry medicine bags containing ceremonial items and have access to a ceremonial pipe and kinnikinnik (a ceremonial "tobacco" consisting of willow, sweet grass, sage and cedar). Potosi does not allow a sweat lodge, sweat lodge ceremony, or fires on the premises. Potosi officials enforce a Missouri Department of Corrections regulation that prohibits hair length beyond the collar for male inmates. Hamilton asserts that prison officials violated his First Amendment right to free exercise of religion by denying him and other American Indian prisoners access to a sweat lodge and by requiring their compliance with the hair length regulation. . . .

Hair Length

Hamilton testified that American Indian males believe that their hair is a gift from the Creator and is to be cut only when someone close to them dies. Hamilton and other American Indian inmates had long hair but were forced to cut it at the Potosi prison. Hamilton testified that at one time his hair was four feet long.

Prison officials testified that long hair poses a threat to prison safety and security. Stephen Long, the Assistant Director of Adult Institutions for the Missouri Department of Corrections, testified that inmates could conceal contraband, including dangerous materials, in their long hair. Long stated that without the hair length regulation, prison staff would be required to perform more frequent searches of inmates, which could cause conflicts between staff and in-

> *"The prison officials' denial of . . . access to a sweat lodge was rationally related to the legitimate penological interests of safety and security."*

mates. Searching an inmate's long hair would be difficult, especially if the inmate's long hair were braided. Long also testified that the prison had tried to control gangs by not allowing them to identify themselves through colors, clothes, or hair carvings. He testified that exempting American Indians from the hair length regulation could cause resentment by the other inmates. He concluded that there was no alternative to the hair length policy because only short hair can easily be searched and remain free of contraband. Finally, Long noted that long hair could also cause problems with inmate identification.

The Sweat Lodge

The sweat lodge ceremony primarily takes place inside a dome-shaped structure constructed of bent willow poles and covered with hides, blankets, or tarps. Rocks heated in a separate fire are placed in the center of the lodge. During the ceremony, several tools are used including an axe (to split the firewood), a shovel (to transfer the hot rocks from the fire to the sweat lodge) and deer antlers. Participants, who are nude, pour water on the hot rocks to create steam, which causes them to sweat. Throughout the ceremony, the lodge remains covered to retain the steam and to keep out the light. The ceremony lasts between one and three hours. When the lodge is not in use, the covers are removed but the willow poles remain intact.

Hamilton testified that the sweat lodge ceremony is instrumental to the practice of his religion because it purifies the participant. Purity, according to Hamilton, is a prerequisite to participating in other religious ceremonies, such as offering prayers and smoking the sacred pipe. Hamilton also testified that participants in these ceremonies must be seated outdoors on the ground. Hamilton stated that if he could not have access to a sweat lodge ceremony, he would not and could not practice any aspect of his religion.

> *"Alternative means remain open to [a prisoner] for exercising his religion."*

Hamilton introduced deposition testimony from prison administrators in a few other states that their respective facilities conduct sweat lodge ceremonies without any major problems. These prison administrators conceded that they were aware of some problems, including rumors of sexual impropriety during the sweat lodge ceremony. No prisoner had filed a formal complaint and the prison guards were unable to observe what actually occurred inside the lodge.

Concerns About Safety and Security

The Potosi prison officials testified that the sweat lodge requested by Hamilton raised concerns of prison safety and security. Specifically, Long testified that the implements requested by Hamilton to conduct the sweat lodge ceremony, such as a shovel and an axe, could be used to assault other inmates and prison guards. Long further testified that problems arise when inmates in a maximum security prison, who are typically prone to violence, congregate in groups.

Alan Luebbers, the Associate Superintendent at Potosi, testified that inmates who work with tools are supervised by prison guards. The secluded nature of the sweat lodge would make such supervision impossible, thus providing the inmates with an opportunity to assault other inmates, make weapons, use drugs, dig a tunnel, and engage in homosexual activity. Normally, a prison guard is posted at religious functions to observe the inmates and ensure their safety.

Gary Tune, the Chaplain at the Potosi Correctional Center, testified that if a sweat lodge were built it would be the only facility devoted to a single religion. Assistant Director Long also expressed concern over allowing Hamilton, an inmate, to decide who may or may not use the sweat lodge. He concluded that providing a sweat lodge may cause resentment among the inmates.

Jodie Jackson, the Chaplaincy Coordinator for the Missouri Department of Corrections, testified that some American Indian inmates at other Missouri state prisons practiced their religion outdoors on the ground without the benefit of a sweat lodge. Those prisoners offered prayers, observed special seasons, and smoked the ceremonial pipe. Jackson testified that Hamilton had not requested permission to practice his religion outdoors in a manner similar to that at other institutions. Jackson stated, however, that the Missouri Department of Corrections would consider such a request if it were made.

The District Court Ruling

The district court found "that the regulations and policies at issue in this lawsuit with regard to plaintiff's practice of his . . . religion substantially [burden] plaintiff's exercise of his religion." The district court held that "[a]lthough safety, security and cost concerns may be shown to be compelling governmental interests in the prison setting, defendants have not shown that the regulations and practices used by the Missouri Department of Corrections are the least restrictive means of furthering that interest." The district court enjoined enforcement of the hair length regulation and ordered the prison officials to allow Hamilton to practice his religion, including a weekly sweat lodge ceremony. In a subsequent order, the district court awarded attorney fees to Hamilton. The district court also stated "that for 6 months after the sweat lodge becomes operational and the ceremony is implemented, participation in the sweat lodge ceremony shall be limited to those who are sincere adherents of the Native American religion or to those who have been approved for participation by majority vote of Native Americans who practice the Native American religion and are scheduled to participate in the ceremony."

> *"Enforcing prison hair length regulations . . . and prohibiting sweat lodge ceremonies do not violate an inmate's constitutional right to free exercise of religion."*

On appeal, the prison officials contend that: (1) Hamilton is not sincere in his adherence to the American Indian religion; (2) the prison regulations and policies do not substantially burden Hamilton's free exercise of his religious beliefs; and (3) the limitations imposed on hair length and sweat lodges are the least restrictive means of furthering the compelling interest of maintaining prison safety and security. The prison officials also assert that under any circumstances, the condition imposed by the district court on who may participate in the sweat lodge ceremony is unprecedented and unreasonable. . . .

Constitutional Analysis

According to the U.S. Supreme Court, prison inmates "do not forfeit all constitutional protections by reason of their conviction and confinement in prison." Moreover, the Court ruled in *Turner v. Safley* (1987) that "federal courts must take cognizance of the valid constitutional claims of prison inmates," which include actions based on free exercise rights protected by the First Amendment.

However, in other cases the Supreme Court determined that "[l]awful incarceration brings about the necessary withdrawal or limitation of many privileges and rights, a retraction justified by the considerations underlying our penal system." The Court continued, "The fact of confinement and the needs of the penal institution impose limitations on constitutional rights, including those derived from the First Amendment, which are implicit in incarceration." Furthermore, the Court found, "issues of prison management are, both by reason of separation of powers and highly practical considerations of judicial competence, peculiarly ill-suited to judicial resolution, and . . . accordingly, courts should be loath to substitute their judgment for that of prison officials and administrators."

An inmate who challenges the constitutionality of a prison regulation or policy that limits the practice of religion must first establish that it infringes upon a sincerely held religious belief. In the present case, we assume that Hamilton's religious beliefs are sincerely held.

According to the Supreme Court in *O'Lone v. Estate of Shabazz* (1987), a prisoner's free exercise claim is "judged under a 'reasonableness' test less restrictive than that ordinarily applied to alleged infringements of fundamental constitutional rights." In *Turner*, the Supreme Court articulated the applicable constitutional test in the context of prison regulations: "when a prison regulation impinges on inmates' constitutional rights, the regulation is valid if it is reasonably related to legitimate penological interests." Prison security is one of these penological interests. Several factors are to be considered when evaluating the reasonableness of a prison regulation: (1) whether there is a valid, rational connection between the regulation and the asserted governmental interest; (2) whether alternative means for exercising the right remain open to the prisoner; (3) the impact of the regulation on prison staff, other inmates, and the allocation of prison resources; and (4) the availability of ready alternatives to the regulation.

No Violations of Rights

We have previously [in *Iron Eyes v. Henry* (1990)] applied the *Turner* factors to an American Indian prisoner's claim that hair length regulations violated his constitutionally guaranteed right to free exercise of religion and concluded that such a regulation passes constitutional muster. Our prior decisions make it abundantly clear that Hamilton's constitutional challenge to the prison hair length regulation must fail. Therefore, we conclude that under the *Turner* criteria, Hamilton's free exercise right is outweighed by the validity of the regulation.

As with prison hair length regulations, we have previously resolved [in *Kemp v. Moore* (1991)] the issue of whether a prison official's denial of access to a sweat lodge violates an American Indian inmate's free exercise right under the First Amendment. In a 1994 case, however, we acknowledged that such a determination "depends upon whether the restriction imposed by prison authorities bears a rational relationship to the furtherance of a legitimate penological interest" (*Thomas v. Gunter*, [1994], in which we concluded that the district court improperly granted summary judgment for prison authorities because their justification for denying the inmate sweat lodge access was based on "security-related limitations," which did not provide a sufficiently specific basis to determine if some rational relationship existed between the denial of access and security). Applying the *Turner* factors to the present case, we conclude that the prison officials' denial of Hamilton's access to a sweat lodge was rationally related to the legitimate penological interests of safety and security at Potosi.

First, prohibiting Hamilton and other inmates from meeting in a completely enclosed area is rationally connected to preventing the type of harm prison officials fear would occur in the sweat lodge. Second, alternative means remain open to Hamilton for exercising his religion, including carrying a medicine bag containing ceremonial items, having access to a ceremonial pipe and kinnikinnik, and praying with other American Indian inmates. Third, accommodating Hamilton's request for a sweat lodge would have an adverse impact on prison staff, other inmates, and prison resources due to the risk of assaulting participants in the ceremony, as well as possible resentment resulting from the erection of an exclusive religious facility. Finally, Hamilton has failed to meet the requirement stated by the Supreme Court in *Turner* to "point to an alternative that fully accommodates the prisoner's rights at de minimis cost to valid penological interests."

Therefore, we hold that the constitutional claim underlying Hamilton's section 1983 action fails. Our prior decisions make it clear that enforcing prison hair length regulations, such as the one at issue in the present case, and prohibiting sweat lodge ceremonies do not violate an inmate's constitutional right to free exercise of religion. Additionally, the applicable constitutional analysis articulated by the Supreme Court in *Turner* supports our conclusion that the prison officials' failure to provide Hamilton with a sweat lodge does not violate his right to free exercise of religion.

The Public Does Not Threaten Native American Religious Activities on Public Lands

by Andy Petefish, Friends of Devils Tower, Devils Tower, Wyoming

About the author: *Andy Petefish is a climber and professional guide who lives at Devils Tower, Wyoming. Friends of Devils Tower is an organization that is opposed to the National Park Service denying otherwise normal and legal access in order to establish a religion on public land at Devils Tower National Monument.*

Access to Devils Tower can never be denied for religious reasons as ruled by a federal judge in June 1996. The coercive "voluntary" June access closure at Devils Tower National Monument to tax-paying Americans out of respect for land-based religious practitioners clearly violates the First Amendment to the Bill of Rights of the U.S. Constitution[1] and Devils Tower National Monument's own management policies.[2]

The National Park Service's closure to, or restriction of, otherwise normal and legally legitimate activities on public land out of respect for any land-based religion, or land-based religious practitioners, forces non-believing American citizens, by act, to adopt the religion for which the restrictions or closures are being implemented. This federal action, by Devils Tower National Monument, on public land blatantly violates the highest law in the land and thus your constitutional freedoms!

The Right to Choose

Friends of Devils Tower is not trying to force anyone to climb or access Devils Tower. Our goal is to protect the individual's right to choose one's religion, without coercion by the National Park Service as given by the First Amend-

From Andy Petefish, Friends of Devils Tower, "Access Fund 'Sell Out' of Rock Climbing at Devils Tower," April 22, 1997 (www.csn.net/freedom/firstamend.html). Reprinted with permission.

ment. We defend our inalienable right to access Devils Tower in June, or any other time, freely, and without fear that our choice to access the Tower now will lead to a mandatory, lengthened, or total access closure (as threatened by the NPS and supported by the Access Fund) at any time in the future because such access is offensive to a particular religious group.

Rock climbing has always been a voluntary activity at Devils Tower. It has never been mandatory for anyone to climb on or access the Tower. No one, or group, is advocating that land-based religious practitioners

> *"Rock climbing, hiking, or just being, are legally legitimate activities . . . and in no way* **prohibit** *the free exercise of any religion."*

must climb on or access the Tower against their faith or belief that such an act is sacrilegious or a desecration. No climber, or climbing group, is advocating that land-based religious practitioners pack up their belongings and hit the road or be denied access to the Tower. Even the notion of such an arrogant and selfish act on public land is beyond reproach for climbers and the rest of the general tax-paying public visiting Devils Tower. But yet, land-based religious practitioners are demanding that rock climbers put their rock shoes, rack, and ropes in their packs and hit the road not only for the month of June but all the time. Furthermore, land-based religious practitioners are advocating that nonclimbing visitors to Devils Tower do the same. . . .

Closure Is Unacceptable

Rock climbing, hiking, or just being, are legally legitimate activities allowed on public lands at Devils Tower National Monument and in no way *prohibit* the free exercise of any religion.

Any illegal closure implemented by the federal government, for even one minute, let alone one month, is unacceptable, and if allowed will only lead to longer closures and eventually the inevitable prohibition of all access, all the time, at Devils Tower and on many other public lands.

Land-based religious practitioners have *never* wanted climbers or anyone else but themselves on the public land at Devils Tower. So how can all the closure sympathizers and observers be so insensitive and hypocritical toward the true wants and desires of land-based religious practitioners by thinking that by not climbing only in June they are truly respecting them and their religious practices?

The truth, and bottom line, is that land-based religious practitioners don't want climbing or any other human activity, but theirs, at Devils Tower at any time. They are not happy with the token one-month temporary closure to humans, and they have made it clear that their ultimate goal is the complete prohibition of all human activity, but theirs, at Devils Tower and on many other public lands.

The True Goal

Small insight into the true goals and manipulations of land-based religious practitioners being used by environmentalists and the NPS to drive tax-paying Americans from national parks and other public lands can be found here in several quotes. The first is from Francis Brown, president for the Medicine Wheel Coalition for Sacred Sites of North America, who wants to prohibit all public access, [except] that of land-based religious practitioners, to Devils Tower and countless other sites in North America:

"Our plan is to shut the climbing down, slowly if that is what it takes."

L.A. Times

"The goal of this meeting should be no climbing for one month on the tower when ceremonies could take place. The ultimate goal should be no climbing at all on the tower."

Land-based religious practitioner, 3/29–30, 1996;
Rapid City, SD (NPS Consultation Meeting)

"Native Americans will never give up the fight for the Black Hills."

Land-based religious practitioner, 3/29–30, 1996;
Rapid City, SD (NPS Consultation Meeting)

"Human Beings climb the tower and interfere with its natural state."

Land based religious practitioner, 3/29–30, 1996;
Rapid City, SD (NPS Consultation Meeting)

"The stake ladder to Native Americans is intrusive to the sacred site. Doesn't the ladder designation contradict the fact that American Indians want to stop climbing on the tower?"

Land-based religious practitioner, 3/29–30, 1996;
Rapid City, SD (NPS Consultation Meeting)

"Native Americans today could be in Washington with a bill asking for no climbing at the tower."

Land-based religious practitioner, 3/29–30, 1996;
Rapid City, SD (NPS Consultation Meeting)

These quotes reveal the true intent of land-based religious practitioners being used by the NPS and environmentalists to stop access at Devils Tower not only for one month, but all the time! Once they get their "foot in the door" they know there will be no stopping them from closing access altogether, not only at Devils Tower, but on countless other public lands.

The mere presence of humans on public land, whether they are climbing, hiking, bird watching, or just being, in no way prohibits the free exercise of land-based religion by anyone. Ask yourself, in what way do the actions, or mere presence, of climbers and other visitors at Devils Tower *prohibit* the free exercise of land-based religious practitioners? They don't. In fact, in 1993 the National Park Service's own lawyers officially stated that accessing the tower does not prohibit the free exercise[1] of land-based religious practitioners.

Land-based religious practitioners being used by, or in partnership with, environmentalists have long sought to gain some exception to the First Amendment knowing full well the "de facto" land ownership benefits they would derive, without tax burden, to control use of public lands if it were granted. Fortunately, the courts and Congress have recognized their manipulative tactics and have upheld the First Amendment without change.

An exception to the First Amendment for land-based religious practitioners would only lead to the eventual loss of their own religious freedom. The First Amendment works only because it applies to all Americans and to all Americans alike regardless of ethnic background or cultural origin.

1. "Congress shall make no law respecting an establishment of religion, or prohibiting the free exercise thereof; or abridging the freedom of speech, or of the press; or of the right of the people peaceably to assemble, and to petition the government for a redress of grievances." *First Amendment.*

2. "Performance of a traditional ceremony or the conduct of a religious activity at a particular place shall not form the basis for prohibiting others from using such areas." *Native American Relationships Management Policy, Final Management Policy, National Park Service.*

Chapter 2

Is Indian Gaming Beneficial to Native Americans?

Indian Gaming:
An Overview

by Anthony Layng

About the author: *Anthony Layng is a professor of anthropology at Elmira College in New York.*

The number of Indian-owned casinos has grown rapidly in recent years and is likely to expand a great deal more in the near future. To understand why so many Native Americans have opted to go into the gaming business and anticipate where this pursuit is likely to lead them, one must view this development as the latest chapter of a long history of economic competition. Indians have competed with non-Indians ever since Europeans began to settle in America, but never before have they had such a conspicuous advantage.

Presently, there are more than 170 high-stakes bingo halls and casinos operating on Indian-owned land in 19 states. Many others are in the planning stage, and more are being promoted. These gaming establishments gross about $6 billion a year, between four and five percent of national gambling industry profits. While Native Americans comprise less than one percent of the American population, because of the peculiar legal status of reservations, they have a competitive edge when it comes to gaming. It is not clear just how long this advantage will last, but the number of reservations deciding to join the casino business is on the rise.

Many on reservations only recently have begun to experience real economic security as gambling casinos and favorable court cases have resulted in windfall profits and expanded employment. Increasingly, Indians no longer see themselves as demoralized victims, but a people who are capable of thriving in spite of discrimination. This newfound confidence is reflected in the popular use of the term "Indian Country," often utilized with evident pride when referring to contemporary life on the reservations.

Indians and even non-Indians now believe that a Native American identity is enviable. In the past, many Native Americans disclaimed their heritage in order to avoid discrimination, but, during the last two decades, there has been a dramatic reversal of such denial. There remains a great deal of concern about all the long-standing social problems that reservations face—alcoholism, poverty, political infighting, etc.—but a spirit of optimism about the future has emerged in Indian Country. . . .

Competing Interests

Most reservations continue to rely heavily on Federal funds for their subsistence and social services. As the Clinton Administration and the Republican-dominated Congress speak of the need for "welfare reform," often a euphemism for cutting aid to the poor, Appalachian whites and inner-city blacks further are inclined to resent the special entitlements that Native Americans receive. Even those tribes which have grown wealthy on casino profits receive hundreds of thousands of dollars of Federal funds.

> *"[Indian] gaming establishments gross about $6 billion a year, between four and five percent of national gambling industry profits."*

Store owners near reservations object to the fact that Indian entrepreneurs are selling gasoline and cigarettes tax free, and state governments are seeking ways to collect revenues on such sales. According to the New York Attorney General, "It's costing the state $100 million a year. Reservation sales [of gasoline and cigarettes] are 30 times over the estimated demands of the reservation populations." In the Northwest, sports hunters and fishers greatly resent restrictions on their recreation that, because of treaty stipulations, do not apply to Indians. Meanwhile, the rapidly growing Indian gaming industry has created an unprecedented potential for wide-scale competition between whites and Indians.

The Indian Gaming Regulatory Act

The rise of Indian-owned casinos is an outgrowth of legislation enacted by Congress in the form of the Indian Gaming Regulatory Act of 1988. This permits Indians to operate casinos if state laws allow any form of gambling. Some states—including Florida, Ohio, Pennsylvania, South Carolina, Virginia, and West Virginia—are responding to the spread and success of these casinos by proposing to legalize white-owned gaming; others are hoping for passage of Federal legislation to remove Native Americans' special rights to own and operate casinos in states where non-Indians lack such rights.

In most of the 35 states that have public lotteries, there is growing awareness that Indian-owned and -controlled casinos effectively can compete with the state for money citizens are willing to gamble away. Accordingly, the National Governors Association strongly favors restricting Indian gambling establishments, claiming that the 1988 Federal gaming law infringes on states' rights, forcing them to grant Native Americans exclusivity in operating casinos. New

Jersey and Nevada, having the largest concentrations of privately owned casinos (in Atlantic City and Las Vegas), are urging the Federal government to establish and impose stricter guidelines for licensing and monitoring Indian gaming. Recently, in states such as Louisiana and Mississippi, private casinos have begun to proliferate.

White owners understand the potential for competition from Indian-owned casinos. When a group of Indians in New Jersey petitioned for Federal status as a tribe, intent on building a casino, the Atlantic City gambling establishment was up in arms. In an attempt to persuade authorities to restrict the Indian gaming industry, real estate mogul Donald Trump, who has a considerable ownership stake in Atlantic City gambling establishments, maintained to the House Subcommittee on Native American Affairs that organized crime is rampant wherever Indian casinos operate.

Many Indian communities that have casinos are enjoying the economic benefits. As a result of gaming revenue, some reservations rapidly are upgrading schools, libraries, tribal industries, and social services. Ada Deer, Assistant Secretary for Indian Affairs in the Interior Department, in contrasting Native American gaming to Atlantic City casinos (including the three owned by Donald Trump), points out that "Indian tribes operate gaming enterprises for public or governmental finance, not for private business profits."

Some reservations enthusiastically are committed to cashing in on this window of opportunity. For instance, the Coushatta Tribe of Louisiana, owners of the 24-hour-a-day Grand Casino Coushatta, plans to build a resort, including a hotel, dinner theater, indoor and outdoor "family fun center," and campground for recreational vehicles.

A Dramatic Success Story

The most dramatic story comes from Connecticut, where the tiny Mashantucket Pequot tribe operates the most profitable casino in the country. In addition to Foxwoods Casino, they are erecting a $100 million museum and cultural resource center. The center is part of a planned resort including present hotels, a Chinese theme park, powwow stadium, and other attractions to be added, all connected by a monorail system.

The New York City architectural firm that designed the National Museum of the American Indian in Washington, D.C., did so for the Pequot museum as well. Among the attractions are a re-created Pequot

"Indian-owned and -controlled casinos effectively can compete with the state for money citizens are willing to gamble away."

village, simulated glacier, Pequot fort, library, media center (housing a Native American cable television network), restaurant, visitors center, archaeology laboratory, public education department, and film theater. The Chinese theme park, to guarantee its authenticity, is being designed by architects in China with plans for a replica of the Great Wall of China, hand-carved marble bridges, and original Chinese art. As if this master plan were not sufficiently ambitious, under consideration is a European theme park.

The original Foxwoods Casino, opened in February, 1992, cost $60 million, provided by Malaysian investors. An expanded casino, accommodating 3,000 slot machines (Connecticut gets 25% of the slot machine profits, about $130 million a year), and hotel ran $240 million. Foxwoods may be the Western Hemisphere's largest casino (floor space is 20,000 feet more than that of the Atlantic City Taj Mahal). Bus service from New York, Boston, Hartford, New Haven, Bridgeport, and New York's Westchester County brings in thousands of customers daily. In addition to gambling and hotel accommodations, there are an 18-store shopping concourse, 1,500-seat meeting hall, swimming pool, health club, and theater complex which has featured stars such as Tony Bennett and Frank Sinatra. The payroll now includes more than 9,000 employees.

> *"Since the [BIA] budget . . . has been reduced . . . , reservations are likely to experience increasing dependence on gaming as a source of financial security."*

All this enterprise had modest beginnings. The Mashantucket Pequot, nearly exterminated in 1637, included only 55 members by 1974. In 1983, they settled a historic land claim and finally gained Federally recognized tribal status. They now have expanded their land from 214 acres to more than 2,000 and have plans to acquire additional property. Yet, they still have only about 320 enrolled members.

A tribe need not be wealthy or large in order to get started in the gaming business. All that is required, in addition to location in a state that allows some form of gambling, is effective leadership and sound council, both of which increasingly are available. So, even in unlikely places like western Iowa, where the Omaha and Winnebago Indians are operating casinos, tribes may generate as much as $1 million a month.

Many tribal representatives interested in exploring the gaming option have consulted with Richard "Skip" Hayward, who has served as the Mashantucket Pequot tribal chairman since 1974. The Menominee Indians of northeastern Wisconsin, since expanding a bingo hall into a casino in 1989, have built a tribal college that includes a program to train any Native Americans who want to manage casinos. Leaders from reservations with casinos occasionally convene to share information and plan collective strategies to protect their common interests. Gaming corporations and other experienced firms readily are available to tribal leaders as consultants and managers. The National Indian Gaming Commission, an independent Federally created agency charged with general regulatory oversight of Native American gaming, screens contractual arrangements between tribes and such corporations.

Nevertheless, most reservations do not have casinos. Of the 550 Federally recognized tribes, less than 20% have sought and received clearance to participate in the casino industry. Some Indian nations such as those of the Shakopee Mdewakanton in Minnesota and the Fort McDowell Apache in Arizona have successful casinos because of their relatively favorable locations, but most reservations are in remote areas, far removed from population concentrations.

Opposition to Tribal Casinos

The construction of some casinos has been resisted militantly by those reservation residents who believe such enterprises are not in the best interests of the traditional culture. Others insist that a gaming contract with the state, granting some jurisdiction over reservation affairs, compromises tribal sovereignty. When the residents of the Navajo reservation, the nation's largest, were asked to vote on gaming, they turned it down. However, their even more traditional Hopi neighbors seriously are considering a casino venture. [The Hopis also voted down a tribal casino.] Opposing sentiments on some reservations have been encouraged by the fact that not all tribal casinos have been successful. Some have generated a great deal of money that has ended up mostly in the hands of outside managers.

In spite of Native American opposition and numerous charges of corruption and crime associated with Indian gaming, the number of tribal-owned casinos continues to grow. The opening of the New York Oneida Indian Nation's $10 million Turning Stone Casino in July, 1993 (fully paid for after just five months), and the construction in 1994 of another casino in northern New York by the Saint Regis Mohawk tribe, where there had been violent opposition, shows that the promise of large profits can overshadow the doubts and hostility from those who philosophically resist casinos.

The Coeur d'Alene Indians in Idaho are planning to create a national lottery that would compete not only with the 36 state lotteries now in operation and the Powerball lottery in 17 states, but also with casinos in other states. Attracted to an initial jackpot of $50 million, customers will be able to participate without leaving home, using an 800 number and a credit card. The Oneidas, who live near Syracuse, N.Y., are attempting to locate another casino at the Monticello Raceway, closer to New York City than Atlantic City is.

In spite of all the present gaming enthusiasm in Indian Country, many tribal leaders realize that Native Americans one day will lose their exclusive advantage, since pending legislation may terminate their peculiar monopoly to operate casinos. There seems little doubt that, as in the case of the rapid spread of state lotteries a few years ago, in some states where tribal gaming is flourishing, non-Indian casinos eventually will proliferate. (As recently as 1990, only Nevada and New Jersey had legal casinos; in 1996, casinos are legal in 25 states.)

Since the budget of the Bureau of Indian Affairs has been reduced and additional cuts in Federally funded programs for Native Americans are all but certain in the next few years, reservations are likely to experience increasing dependence on gaming as a source of financial security. Yet, with rising competition from non-Indian sources, most reservation casinos are likely to decline rapidly.

Early in the twentieth century, some western reservations became wealthy from oil revenues. Remember those old pictures of Indians wearing top hats and sitting in their brand new cars? Once their oil wells ran dry, they soon returned to poverty. Because all this money from oil companies simply was distributed to members of the tribe, it quickly dissipated. Those reservations that are economically dependent primarily on gaming, who do not use their casino profits wisely to develop economic alternatives, could return to being primarily dependent on Washington again, only to discover that the Federal government no longer is able or willing to meet their needs.

Indian Gaming Revenues Provide Many Needed Services

by Dennis McAuliffe Jr.

About the author: *Dennis McAuliffe Jr. is a staff writer for the* Washington Post.

It is 8:30 on a Monday morning at a casino that never closes. Snow is burying the dozen cars parked outside the Turning Stone Casino on the Oneida Indian reservation. Inside, the give-and-take of chips and cards blurs the green-felt surfaces of a half-dozen blackjack tables. A roulette wheel revolves in slow motion for a lone hopeful. A man with a cigar and a woman with a cigarette sit at smoky screens of video gambling games, including one called Indian Gold. A man is snoring in a corner of the casino coffee shop. Whatever he is sleeping off, it is not a night of drinking. The Oneida Indians, out of distaste for liquor, run the only casino in the country that is alcohol-free.

Turning Stone's 15 patrons this morning, and the 7,000 people who visit the central New York casino each day, and the millions who each year visit the 220 Indian gambling businesses now operating around the country, are more than mere gamblers.

A Winning Hand

They are the pioneers of a new era in U.S.-Indian history, creating more than $4 billion in new income annually for Indians and transforming the relationship between government and tribes. Gambling has given many tribes something that a century of federal policy has failed to deliver: a winning hand in creating economic development. Revenue from casinos and high-stakes bingo halls has seeded other tribal ventures, from buffalo-motif T-shirts to T-bones of buffalo meat. According to Indian tribal leaders, gambling's success is building something else on reservations that money alone cannot buy: rising pride and can-doism.

How history will judge gambling's new deal for Indians, however, is still a roll of the dice. As in the nineteenth century, battle lines have been drawn around Indian land. The "new buffalo," as Indian gambling is often disparagingly called, has attracted a new generation of Buffalo Bills, and they have opened fire from state capitals to Capitol Hill. Indians themselves are united over gambling only in their blanket opposition to non-Indian criticism of the issue. The nation's 557 federally recognized tribes have split between casino haves and have-nots, and the growing wealth of the former group, still a minority, has made the poverty of the larger, latter group appear more acute.

> *"Gambling's success is building something else on reservations that money alone cannot buy: rising pride and can-doism."*

Gamblers are the crutches with which many tribes are lifting themselves out of dependence on the federal government, and out of more than a century of poverty. And for the government, gambling—fraught as it is with questions of immorality and fears of illegality—may become a way to forgo new Indian program spending, or cut it back.

Congress has allowed tribes to venture into gambling only if they spend their profits—gamblers' losses—on the social, welfare and economic-assistance programs historically regarded as Washington's responsibility to Indians under treaties and the ensuing federal trust relationship with the tribes. Only after covering these needs can Indian leaders pay out gambling profits to tribal members, and only 23 tribes now do so.

The social spending is strictly specified by Congress: Gambling dollars feed, house and nurse elderly Indians; provide health care for Indian infants, day care for Indian toddlers and after-school activities for Indian children; send Indian teenagers to college; build clinics, and counseling and cultural centers; repair roads; and erect modern, often modular, houses to replace the mobile homes that Washington sent to tribes.

High-Stakes Bingo

It was, in fact, the fate of two of these aging government-issue trailers on the Oneida reservation that sparked the Indian gambling phenomenon.

The way Oneidas tell the story, Indian gambling rose from the ashes of a trailer fire in 1975.

The reservation had no fire company of its own and two Oneidas died in the two-trailer blaze, says Oneida Nation Representative Ray Halbritter, 45, the tribe's Harvard-educated leader and nephew of both victims.

To prevent such tragedies in the future, Halbritter says, the Oneidas decided "to raise money for our own fire department"—and to do it the way "all the fire departments" raise money.

Bingo.

Played in a double-wide trailer, the Oneidas' game offered prize money exceeding New York limits. State bingo regulations did not apply to them, the Oneidas insisted, because they are an Indian nation; their recognized right of sovereignty entitled them to run their own game, and to offer a pot enticing enough to draw non-Indians—and their money—to a place they otherwise might never visit.

"The Seminoles got wind of it" and started their own high-stakes bingo game in Hollywood, Florida, Halbritter says. The Madison County, New York, district attorney promptly shut down the Oneidas' operation. Local authorities also tried to put the Seminoles' game out of business, but the Seminoles took them to court and won. *Seminole Tribe v. Butterworth,* a landmark 1981 case, was the first of several tribal victories over state governments.

The legal skirmishing culminated in a sweeping 1987 U.S. Supreme Court decision that effectively legalized casino gambling on reservations and sent state governments reeling.

> *"Gamblers are the crutches with which many tribes are lifting themselves out of dependence on the federal government, and out of more than a century of poverty."*

The court ruled that a state could not ban Indian gambling unless it banned all forms of gambling for all its citizens. Moreover, the court reaffirmed tribes' right of limited sovereignty, which it first recognized in 1832. Federal and state governments, the court said, have no regulatory jurisdiction on Indian reservations, and therefore they cannot tax a tribe's profits or wealth.

The negative reaction from states pursuing their own gambling enterprises, notably Nevada, put pressure on Congress and led to the 1988 Indian Gaming Regulatory Act.

The new law gave the states a substantial role in deciding how and where tribes could run gambling operations. Before Indians could offer casino-style games that involve betting against the house, the tribe had to secure the state's permission in the form of a negotiated agreement, or compact.

Some states have resisted tribal efforts to negotiate compacts, resulting in a dozen more court cases. Other states have insisted on a share of tribes' casino profits, in lieu of lost tax revenue. The Mashantucket Pequots, by far the most successful casino tribe in the country, give the state of Connecticut a 25-percent cut of their slot-machine revenue—a large portion of the casino's estimated $1 million a day in profits.

Gambling Revenues

Since the act, about 200 tribes have set up 220 gambling operations, including about 126 casinos in 24 states. The Oneidas opened Turning Stone Casino in 1993.

"It all came full circle back to the Oneidas," Halbritter says.

In 1975, on their bingo game's first weekend in business, the Oneidas counted a profit of $150; in 1994, gambling tribes raked in an estimated $4.2 billion— about 10 percent of the U.S. gambling industry.

These profits have underwritten an explosion of entrepreneurial enterprises, according to the National Indian Business Association in Albuquerque, which lists more than 24,000 Indian-owned and -operated businesses in more than 100 categories.

According to Indian leaders, gambling revenue effectively allows the federal government to save money on Indian programs. Rick Hill, an Oneida Indian from Wisconsin who chairs the National Indian Gaming Association, told Congress, "Indian gaming serves to reduce the federal deficit by lowering welfare dependence and by assisting with many unfunded and underfunded federal obligations."

> *"[Gambling] profits have underwritten an explosion of entrepreneurial enterprises."*

In enacting the Indian Gaming Regulatory Act, Congress did not intend to substitute gambling for government as the treasury of tribes. According to an inspector general's report, the law's spending requirements stemmed from Congress's desire to head off Mafia meddling and to ensure that tribes and their members would receive direct benefits from the gambling operations. The act stipulates that tribes must receive at least 60 percent of the profits from their casinos, nearly all of which are managed by non-Indian commercial companies, including big casino operators such as Harrah's.

Budget Cuts

Nonetheless, congressional appropriators took note of the new-found wealth of many tribes in defending proposed cuts in the budget for the Bureau of Indian Affairs (BIA). Republican Senator Slade Gorton of Washington, chairman of the Appropriations Committee's subcommittee on the Interior, wrote in a *Washington Post* op-ed article in September 1995: "Indians are not wholly dependent on federal government for their income. Many tribes run revenue-generating activities such as gambling operations."

Noting that the current Interior appropriations bill requires the BIA to report to Congress on the gambling revenue of all tribes, George T. Skibine, director of BIA's Indian Gaming Management office and an Osage Indian of Oklahoma, says: "Clearly the purpose of that report is . . . for Congress to start gauging whether they should take into consideration gaming revenues in making their appropriations."

Not all tribes have anted up to gamble, however. Many are hamstrung by isolated locations. Others have chosen to avoid the lengthy legal fights with state authorities that often accompany the start-up of new gambling operations.

Some tribes, such as the Navajos of Arizona and New Mexico who occupy the largest reservation in the United States, and their neighbors, the Hopis, have rejected gambling for moral reasons.

Halbritter, while saying that the Oneidas traditionally gambled as part of some tribal ceremonies, admits to feelings of unease about the tribe's venture into the casino business.

Gambling Is Not a Panacea

"We'd rather do something besides gaming," he says. "We don't like the idea that people [can become] addicted to it. It's a vice for people that's uncontrollable. [But] there's a lot of things that aren't controllable, like caffeine [and] smoking."

Before the casino opened, Oneida tribal social workers underwent training to treat gambling addiction. Among Oneidas seeking help for addictions, however, fewer than 1 percent have sought treatment for gambling problems, according to the Oneida Family Services Department.

Most Oneidas, like other Indians, do not spend much time or money at the gaming tables. America's 2 million Indians make up less than 1 percent of the U.S. population, so Indian casinos must draw most of their customers from outside the reservations to make serious money.

"What's happened, I think, is 90 percent of the perception about Indian people is being generated by maybe 1 percent of the population of Indian people," Halbritter says. "A few Indian people, groups, are doing amazingly well, and that perception is being broadcast to an extent that it's warping the true condition of Indian country."

Many Indian leaders say they fear that non-Indians are blind to differences among tribes and lump all Indians into one category: rich, and thus undeserving of federal assistance. The misperception is molded in part by persistent media focus on the phenomenal success of the Mashantucket Pequots in Connecticut. Their Foxwoods Resort, which serves 45,000 meals a day, is said to be the largest casino in the Western world.

Gambling has not improved the lot of most Indian people, who remain "at the bottom of the socioeconomic ladder," according to Ada E. Deer, assistant secretary of the Interior for Indian affairs and a Menomini Indian from Wisconsin. Almost 32 percent of Indians live in poverty, compared with 13 percent of the general U.S. population; nearly 15 percent are unemployed. Other statistics from the last U.S. census—higher rates of liver disease, diabetes, suicide, homicide and accidental death—also point to a society still in distress.

The small Hydaburg tribe of Alaska, which has no gambling operation on its reservation, offers a contrast to the Pequots and other successful gambling tribes. "We have no income and no resources at this time," says tribal President Charles N. Natkong Sr. "Our unemployment rate is a chronic 50 to 55 percent . . . and the federal budget picture for contracts and/or grants looks more bleak with each passing month."

Natkong's remarks were contained in a thank-you letter to the Coeur d'Alene tribe of Idaho, which has offered non-gambling tribes a 5 percent share of gross revenues from its proposed National Indian Lottery. The Coeur d'Alenes would operate the lottery from a phone bank on their reservation, and players would bet via toll-free numbers using credit cards. The proposal has run into stiff opposition from officials in states that run lotteries.

A Possible Backlash

Halbritter and other Indian leaders worry that the success of Indian gambling will provoke a backlash and the possibility that history will repeat itself. Their fear is this: As more tribes join the casino wave, the Indians' new buffalo will run a greater risk of going the way of the old one, and this time extermination could come with just a swipe of a pen.

Already senators and representatives have proposed amendments to toughen the 1988 Indian gaming act; Democratic Representative Robert G. Torricelli of New Jersey, denouncing reservation gambling as "untaxed, unregulated and out of control," has suggested a two-year moratorium on new Indian casinos.

In 1995, the House Ways and Means Committee unsuccessfully sought to slap the 35 percent corporate tax rate on Indian casinos.

> *"Gambling revenue effectively allows the federal government to save money on Indian programs."*

Opposition to Indian gambling generally has centered on the tax-free status of tribes; critics say this has stacked the cards in favor of gambling tribes over their commercial competitors and deprived states of tax revenue from tribal casino profits. But the Oneidas and other gambling tribes say the tax argument ignores the tax-paying jobs that Indian casinos have created.

The Oneida casino, which opened in July 1993, employs 1,500 people. The National Indian Gaming Association says Indian casinos have created 140,000 jobs nationwide, about 85 percent held by non-Indians.

"Indians are held to a double standard," Deer says. "On the one hand, [non-Indians] say, 'Okay, come on, you Indians, pull yourselves up by your bootstraps.' And then when Indians did find a bootstrap—most of the time these bootstraps are missing—and that bootstrap was gaming, and then some succeeded, then people are saying, 'Whoa, we didn't really mean that.'"

New Housing from Gambling Profits

Ruby Collett, a 70-year-old Oneida Indian great-grandmother, cannot believe her good fortune. She shows a visitor her new home, a two-bedroom, two-bathroom dream-come-true. It is equipped with a modern kitchen and a washer-dryer nook, a ceiling fan, a garage and cedar siding. "Never in my life did I dream I would have a house like this," Collett exclaims, adding with a chuckle, "Especially after having six kids!"

Collett's year-old home is one of 10 units that the 1,100-member Oneida tribe has built with casino profits—"enterprise funds," they call it—to house their elderly. The units are tucked into a hillside of rolling pasture on Oneida land about five miles from the casino.

Each house is outfitted for the handicapped, including an automatic fire extinguisher system. Collett's bedroom window overlooks 20 other new houses, the Village of White Pines. Her son and a niece live there in single-family modular houses wired with fiber-optic cable to facilitate computer messaging among the residents and enable house-bound parents to perform office work at home, says Dale Rood, a computer technician and member of the Oneidas' governing tribal council.

> *"Indian casinos have created 140,000 jobs nationwide, about 85 percent held by non-Indians."*

The way the Oneidas financed their new houses is a process other gambling tribes have adopted. The Oneidas received a basic grant for reservation housing from the Department of Housing and Urban Development, then matched that amount with casino money to build units more to their liking.

"If we went with strictly HUD money, what you'd see is a tin box," Rood says.

Oneida "enterprise funds" paid for 57 upgrades to each modular unit, including basements, porches and sliding doors for the single-family houses, and the cedar siding and garages for all the units, Rood says.

Enhancing Government Assistance

The Oneidas, who do not make per-capita payments of casino profits to tribal members, similarly enhanced other forms of government assistance, mainly in family services—a second meal a week for the elderly lunch program, for example.

The tribe built a 5,000-square-foot clinic for health care furnished by the federal Indian Health Service. Oneidas once had to trek 40 miles to a clinic on the Onondaga reservation south of Syracuse; now, about 2,300 members of 15 tribes in a six-county radius travel to the modern Oneida facility.

"Enterprise-funded" scholarships have sent 38 Oneida youngsters to college—up from two before the casino—and 32 to vocational schools; about 70 tribal members are attending Oneida language classes; and 27 preschoolers receive an introduction to Oneida language and culture at a newly opened daycare center, soon to be replaced by a 32,000-square-foot, futuristic C-shaped, elder/child day care center in White Pines village.

At the casino, the Oneidas are building a $50 million, 227-room hotel—to supplement a 175-spot recreational vehicle park—and recently opened a 12-pump gas station that sells gasoline free of federal and state taxes. To placate local gas distributors, the Oneidas keep prices only 7 to 10 cents cheaper than at "regular" gas stations. The Oneida station also sells tax-free cigarettes.

And whenever a local farm goes on the block, the Oneidas buy it. In a reversal of a historical trend, an American Indian tribe is gaining ground: The Oneida Nation has grown from its 32-acre reservation to nearly 4,000 acres.

Many of the old trailers—leftovers from federal flood assistance donated to the Oneidas more than 20 years ago—are still occupied. But they now line a paved road that leads to a new community swimming pool and playground, sports fields, and a $500,000 youth recreation and study center.

"Our future depends on our ability to take care of ourselves, not on our ability to get anybody else to look out for us by either giving us money or having a law that protects you," Halbritter says. "We've really got to, number one, develop our own empowerment. Gaming gives us one step in that direction."

Indian Gaming Promotes Native American Sovereignty

by **William Thompson and Diana R. Dever**

About the authors: *William Thompson is a professor of public administration at the University of Nevada in Las Vegas. Diana R. Dever is a professor of social science at Mohave Community College in Bullhead City, Arizona.*

Editor's note: The following viewpoint is the first of a two-part series by the authors on sovereignty and Native American gaming. In the second part, the authors examine the ways gaming may inhibit the efforts of Native Americans to restore full sovereignty.

Sovereignty: "The supreme power of the state, exercised within its boundaries, free from external interference."   —*The American Political Dictionary*

Fully sovereign indigenous nations existed and thrived in North America long before Europeans came to the continent. But with the passing of five centuries, the condition of sovereignty for the Indian nations declined. However, in recent decades, the Euro-American (non-Indian) community has endorsed a restoration of Native American self-determination that is so much an element of sovereignty.

Presidents from Lyndon Johnson to Richard Nixon to Ronald Reagan espoused self-reliance and self-governance for Native Americans by endorsing passage of a series of bills with that purpose in mind. The Indian Gaming Regulatory Act (IGRA) of 1988 is a key measure in the struggle for sovereignty. In passing the Act, the United States Congress declared its purpose was "to provide a statutory basis for the operation of gaming by Indian tribes as a means of promoting tribal economic development, self-sufficiency and strong tribal governments." Presidents and Congress want enhanced sovereignty for tribes. Gaming has been identified as a major tool in the battle to restore conditions of enhanced sovereignty.

From William Thompson and Diana R. Dever, "A Sovereignty Check on Indian Gaming," *Indian Gaming Magazine*, April 1994. Reprinted with permission.

Gaming has existed as a tool for restored sovereignty since 1988. It is time we take a sovereignty check. It is time we begin to ask just how effective Native American community gambling has been in reestablishing meaningful sovereignty, and how effective we can expect it to be in achieving such goals in the future. . . .

Money Promotes Sovereignty

A politician once said, "Money is the mother's milk of politics." He could just as easily have said, "Money is the mother's milk of sovereignty." Money allows people to survive. If the people of a nation cannot survive, they cannot be sovereign, for sovereignty demands a continuity for a people. Survival means food. Sovereignty means housing and it means medical care. Today, whole nations of people die slow deaths as disease and famine grind life out of them. Money is a solution to this basic condition for sovereignty. Money from gambling activities has been placed into food, housing and health programs that were suffering severe budget cuts at the hands of federal authorities. Survival is also threatened by substance abuse—namely, drugs and alcohol. Gaming revenues are used for abuse treatment and also prevention programs.

Gaming Means Economic Opportunity

Without opportunity, populations disperse, much as the migrating Euro-Americans were dispersed from their Old World homes due to economic deprivations in the 17th, 18th and 19th centuries. Without jobs in their homelands, peoples gave up their nationalism in exchange for a new American nationalism. Gaming has brought jobs to Native American lands, and these jobs have given tribal members employment and an incentive to return to their homelands, thereby renewing their native nationalism.

The Oneidas of Wisconsin employ more than 1,000 people in their casino. This opportunity represents not only employment, but also a "chance" for members of the tribe. The tribe's casino near Green Bay is the 11th largest employer in the area. One tribal member asserted that "everybody needs a chance to prove themselves . . . the advantage we have now is the exposure of our talents—to prove that Native Americans can succeed in business." Non-Indians in the Green Bay area used to job discriminate against Native Americans. However, now the

> *"[Indian] gaming has been identified as a major tool in the battle to restore conditions of enhanced sovereignty."*

"curtain of racial prejudice . . . is finally coming down," said the Oneida tribal member. "They look at the Oneidas as contributing members of the community, no longer as people on welfare."

Minnesota Native American casinos are among the leading five employers in all the counties in which they are geographically located. The Mashantucket Pequot's casino of Ledyard, Connecticut, is the second-largest single employer in the state.

Moneys from gaming opportunities have been invested in non-gaming enterprises in order to gain a diversity of employment and to secure a more stable economic basis for the future. Arnold Sowmick, chief of the Saginaw Chippewa Tribe in Mt. Pleasant, Michigan, indicated that with gaming his tribe is "branching into manufacturing" and other ventures. "It's a whole new ball game . . . you can see it all around, but where I like to look is at our young people. They're outgoing and confident and they present a positive image. It hasn't always been that way. . . . People will listen to us now who wouldn't before. That old saw about 'money talks' is true." He added that the tribe has gained credibility by demonstrating that it can operate businesses.

> *"Money from gambling activities has been placed into food, housing and health programs that were suffering severe budget cuts at the hands of federal authorities."*

The best benefit from gaming revenues is that they are invested by Native Americans under the control of tribes. Other funds that have come to Native Americans from other sources have often been managed and controlled by Euro-American governments and used in manners not chosen by the tribes and often not to the benefit of tribal members.

Gaming Allows a Choice of Economic Development

Before gaming funds came along, many Native Americans felt pressured to accept any economic opportunity. Accordingly, they were enticed to allow their lands to be strip-mined, grazed or timbered in non-ecological manners, and polluted with garbage and industrial wastes. Efforts were made to use lands as dumping grounds for nuclear waste materials. One Nevada tribe even seriously explored the prospect of allowing a brothel on its lands.

Lance Hughes, director of the Tahlequah, Oklahoma-based Native Americans for a Clean Environment, said that 40 tribes across the United States had been approached by the waste disposal industry. "It's big money," Hughes said. "It's the biggest money there is right now . . . they pick on the poorest of the tribes."

Gaming revenues permit a more reasoned consideration of good economic opportunities. Additionally, where past choices forced by economic necessity led Native Americans to accept business ventures that disturbed their lands, the moneys from gaming can now be used to clean up past degradations of lands.

A Milwaukee, Wisconsin, Potawatomi Nation bingo hall used gaming funds for books, computers, new desks, a roof, remodeled halls and plumbing for an Indian Community School. Bake sales were formerly held simply to make ends meet. The school now serves the urban Native American population of Milwaukee with both cultural and vocational education.

The Mashantucket Pequots were, at the time of European contact, a nation of 13,000 thriving on a land area of 2,000 square miles. European contact was not kind to them. Disease and massacres left the tribe with only 200 members and 213 acres of land. Gaming revenues have been used to hire archaeologists to help identify traditional lands. Thus far, the tribe has been able to purchase back 1,500 acres of this land. Lost lands may be the most vital symbol of lost sovereignty, and now, through gaming, this measure of sovereignty is being returned.

Tribal gaming has also been focused on cultural restoration activities. The Pequots plan to spend millions on a museum building that will chronicle their history. Many tribes are turning gaming revenues into education programs designed to reestablish their languages.

Sovereignty Is Political

Gaming revenues have allowed Native Americans to assert an array of legal issues in courts and in front of other policy makers. The costs of court cases on gaming negotiations have been secured in many cases from gaming operations. Gaming also provided a catalyst for the creation of the National Indian Gaming Association in 1983. The Association has participated as a serious lobbying group within Euro-American political systems in order to assure that legislation and regulations pertaining to tribal gaming preserves "the integrity and rights of tribes to be governed by their own laws, exclusive of state jurisdiction."

IGRA precludes state or local taxing of Native American gaming enterprises. However, with their wealth of gaming funds, Native Americans have brought several economic benefits to local and state governments. Tribal employment of members and others has enhanced local tax bases and resulted in reduced welfare rolls.

Additionally, Native Americans have given state and local governments payments in lieu of taxes for services they would otherwise receive at no cost. Michigan and Connecticut tribes have agreed to pay sums of money to the Euro-American governments in exchange for an understanding that they would have certain exclusive gaming rights. Michigan tribes will pay revenues equaling eight percent and two percent of slot wins to the state and local governments, respectively, if the state agrees that no one else will have slots in the state. Direct power—sovereignty—of the tribe over local governments will be secured to a degree, since tribes will be able to tell local governments how they must spend their two-percent share. Connecticut's Pequot Tribe will give the state $100 million this year and 25 percent of slot revenues in the future for a similar exclusivity arrangement. The most basic

> *"Lost lands may be the most vital symbol of lost sovereignty, and now, through gaming, this measure of sovereignty is being returned."*

benefit of these agreements is that it makes it very difficult for states to authorize competitive commercial gaming in these circumstances; by doing so, the state would immediately lose large sums of revenues from the tribes. It is the state governments that have relinquished "sovereignty" to the Native American nations within these agreements.

Sovereignty Forces Negotiation

IGRA has lent itself to an expansion of Native American sovereignty by requiring state governments to work one-on-one with tribes on an equal footing. Money also gives tribal councils a stability that permits responsible government. The councils are making decisions about their own resources, not simply deciding how to spend handouts from others. This control builds a pride of accomplishment that will be essential in the full restoration of national sovereignty.

Indian Gaming Helps the Economy

by New Mexico Indian Gaming Association

About the author: *The New Mexico Indian Gaming Association is comprised of tribes that promote Indian gaming in New Mexico.*

Gaming on reservations has emerged in New Mexico and throughout the Nation as a means for tribal communities to climb out of the most dismal economic conditions that exist anywhere in the Nation. Formidable obstacles impede economic improvement on the reservations, and, to date, they have proven largely insurmountable. Gaming on reservations simply must be considered against this defining backdrop.

Economic Development Is Needed

It is helpful, therefore, first to discuss the economic climate in which New Mexico Indian gaming exists. New Mexico is one of our poorest states, ranking forty-sixth in the nation in per capita income. In New Mexico, as in virtually every other western state, Indian people are the poorest of the poor. According to the 1990 census, the average per capita income of New Mexico Indians was $5,141. Of 34,170 Indian households in the state, 17,417 (51%) earned less than $15,000 in annual income. Of 27,883 Indian families in the state, 12,092 had income in 1989 below the poverty level. That translates to 60,431 Indian people, 46% of the state's total Indian population, living in poverty; 26,643 of these poor are children.

Other measures of economic well-being tell an equally grim story. Of 63,991 Indians age 25 or older, 13,484 had less than a ninth-grade education, and another 13,287 failed to finish high school. Only 58.2% of adult Indians were high school graduates; only 5.8% had college degrees. Twenty-three percent of the state's Indian homes lack complete plumbing facilities. The numbers are even worse in New Mexico's Third Congressional District, in which the majority of New Mexico's Indian reservations are located.

Clearly there is a compelling need for economic development on New Mex-

From the New Mexico Indian Gaming Association, "Position Paper of the New Mexico Indian Gaming Association on Proposed Amendments to the Indian Gaming Regulatory Act," July 1995. Reprinted with permission.

ico's Indian reservations. Many of the most impenetrable barriers to reservation economic development are the direct result of state government interfering in reservation affairs, sometimes with federal acquiescence. For example, the state routinely claims the authority to tax reservation enterprises, even where the tribe and federal governments are taxing that enterprise and the state provides few or no services to either the enterprise or the Indian community. This results in a ruinous double or triple tax burden on reservation enterprises that discourages the initial investment of capital and inhibits the growth of existing businesses. Similarly, the states claim the authority to impose

> *"For many tribes, Indian gaming is the first successful Tribal enterprise that provides confidence and capital to venture into other businesses."*

their environmental laws, their liquor laws, and their zoning laws to reservations, thereby either discouraging investment in or prohibiting altogether activities that might profit an Indian community. We are dismayed that the states would attack the highly profitable business of Indian gaming in light of the states' uninterrupted history of discouraging reservation economic development through attempts to apply state laws, in addition to federal and tribal laws, to tribal development projects. Only a few tribes have had the resources to fight these state laws in court but, when they have, tribes often have won. In light of this history, we cannot accept the states' statements that they are concerned with economic conditions in Indian communities.

Gaming Provides Jobs

One of the few bright spots in the bleak picture of Indian economies is Indian gaming. Of the twenty-two Indian tribes in New Mexico, ten have tribal gaming operations located on their Indian lands. All of the tribal gaming operations are 100% tribally owned and operated. Several of the gaming operations were started with outside investors spending several million dollars in New Mexico on construction and start-up costs. For many tribes, Indian gaming is the first successful Tribal enterprise that provides confidence and capital to venture into other businesses. Tribal members employed by the gaming operations are gaining experience at every level of the operations. For many tribal members, this is their first job, and the experience they gain at gaming operations prepares them to compete in the larger job market. In addition to tribal members we each employ, we provide employment to individuals from surrounding Indian and non-Indian communities. Based upon data gathered by the Center for Applied Research in Denver, Colorado, tribal gaming has created directly 2,650 jobs in New Mexico for both Indians and non-Indians. These jobs mean that employees can provide the basic necessities of life: food on their tables, shelter for their families, school supplies and clothes for their children. The multiplier effect (the impact of employees' income that is spent by employees on goods and services in the community) of these jobs, plus jobs related to our purchasing of goods and services, translates into over 13,000 jobs in the State of New Mexico. Our annual payrolls exceed $46,000,000, and we purchase over $69,000,000 worth of goods and services, primarily from surrounding non-Indian communities. (The multiplier effect of these expenditures is in excess of $215,000,000.) Through our promotional out-reach, we have transported and attracted customers from all across the nation. With few exceptions, these gaming customers stay at hotels, eat at restaurants, and spend money in shops located off our reservations.

In addition, we make contributions to Indian and non-Indian charitable and non-profit organizations. One gaming tribe, for example, has donated well over 1 million dollars to various charitable organizations since beginning operations in 1986. Unlike commercial non-Indian gaming profits, which go into the pockets of the few, the profits from our tribal gaming enterprises go to our tribal governments' general funds and support tribal government services, programs, and projects that benefit our people. These revenues provide salaries for our employees and repair and maintenance of our community facilities, such as sewer and water systems. These revenues provide funds for training and education programs, fire and law enforcement departments, and a variety of other programs and services. These revenues provide investment capital for business acquisitions and reduce unemployment and the financial burden that unemployment brings. . . .

What Should Be Done

The reason so many tribes have turned to gaming is that the tribes have few viable economic development options. As discussed above, we believe that our inability to develop viable reservation economies is in large part due to state efforts to tax and regulate economic activities on our lands. We also note terribly unfair federal laws that either give states jurisdiction over Indian lands or allow the states economic advantages that we are not granted. If the states are genuinely concerned about the development of viable reservation economies, let them support legislation that levels the playing field between tribes and

> *"[Indian gaming] jobs mean that employees can provide the basic necessities of life."*

states, gives the tribes the same tax advantages the states enjoy, guarantees fair forums for the resolution of tribal-state disputes, and guarantees tribes the same ability states have to create a legal and regulatory climate that encourages economic growth. Rather than attacking Indian gaming, Congress should:

- Prohibit state taxation of any person, property, or activity that the tribes have jurisdiction to tax;
- Prohibit the application of state and local environmental and zoning laws to persons, property, and activities within Indian country;

- Amend the Internal Revenue Code to allow tribes to issue tax-exempt bonds for the same purposes that states may do so, and modify the volume caps on such bonds to reflect the small populations and greater need for capital in Indian communities;
- Amend Public Law 280 to require states, upon the request of an Indian tribe, to retrocede any jurisdiction they may have acquired under the statute;
- Repeal the McCarran Amendment, which gives state courts jurisdiction to adjudicate tribal reserved water rights; and
- Ensure that tribes are given equitable shares of federal funds for highways, sewage treatment facilities, solid waste facilities, drinking water systems, and other critical infrastructure.

Taking from the Tribe

In our judgment, the issue is a simple one. The states claim the issue is one of morality or infiltration by organized crime or state sovereignty. It is nothing of the sort. The issue, pure and simple, is competition for resources. It is the same battle we have fought with the states for two hundred twenty years. Indian tribes have always had something the states want. First it was our land; then it was our water; then it was our timber, our fish and game, and our oil and gas; then it was our tax revenues. Now it is our gaming revenues. The states have always couched the issue in terms of "what is good for the Indians." As discussed above, after two hundred twenty years of the states dictating "what is good" for us, our people are poor, ill-housed, and under-educated. We encourage all Americans to see this battle for what it is: yet another effort by the states to take from the tribes.

Indian Gaming May Promote Compulsive Gambling Among Native Americans

by Don A. Cozzetto and Brent W. LaRocque

About the authors: *Don A. Cozzetto is an associate professor and director of graduate programs in the Department of Political Science and Public Administration at the University of North Dakota. Brent W. LaRocque is a member of the Turtle Mountain Chippewa tribe and a criminal investigator with the Bureau of Indian Affairs Division of Law Enforcement Services in Albuquerque.*

The theme of this viewpoint is that greater tribal self-rule, though favored by tribal populations and a goal of federal Indian policy, comes with a social price. Exercising tribal sovereignty, North Dakota tribal governments, along with other tribal governments across the country, initiated reservation "high-stakes gambling." These tribal "high-stakes" gambling enterprises have been praised as examples of successful tribal self-rule and reservation economic development, but that is only part of the story. The other side of the story is that self-rule is accompanied by potential increases in reservation social problems, and, in this case, the problems can be exacerbated by unanticipated gambling-related social dysfunctions.

This viewpoint explores a relatively new and uncharted component of Indian gaming. Through primary empirical research, we examine whether there appears to be a positive correlation between the rapid growth in the numbers of tribal casinos and the incidence of pathological gambling activity in two North Dakota Indian tribes—the Devils Lake Sioux of the Fort Totten Reservation and the Chippewa of the Turtle Mountain Reservation. We then compare the rate of pathological gambling activity in the Indian population to the rates for the general population of North Dakota as well as the rates for the general population of Fort Totten, North Dakota, and Belcourt, North Dakota, the major communities on the two reservations. The viewpoint concludes with a discussion of alternative strategies that might be employed to address compulsive gambling behaviors.

The Benefits of Indian Gaming

Promoting economic development and attaining a greater degree of political and fiscal self-sufficiency has been a major challenge for the nation's original peoples in general and for Indian tribes in the state of North Dakota in particular. Casino gambling on Indian reservations is the latest in a long history of attempts to empower tribal communities. The objective is that tribal governments utilize revenues from casino operations to invest in the tribal infrastructure, to create employment opportunities for tribal members, and to address social problems on the reservations.

The direct and secondary economic benefits that have accrued to many tribes as a result of gaming revenues are indeed impressive. In 1994, total revenues nationally from Indian gaming exceeded three and one-half billion dollars. As of 7 July 1995, there were 123 tribes with approved class III tribal-state gaming compacts.

It should be noted at the outset that the majority of individuals who frequent tribal casinos located close to urban areas are non-Indian and that the majority of Indians on reservations do not gamble at their casinos. In rural states like North Dakota, however, geographic location becomes an important variable. The two tribal casinos that are the subject of this study are located hundreds of miles from any major population center. There is therefore a higher degree of unwillingness on the part of non-Indians who are not residents of North Dakota or of the communities along the Canadian border to travel these great distances to gamble, when similar facilities offering more amenities are located in urban areas closer to their place of residence. Moreover, high unemployment rates on the North Dakota reservations may explain the propensity for members of the tribes to gamble at the casinos.

> *"Traditional [Indian] gambling differs distinctly from casino gambling."*

Although there is considerable variation from day to day, during the period of this study the ratio of Indians to non-Indians was much higher on weekdays than on weekends. We also observed that the ratio of Indian to non-Indian gamblers was higher at the Turtle Mountain Reservation than the Fort Totten Reservation. This may be explained in part by the fact that Fort Totten is much closer to a larger, predominantly white community (Devils Lake) than is Turtle Mountain. Moreover, the Turtle Mountain Reservation has a larger Indian population than does Fort Totten. Another interesting difference is that alcohol is served at the Belcourt casino, but it is not served at the casinos on the Fort Totten Reservation.

Reservation Profile

Before examining the results of this study, we will present a brief discussion of the history and demographic characteristics of the Devils Lake Sioux tribe (Fort Totten) and the Turtle Mountain Chippewa tribe (Belcourt). The Devils Lake Sioux Reservation in north-central North Dakota encompasses 50,154 acres, while the Turtle Mountain Chippewa Reservation located in northeastern North Dakota covers an area of 35,379 acres. The map (below) shows the geographic location of the two reservations.

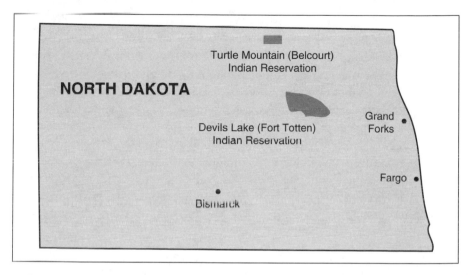

The Sioux population on the Devils Lake Reservation numbers 2,676. The Turtle Mountain Chippewa Reservation population is 4,808. The median income for all North Dakotans is $23,123. The median income on the Fort Totten Reservation is $15,394; on the Turtle Mountain Reservation it is $12,020. The unemployment rate for non-Indians in North Dakota is 4.5 percent. At Fort Totten and Turtle Mountain, the unemployment rates are 23.5 percent and 33 percent, respectively. The median age for the reservation populations is 18.2 years for Fort Totten and 22.3 years for Turtle Mountain.

Traditional Versus Contemporary Indian Gaming

Historically, gambling among Indian tribes is not uncommon. Tribes have a long history of wagering on sporting contests such as horse racing, running, and arrow-throwing as well as traditional games of chance. However, traditional Indian betting was certainly not organized, emphasized, or depended upon by tribal society to the extent characterized by the opening of casinos on Indian reservations. In most instances, traditional wagering occurred during tribal ceremonies, celebrations, or other special events. Tribal life was also not complicated by a monetary system or by modern forms of government, which encourage competition for the accumulation of scarce resources.

Traditional Indian culture dictated a very prudent and minimal use of environmental resources necessary to exist. The very concept of gambling in contemporary society rests on the hope of accumulating vast monetary resources in a short period of time. This contemporary view is fast becoming an institutionalized aspect of tribal culture. Some tribal leaders proclaim casino gambling as the "new buffalo," a cure-all for the economic woes that plague most tribes in the United States. Conflict has arisen among some tribes over casino gambling and its possible effect on Indian culture.

> *"Three separate studies . . . found significantly higher rates of pathological gambling in the Indian population than in the non-Indian population."*

It is important to note that traditional gambling differs distinctly from casino gambling in two other important respects. First, an important distinction lies in the contrast between traditional and contemporary Indian societies. Prior to contact with European culture, traditional tribal societies were not afflicted with dysfunctional social behaviors such as alcoholism, suicide, and poverty to the degree that they are today. Second, as Rachel A. Volberg and Eric Silver note, "research shows that continuous forms of gambling, with rapid cycles of stake, play and determination, are more likely to lead to problematic involvement than non-continuous forms of gambling. Pull-tabs, bingo and casino-style games are all continuous forms of gambling."

The Indian Gaming Regulatory Act

The genesis for the development of Indian casinos is a 1987 Supreme Court decision in *California v. Cabazon Band of Mission Indians*. The case involved a dispute between an Indian band and the state of California over the band's gambling operations. The band claimed that it had sovereign jurisdiction on reservation lands. The Court decided in favor of the band, upholding the right of Indian tribes to conduct gambling operations in states where gaming was already legal. This court ruling was the catalyst for the Indian Gaming Regulatory Act (IGRA) passed by Congress in 1988. The act provides the statutory basis for tribes to conduct gambling on Indian land. Indian land is defined as land that is part of an Indian reservation or off-reservation land held for an Indian tribe in trust by the federal government. Three categories of gaming are covered under this legislation, although class I gambling (social and traditional games) is not subject to the regulatory scheme established by the IGRA. Class II designates bingo, keno, pull-tabs, and card games. Class III provides for casino gambling and parimutuel betting. The legislation dictates that Indian tribes can conduct gaming operations only in states where non-Indians are already permitted to gamble.

The IGRA further requires those states that currently allow class III gaming to enter into compacts with Indian tribes who also wish to operate class III facilities. Under federal law, the tribes can initiate action in federal court seeking a court order compelling state governments to negotiate compacts in good faith. If a compact still cannot be reached, a court-appointed mediator selects a compact most consistent with federal law. Federal law also prohibits states from imposing fees or taxes on Indian gaming unless the tribe agrees during the compact negotiation process to pay such fees.

Both the Turtle Mountain band of Chippewa and the Devils Lake Sioux tribe opened casinos after entering into gaming compacts with the state of North Dakota in October 1992. Prior to that time, both tribes operated bingo facilities. Casinos on both reservations offer video gambling and slot machines. The Turtle Mountain casinos also offer blackjack and Indian dice. Poker and crap tables are available at the Sioux casino. In other words, both casinos offer high-stakes gambling.

Race and Compulsive Gambling

Several studies have been conducted over the past fifteen years on pathological gambling behaviors in the general population. As a result, we now know that addiction rates in the general population (non-Indian) range from 3.5 percent to 4.5 percent. The problem is that there is little in the way of empirical research relating specifically to pathological gambling in minority communities in general and the Indian community in particular. For example, the Minnesota Institute of Public Health compiles data on the numbers of compulsive gamblers seeking assistance through the compulsive gambling hotline, including information on variables such as gender, age, and occupation. However, no data is collected on race. This is despite the fact that race may be an important variable in trying to determine whether pathological gambling affects certain segments of society in a disproportionate manner. In North Dakota, no data are collected.

One possible reason for this paucity of research on the effects of gambling on minority communities is that race might then be used as a political tool. White people might claim that gambling is an "Indian problem" in the same manner that some people argue that increases in violent crime rates in the nation's cities are attributable to the African-American community. Indians might counter that these accusations represent yet another form of racism and yet another attempt by the dominant society to destroy Native American culture through assimilation.

> *"The . . . rate [of gambling addiction] in the Indian population was found to be 14.5 percent, compared to 3.5 percent in the general population."*

Two [other] research projects, in addition to this one, attempt to assess these dysfunctional behaviors specifically in the Indian population in upper Midwest states. Three separate studies conducted by the Indian Health Service (IHS) on an Ojibway reservation in Minnesota found significantly higher rates of pathological gambling in the Indian population than in the non-Indian population. The studies included a school survey of students aged twelve to nineteen years, a telephone survey of adults ranging in age from twenty to eighty-six years, and systematic sampling of active adult gamblers at various gambling sites, a methodology similar in part to the one used in this North Dakota case study.

> *"A trend [of pathological gambling behavior by Native Americans] is emerging that should concern tribal leaders in rural states."*

The adolescent survey and the adult survey of active gamblers showed significant differences between pathological and potential behaviors in the Indian population compared to non-Indian peer populations. The study also notes that there appears to be a correlation between alcoholism, poverty, and unemployment rates on reservations and the potential for increased gambling problems.

A second study commissioned by the North Dakota Department of Human Services presented findings similar to those of the IHS study described above. The combined lifetime pathological and probable rate in the Indian population was found to be 14.5 percent, compared to 3.5 percent in the general population. Using the 1990 census data for the state, the report predicts that as many as 3,700 Native American adults in North Dakota suffer from compulsive or potentially compulsive gambling behavior.

The Study

Five separate samples were generated for the purposes of this study. For comparative purposes, a random sample of 504 adult North Dakotans was generated from the population of North Dakotans. A second random sample of 250 residents of Fort Totten was generated. A third random sample of 250 residents of Belcourt was generated. The fourth sample was a quota sample of one hundred members of the Turtle Mountain band of Chippewa at the tribal casino in Belcourt. The fifth sample was a quota sample of one hundred generated from members of the Sioux tribe at their casino near Devils Lake. Care was taken to ensure consistency in representation of males and females in the samples. With the quota samples, all respondents were asked to identify their tribal affiliation to ensure that non-Indians were not included.

The South Oaks Gambling Screen (SOGS), an instrument validated by the American Psychiatry Association (APA), was administered to assess the prevalence of pathological and potentially pathological gambling behaviors in the North Dakota general population, in the general populations on the two reservations, and in the population of Indians who actually gamble at the reservation casinos. The SOGS questions respondents about a number of behaviors concerning gambling activity, sources of funds used to gamble, whether the individual has been criticized about gambling behaviors, whether the individual feels guilty about the amount of gambling, and so forth. If the respondent answers affirmatively to five or more of the questions that are indicative of compulsive behavior, that respondent is considered to be a pathological gambler. Pathological gambling is defined by the APA as "chronic and progressive failure to resist impulses to gamble, and gambling behavior that compromises, disrupts, or damages personal, family, or vocational pursuits." Those responding affirmatively to three or four of the indicator questions are considered potentially pathological gamblers. In other words, they exhibit all of the signs that will result in compulsive behavior in the future if they continue to gamble today. The instrument used for this study included two additional demographic questions about gender and age. The instrument was pretested to ensure that the questions contained no cultural bias. . . .

A High Rate of Compulsive Gambling

Analysis of the data from the general population of North Dakotans reveals a state-wide compulsive gambling rate of 6 percent. The national average ranges between 3.5 percent and 4.5 percent. . . . Forty-eight percent of those individuals who showed signs of compulsive gambling behavior were men. The age distribution was random.

The compulsive rate for the Fort Totten general population sample was 14 percent; for the Belcourt general population sample it was 10 percent. . . . In Belcourt, 80 percent of the compulsive gamblers were men, and 20 percent of the total number of those individuals in the Belcourt general population sample were under thirty years of age. In the Fort Totten general population sample, 58 percent of those who exhibited compulsive gambling behavior were male, and the age distribution for all respondents in this category was random. . . .

The data indicates that 23 percent of the Chippewa are compulsive gamblers, with another 19 percent probable pathological gamblers (combined rate 42 percent).

In the compulsive category, 74 percent are women, 65 percent of compulsive pathological gamblers are under thirty years of age, and 73 percent of those under thirty are women. The percentages are similar in the potential category.

Respondents in the Devils Lake casino sample exhibited a compulsive rate of 29 percent and a potential rate of 30 percent (combined 59 percent). The disproportionate impact on women and individuals under thirty years of age is consistent with the findings for the Turtle Mountain Chippewa. . . .

Compulsive Gambling Is Harmful

This is the third study conducted in two years that indicates a significant difference in pathological and potentially pathological gambling behavior in the Indian population relative to the general population, although compulsive rates in the North Dakota general population are slightly higher than the national average. Although more research is needed, it seems clear that a trend is emerging that should concern tribal leaders in rural states like North Dakota. As more and more reservations negotiate compacts with state governments to construct casinos, additional studies will be needed to determine any changes in the pathological gambling rates for Indians and non-Indians.

An important question is, Who will fund additional studies to assess the long-term effects of this problem on tribal communities in states like North Dakota? Equally important issues are how professional treatment will be provided, how these treatment programs will be funded, and what role tribal governments will play in the process.

> *"Untreated pathological gambling behaviors on Indian reservations . . . could destroy what remains of tribal culture."*

We believe that discussions concerning these questions are not simply part of the social policy debate that relates to a number of severe problems on Indian reservations in North Dakota. In fact, that type of narrow focus diminishes their importance. Indeed, the issue of how pathological gambling in the North Dakota Indian population will be addressed goes beyond the social dysfunction debate. It lies at the heart of Indian self-determination for the Turtle Mountain Chippewa and the Devils Lake Sioux.

North Dakota Indian tribes have been demanding more autonomy in the operation of service programs and a further devolution of responsibility from the Bureau of Indian Affairs (BIA) to tribal government. Surely an important component of increased self-government and self-determination relates to tribes assuming a proactive role in promoting the social as well as the economic well-being of their members. Tribal government is the beneficiary of gaming revenues and therefore must assume primary responsibility for the social costs related to gambling. Tribal leaders must accept the fact that compulsive gambling is a problem on the two reservations in question and that tribal government, not the federal government, must address this problem.

The long-term externalities [secondary costs] associated with untreated pathological gambling behaviors on Indian reservations such as Fort Totten and Belcourt could destroy what remains of tribal culture. Moreover, current tribal leadership may be guilty of exacerbating the social dysfunctions on the reservations—a malfeasance heretofore attributed exclusively to non-Indian leaders. The placement of large advertisements in the tribal newspaper enticing tribal members to spend their treaty payments in the local casino is a case in point.

Long-term compulsive gambling can lead to the further deterioration of tribal social institutions such as collectivity, family, and the important role of elders. Compulsive gambling can also cause increases in suicide rates, divorce rates, and alcoholism. This decay can ultimately harm economic development, because economic development and social development are not mutually exclusive. Future business partnerships and investments in the reservation infrastructure may be constrained by these social dysfunctions.

Policy Recommendations

Recent federal legislation reflects the view that tribal government should take a more proactive role in addressing social problems such as pathological gambling. The Indian Mental Health Demonstration Grant Program offered by the Indian Health Service (IHS) provides for partial funding of community-based health services to Indians (USCA). Tribal governments are required to share costs of planning, developing, and implementing the program. Unlike most past policies for Indians, the onus is placed on tribes to take the initiative by, first, expressing a desire for mental health services through IHS and, second, funding 25 percent of the program.

Perhaps the most important feature of this new policy is its emphasis on the use of mental health approaches that seek to maintain traditional Indian values and culture. There is a growing movement in the mental health counseling literature away from conventional psychological approaches and toward integrated interventions that recognize Indian traditions. This approach weaves conventional practices with a holistic and spiritual healing system. Not only does an integrated approach offer a greater likelihood for success through counseling intervention; it seeks to strengthen traditional Indian culture debased by the application of past assimilation policies. We believe an important indicator of tribal governments' ability to govern effectively will be their response to the challenge of providing

"Long-term compulsive gambling can lead to the further deterioration of tribal social institutions."

assistance to those negatively affected by tribal policy choices such as the introduction of casino gambling.

Tribes need to invest in research concerning treatment alternatives that are applicable to the Indian community, and they need to develop an internal capacity to provide education, treatment, and prevention programs for pathological gamblers that are sensitive to the needs of their citizens. This first requires recognition that a problem exists, development of long-term strategic plans to address the problem, and allocation of resources for research, training, and treatment to confront the problem.

A Serious Problem

This viewpoint has examined the rate of pathological gambling in the general population of North Dakotans, in the general populations of the Turtle Mountain Chippewa and the Devils Lake Sioux, and in the population of Chippewa and Sioux who gamble at reservation casinos. The data were then compared to national pathological gambling rates.

The results showed that the compulsive gambling rates for categories of respondents was higher than the national rate of between 3.5 and 4.5 percent. The problem was particularly acute in the Indian respondents who gamble, and the problem was most dramatic in Indian women under thirty.

Obviously, the results of a study focusing on two Indian tribes in a single state cannot be generalized beyond the two reservations in question. However, more research is needed into pathological gambling on Indian reservations, particularly in light of the growing number of reservation casinos. A comparative database is needed to assess the situation on a national basis.

Tribal casinos are now a part of an emerging policy debate on the growing prevalence of compulsive gambling in the Native American population. This case study of the Turtle Mountain Chippewa and the Devils Lake Sioux tribes of North Dakota lends further empirical justification to the fact that a serious problem appears to exist, at least in North Dakota. Tribal leaders at the Belcourt and Fort Totten reservations need to take a proactive role in assessing the situation and devising strategies to deal with the problem before it worsens.

Indian Gaming Could Destroy Native American Culture

by Clay Akiwenzie

About the author: *Clay Akiwenzie is a member of the Saugeen Ojibway tribe of the Cape Croker Reserve in Ontario, Canada.*

Gaming will give tribes more money which will enable them to diversify and realize the long sought-after goal of individual tribal sovereignty. At least, that is the succession of events that proponents of Indian gaming would like us to believe. While the allure of more money in communities that generally have precious little industry, nearly no liquid assets, and extremely high unemployment is fairly easy to see, what is often missing from a thorough discussion of gaming is a clear understanding of basic issues like what sovereignty actually means, how best to achieve it, and who exactly "counts" as Indian? These sort of basic questions about the terminology used in this debate are often side-stepped altogether when more pressing questions come up, like: Where is all of this money actually going? Who decides where it goes? And of course, most importantly, when do I get mine? Among other things, the rising tide of crime on Indian reservations that have already instituted gaming, from the Mashantucket Pequot in Connecticut to the Fort Regis Mohawk in New York to the Clear Lake Pomo Indian Colony in California, would seem to indicate that perhaps Indian gaming does not represent the panacea for Indian country that we have been led to believe.

A Disaster in the Making

The problems are practically uniform throughout Indian country. Disorganized, factionalized, and historically poor communities with limited infrastructure and little-to-no experience managing large sums of money are now being confronted with the daunting task of effectively managing a multimillion dollar

From Clay Akiwenzie, "A Modern 'Small-pox' for Native Culture," *Thinker*, November 1, 1995. Reprinted with permission.

corporation. Given the obvious enticements of Indian gaming, it should come as no surprise that many of the actual members from these reserves have accepted gaming with a less-than-perfect understanding of what they were getting into and perhaps have made some less-than-ideal management decisions. This poor understanding of what gaming and sovereignty actually mean portends disaster for a disturbingly large number of tribes.

However, vague concepts and ideals aside, former proponents of Indian gaming have been echoing each other with warning calls to tribes pondering the plunge into the business of high stakes gambling. Beverley Louis, a registered band member of the Sault St. Marie Band of Chippewa Indians, noted in her letter to the editor in the July 6, 1995 edition of *Indian Country Today* that while her "tribe has grossed billions of dollars since the conception of casinos, . . . our people—our true Native Americans—remain indigent, disgracefully poor. We have no idea where the money is going, and diligent inquiry into this matter is met by silence—or in the alternative misrepresentations." Ms. Louis repeated references to the disparity of wealth and subsequent friction between what she describes as the "true Native American," or full-blooded Indians, and the increasingly large numbers of migrating mixed breeds is a massive problem for nearly every single reservation in North America.

While the membership issue may seem like a completely separate issue from gaming, this power to decide who does and does not belong to the group becomes an absolutely crucial

> *"Indian gaming does not represent the panacea for Indian country that we have been led to believe."*

and potentially divisive issue when you start talking about gaming and the distribution of profits. Although there are federal guidelines for membership criteria, each reserve implements its own membership criteria as an exercise of tribal sovereignty and self-government which the feds in turn refer to when allotting federal funding. The point being that membership roles, federal funding, and the distribution of wealth are all intimately connected, and whoever controls membership also controls the future of the Nation. Often, the irony of the situation is that the people who justify the continued existence of Indian Nations as distinct Nations (i.e., the people who keep the traditions alive), are often left out in the cold when the profits are divvied up.

Sovereignty

One issue that always comes up with gaming is the issue of sovereignty and its relation to Indian gaming. Proponents of gaming invariably point to gaming as a means to the ultimate end: real, not just quasi-sovereignty, but real sovereignty for Native peoples. Few, however, have a clear understanding of what sovereignty would actually mean to Indian tribes. For example, does sovereignty mean an end to the federal fiduciary relationship between Indians and the Federal government? What will sovereignty mean to the trust status of Indian lands? Will sovereignty legitimate us as Nations, states, or municipalities? Are we, as a collective group of Native peoples, ready for tribal sovereignty and all of its implications? If we aren't, and if gaming moves already unstable Nations towards some uncertain and undetermined fate, then all of this talk about sovereignty and economic independence may turn out to be another classic example of counting your chickens before the eggs are hatched.

> *"Casinos on Indian lands . . . could prove the most destructive . . . element introduced to Native culture since Christopher Columbus brought the smallpox."*

Another similarly discussed, but never resolved, issue in Indian country is how best to balance traditional cultural practices and moral belief systems with economic development. This idea of balance has been central to the debate over gaming on the Hopi Reservation in Arizona as well as on the Navajo Reservation which surrounds them. Both Nations have chosen to reject gaming as a source of revenue because for them the question takes on an either/or sensibility. Either you value your culture and moral values above all else, or you support economic development with the knowledge that culture will be inevitably compromised to one degree or another. While this may seem rigid and anti-progressive to some people, it is a very real concern to many of the traditional people whose reality exists outside the world of profit margins and economic theory.

An Unsure Bet

So, does gaming on reservations represent a new hope for an economic resurgence in Indian country? Maybe, but at best, it's still an unsure bet, and tribes should know the risks before entering into any agreement with any outside corporation, investors, or government. I want to be clear that I'm not saying that Indians have to be poor in order to be "real" Indians, or that casinos are "bad," so we shouldn't have them. However, it is my fear that many tribes have rushed into these ventures without a clear understanding of what they wanted to gain from their involvement with gaming, aside from the vague assumption that more money means less problems.

Finally, without the right leadership, discussion, and understanding of gaming and all its implications, the ubiquitous construction of casinos on Indian lands across the continent could prove the most destructive and divisive element introduced to Native culture since Christopher Columbus brought the smallpox.

Organized Crime May Infiltrate Indian Casinos

by Robert G. Torricelli

About the author: *Robert G. Torricelli is a U.S. representative from New Jersey.*

> *Editor's note· The following viewpoint is an excerpt of Robert G. Torricelli's testimony before the House of Representatives' Subcommittee on Native American Affairs on October 5, 1993.*

What we have seen since 1988—the proliferation of over 175 commercial Native American gaming establishments in 26 states—has enormous consequences to our social fabric and our law enforcement capabilities.

What we have seen is the spread of deregulated casino gaming across the country without the citizens of the United States or their elected representatives ever having made the decision to let that happen. As a representative from one state that does allow high-stakes casinos, I believe that is the wrong way to proceed.

Gambling in New Jersey was a very difficult public policy decision. It was made only after careful consideration by the people of New Jersey and their elected officials, and it was accompanied by an amendment to the state's Constitution. I believe that decisions to allow casino gaming on Native American lands should undergo the same public scrutiny and the same input from affected communities.

But the purpose of today's hearing is not to discuss whether we should allow the further proliferation of these casinos. The purpose, instead, is to discuss whether these casinos are properly regulated and whether they pose an irresistible invitation to organized crime.

Comprehensive Gaming Regulations

I believe that if one compares the regulation of casino gaming in New Jersey with the regulation of tribal casinos, there is great cause for concern.

From Robert G. Torricelli's testimony in *Implementation of Indian Gaming Regulatory Act: Oversight Hearing Before the Subcommittee on Native American Affairs of the Committee on Natural Resources, House of Representatives*, 103rd Cong., 1st sess., October 5, 1993, Serial no. 103–17, Part V.

Atlantic City's casinos operate under *the most comprehensive system of gaming regulations in the world*. In developing its regulations, New Jersey officials sought considerable input from their counterparts in Nevada. We took what worked best in Las Vegas and adopted it for our own, and we went above and beyond Las Vegas' regulations where we thought it was necessary.

New Jersey spends $60 million each year to fund two government agencies that enforce its regulations. Virtually all aspects of casino operations, from who can be involved to the specific dimensions of a chip, are strictly enforced.

> *"Operators of tribal casinos are hired by the tribes themselves, and often undergo no background investigations."*

In Atlantic City, background checks are conducted on any individual who handles any money or who is involved directly in the games. These checks are so thorough that the owners of the Hilton Hotel chain were originally turned down for a license because the company had some dealings that were not sufficiently explained to state regulators.

New Jersey's casinos are also subject to the Bank Secrecy Act, which requires meticulous reporting and recordkeeping of cash transactions. In fact, every single dollar is accounted for and reported back to the state.

Loose Regulations

Tribal casinos, on the other hand, are regulated by the tribes themselves. The Federal Government is severely limited in the amount of oversight it can provide, and the states can only monitor the games subject to conditions laid out by a tribal-state compact.

The federal Indian Gaming Commission does have oversight responsibilities for Class II gaming, such as bingo. But the Commission has a *$3 million budget and a staff of 24 to oversee more than 100 class II Indian gaming operations* across the country. By contrast, New Jersey gaming regulators, who have responsibility for *12 gaming operations in one city, have a $60 million budget and 985 employees*.

Operators of tribal casinos are hired by the tribes themselves, and often undergo no background investigations. To illustrate how inadequate background checks can be, an individual who headed the management firm for gaming operations on the Barona Rancheria reservation in San Diego was twice turned down for a license by the Nevada Gaming Control Board.

Furthermore, these casinos are not subject to the Bank Secrecy Act. The danger of this situation has attracted the attention of former Treasury Secretary Lloyd Bentsen, who has stated support for making tribal casinos subject to the Act, and who wrote that "without adequate recordkeeping, internal controls, and currency reporting, Indian gaming has . . . potential to be an attractive target for money laundering."

111

We are already beginning to lee the negative consequences of this loose regulation.

- In a report issued in December 1992, the Inspector General for the U.S. Interior Department said gaming revenues of over $12 million may have been improperly diverted from tribes to operators and suppliers, principally because of theft and mismanagement by contracted operators of gaming establishments. In the September 29, 1993, *Boston Globe*, the author of that report stated that "those places are sitting ducks for fraud."
- On the Rincon Reservation outside of San Diego, three reputed mob leaders from Chicago and two local men were convicted of conspiracy to launder money and defraud the tribe.
- There have been repeated allegations of ties between the Seminole Indian Tribe's bingo operation in Florida and organized crime. Both the Interior Department and the Attorney General of Florida have begun investigations. And the FBI recently reported that ties do indeed exist.
- The Cabazon tribe in California hired a member of a local crime syndicate to run its casino. A tribal official who accused the manager of skimming profits was forced out of office and found dead two months later. While the case has not yet been solved, investigators believe that the murder was mob related.

> *"The only reason we have not seen even more evidence of ties between organized crime and tribal casinos is that no federal regulatory apparatus exists to police it."*

- New Jersey's Ramapough Mountain Tribe signed a contract with the Rory Management Company (RMC). In return for spending millions of dollars on lobbying efforts to secure federal recognition for the tribe, RMC would be allowed to co-own and operate a high-stakes bingo hall and casino on tribal land. Robert Frank, RMC's president, was sued less than a year later for $6 million for alleged fraud and embezzlement scheme at a California Indian bingo hall. He was subsequently the subject of a criminal investigation for fraud, interstate money laundering, and possible ties to organized crime.
- The FBI is currently investigating Angelo Medure, who manages a casino for Minnesota's White Earth Band of Chippewa Indians. Medure is a business associate of Henry Zottola, who works for the Genovese crime family. It is suspected that these men are laundering money for that crime family. . . .

The Tip of the Iceberg

Some will say that these are isolated instances, or that they are only rumor and hearsay. But the fact is that since the 1988 passage of IGRA [Indian Gaming Regulatory Act], tribal casinos have opened in 26 states, and reports of corruption or ties to organized crime have already surfaced in 10 of them.

Anyone who honestly examines the manner in which tribal casinos are currently managed and regulated—and the ability of organized crime networks to exploit this situation—can only come to the conclusion that what we are seeing today is the tip of the iceberg. In fact, I am willing to submit that the only reason we have not seen even more evidence of ties between organized crime and tribal casinos is that no federal regulatory apparatus exists to police it or look into it.

Tightening the Regulations

I have introduced legislation—HR 2287, the Gaming Integrity and State Law Enforcement Act—that will address these problems. Similar legislation has been introduced by Senators Harry Reid and Richard Bryan in the other body. [Neither bill made it out of committee.]

- HR 2287 will give states the right to reject forms of gaming on tribal lands that are not allowed elsewhere in the state and give states that do allow tribal gaming more power to negotiate regulatory controls in gaming compacts.
- It will make it the responsibility of the Attorney General of the United States to ensure that adequate background checks are conducted on individuals affiliated with tribal casinos before those individuals begin work at a casino
- It will also address Secretary Bentsen's concerns by making Indian gaming establishments subject to the same financial reporting requirements as other businesses in the United States.

Some have already branded my legislation as an effort simply to protect the economic interests of New Jersey and Nevada. I will not deny that the economic health of Atlantic City's casinos is crucial to the economic health of New Jersey, and that I have an interest in looking out for my home state. But I would also point to cosponsorship of this legislation by Members and Senators from California, Wyoming, Florida, Arizona, Kentucky, Wisconsin, New York and New Hampshire.

Those with open minds will also see that this legislation comes from people who know gaming, and who see better than anyone else the dangers posed by loosely regulated casinos. We know that Native Americans themselves want to prevent criminal elements from infiltrating their operations. We also know that gaming is the most productive engine of economic development that many tribes have ever experienced. We're simply trying to use our own experience to better protect them.

We also understand better than anyone the stakes that are involved if just one tribal casino is found to be under mob influence, or if just one tribal casino is found guilty of fixing games. The ramifications would not be limited to tribal casinos, but would reverberate throughout the entire industry. We cannot allow a few unscrupulous individuals to destroy an industry that has been built very carefully over several decades and that is the economic lifeblood of two states.

Indian Gaming Will Hurt the Economy

by Donald Trump

About the author: *Donald Trump is a real estate investor who owns three casinos in Atlantic City, New Jersey.*

Editor's note: The following viewpoint is an excerpt of Donald Trump's testimony before the House of Representatives' Subcommittee on Native American Affairs on October 5, 1993.

I'm Donald Trump. I'm from New York where I develop, restore and create new properties and hotels. I also operate three casinos in Atlantic City under license from the state of New Jersey and that is why I am here today. Those casinos have stockholders and bondholders other than myself. As Chairman of the Board of these casinos, I represent their interests as well.

Much has been said about the big casino interests—people like Donald Trump taking on America's native people. Trump and all the moneyed muscle crowd attacking minorities. That isn't the case at all. In a sense, this has little to do with the Indians. Neither I nor my colleagues in the industry oppose the right of our first countrymen to seek economic determination and to secure their futures. As you know, many people in our industry are helping Indian tribes accomplish that goal.

I am not here to quarrel with Indians. But I and others do have a quarrel with the federal government. And when it comes time for a single citizen to stand up to the power and resources of Washington, all of us, including Donald Trump, are just members of John Q. Public. A little guy against the biggies.

But America is a great country and even little guys, in this case even Donald Trump, have some rights. And states also have some rights in our constitutional system. We believe that in this case the rights of Donald Trump, the residents of New Jersey and the state itself are quite synonymous.

From Donald Trump's testimony in *Implementation of Indian Gaming Regulatory Act: Oversight Hearing Before the Subcommittee on Native American Affairs of the Committee on Natural Resources, House of Representatives*, 103rd Cong., 1st sess., October 5, 1993, Serial no. 103–17, Part V.

Economic Partners

As stated, I operate three casinos in Atlantic City. Actually, although a lot of people seem to think I know little about the business, I am the largest individual casino operator in the world. I say that modestly as you would expect.

However, in New Jersey, I and my colleagues don't merely operate casinos for our own fun and profit. We are economic partners with the state. The first 9.25 percent of every dollar we take in goes to New Jersey—off the top—off our gross, not our net. Eight percent of that goes to support the Casino Revenue Fund (CRF). This is a state program we fund which supports seniors and the disabled. It allows seniors to buy prescription drugs for $5.00, offsets their property taxes, helps reduce their electricity bills and provides other services like home health care. It offers our seniors and disabled both security and dignity.

In 1992 New Jersey casinos provided $255 million to this fund. Since 1978, when Atlantic City's first casino opened, our industry has provided $2.5 billion to the CRF.

The next 1.25 percent of gross casino revenue goes to a state agency, the Casino Reinvestment Development Authority (CRDA). We are the sole funding source of that organization. In 1992, we provided $40 million to the CRDA, which invests these funds in public projects throughout New Jersey. Through 2009, it is estimated the CRDA will invest $654 million in Atlantic City, $413 million in southern New Jersey and $297 million in northern New Jersey.

> *"[Atlantic City's casino gambling revenues] build housing, day care centers, senior citizen complexes and shopping centers."*

This money has and will continue to build housing, day care centers, senior citizen complexes and shopping centers in all of the state's urban areas. It's a lot of money, and it's for worthwhile causes.

Some 75,000 New Jerseyans and their families are working because of our business; more than 43,000 directly in Atlantic City. We employ well over half of the city's entire work force. In 1992 alone we paid more than a billion dollars in wages and benefits to our people.

More than $5 billion of investment—that's right, $5 billion of private capital—has made Atlantic City the economic base of the entire southern half of New Jersey. We represent over 4 percent of the state budget.

Stiff Regulation Requirements

We have accomplished all this under the most restrictive regulatory standards in the country. We are the most highly regulated business in any capacity in any venue. We pay the state over $60 million annually for our own regulation. That's correct—we pay to regulate ourselves although state regulation is separate and apart from us and beyond reproach.

As I said, our regulation is stiff. Each of my businesses is relicensed on a biannual basis. As of now, I must personally requalify each year. All key employees must do so. This is no easy process. Every activity and transaction are checked by the State Police: some eighty pages of documentation; associations, personal and business checks; family background; and resources. It is totally pervasive. Actually, I am told that some of the owners of sports franchises in our country would not qualify for licensure in New Jersey's casino industry.

> *"A scandal in any Indian casino operation would reflect on us, rub off on our industry."*

I can state without fear that we are solid corporate citizens operating a clean and honest entertainment business. Both we and New Jersey are proud of this record and rightfully so.

Do you wonder, therefore, why we are so deeply concerned, even paranoid, that Indian tribe operations are not similarly regulated? Do you know what would happen to our reputations, our businesses, if organized crime gained a foothold in any of the Indian operations? I am not suggesting that organized crime has done so, although there have been numerous articles in the press that this has happened. It is the mere possibility that scares us. A scandal in any Indian casino operation would reflect on us, rub off on our industry. Our honesty, our integrity, our reputations would be compromised at once. It is an old story—guilt by association. Years of work down the drain. We know that Indian tribes want clean and honest operations. However, we also know that people involved in advising some of the tribes, those operating and funding certain of their operations, are not subject to the strict licensing and qualifying regulations in place in New Jersey and other states. Yes, we are concerned, very concerned. The federal government has unleashed a process without regard to the economic or social consequences to the state in which the activity takes place.

However, I am not in law enforcement so I will let the law enforcement people discuss these matters.

The Economic Effects of Indian Casinos

I am here to talk about what could happen in New Jersey if this process were applied there. I would like to trace for you what would happen to us, our employees and their families, our seniors and disabled if the federal government unilaterally determined to recognize an Indian tribe in northern New Jersey near New York City. Please note I used the word would; not what could happen.

First of all, an Indian casino operation in northern New Jersey would be the economic death knell to Atlantic City. Much of our market, which we and the state, our economic partner, have worked hard to create and protect, would disappear. No one will ride two hours in traffic to do the same thing that they could do in fifteen minutes or a half hour. We would lose jobs—a lot of them because casinos would be forced to close in a dwindling market.

New Jersey's public investment in a new convention center, in airport development, would be seriously compromised. Millions spent on new infrastructure and highway development would have been wasted. Atlantic City, even today, is a state resource and treasure which would be immediately undermined.

Let's forget Donald Trump and the casino industry for a moment. What about New Jersey's citizens? Certainly the millions for seniors and the disabled and reinvestment would decrease quite measurably. The money will not be replaced by an Indian casino.

What about the state? Would New Jersey be able to assure itself that its public policy of strict regulation would be maintained? Not to the extent that it now controls the regulation of gaming in Atlantic City. Under existing laws, no state has prerogative over Indian gaming. Therefore, the state would be powerless to carry out its regulatory policy over these operations. It is quite a dichotomy. New Jersey, which has prided itself as the state with the strictest form of casino regulation, could be forced to accept lesser standards for Indian tribes operating within its state. Such is the nature of State-Indian compact negotiations where states are forced to accept less than optimum regulatory measures out of fear that they will be sued by Indian tribes for not negotiating in "good faith."

The Rights of the Workers

And what about workers? Did you know, for example, at the 1993 AFL-CIO meeting in San Francisco that some of our largest unions, the Service Workers, the Seafarers, the Operating Engineers and the Restaurant and Hotel Workers joined to form the Riverboat and Indian Gaming Service Trade Council? The purpose of the council is clear-cut—to protect workers. Do you know why? Because federal laws, like the Taft-Hartley, like the jurisdiction of the National Labor Relations Board, do not apply. They also cease to exist at the tribal land doorstep. At present, union workers, even in states like New Jersey, would have no federally or state-protected rights or the ability to organize in casinos operated on tribal lands. The unions hope to do something about this. They hope to gain the right to recognition, the right to organize if they so choose. Quite frankly, I hope they have better luck than we have had so far.

> *"An Indian casino operation in northern New Jersey would be the economic death knell to Atlantic City."*

So, gentlemen, the issue is really not Donald Trump and the moneyed casino interests against various Indian tribes. The issue is whether our government, in recognizing the legitimate rights of our native Americans, will simultaneously assure that the rights of our state's own citizens, our workers, our seniors and, yes, even Donald Trump, are not bargained away or stomped upon in the process.

Chapter 3

How Should Tribal Resources Be Used?

Native American Resources: An Overview

by David Rich Lewis

About the author: *David Rich Lewis is an associate professor of history at Utah State University in Logan.*

Traditionally Native Americans have had an immediate and reciprocal relationship with their natural environments. At contact, they lived in relatively small groups close to the earth. They defined themselves by the land and sacred places, and recognized a unity in their physical and spiritual universe. Their cosmologies connected them with all animate and inanimate beings. Indians moved in a sentient world, managing its bounty and diversity carefully lest they upset the spirit "bosses," who balanced and endowed that world. They acknowledged the power of Mother Earth and the mutual obligation between hunter and hunted as coequals. Indians celebrated the earth's annual rebirth and offered thanks for her first fruits. They ritually addressed and prepared the animals they killed, the agricultural fields they tended, and the vegetal and mineral materials they processed. They used song and ritual speech to modify their world, while physically transforming that landscape with fire and water, brawn and brain. They did not passively adapt, but responded in diverse ways to adjust environments to meet their cultural as well as material desires.

Euroamerican Contact

The pace of change in Indian environments increased dramatically with Euroamerican contact. Old World pathogens and epidemic diseases, domesticated plants and livestock, the disappearance of native flora and fauna, and changing resource use patterns altered the physical and cultural landscape of the New World. Nineteenth-century removal and reservation policies reduced the continental scope of Indian lands to mere islands in the stream of American settlement. Reservations themselves were largely unwanted or remote environments of little perceived economic value. Indian peoples lost even that land as the General Allotment Act of 1887 divided reservations into individual holdings.

By 1930, this policy contributed to the alienation of over 80 percent of Indian lands—a diminishment of land, resources, and biotic diversity that relegated Indians to the periphery of American society.

By the beginning of the twentieth century, Native Americans controlled mere remnants of their former estates, most in the trans-Mississippi West. Relatively valueless by nineteenth-century standards, their lands contained unseen resources of immense worth. This single fact informs nearly all Native American environmental issues in the twentieth century. Land, its loss, location, and resource wealth or poverty, the exploitation and development of that land, and changing Indian needs and religious attitudes all define the modern environmental debates.

By the beginning of the twentieth century, agriculture and grazing had fundamentally changed the face of Indian lands. In Oklahoma and on the high plains, Indians and agents cleared, plowed, and planted large areas in a succession of monoculture crops. Overcropping marginal lands, drought, the Dust Bowl, the Great Depression, isolation, and the vagaries of the American market economy led to the wide-scale abandonment of Indian agriculture after World War II. Likewise, the adoption of domestic animals radically changed the landscape and biotic diversity of reservations. In the 1930s, the government instituted drastic livestock reduction and reseeding programs on southwestern reservations. Range scientists introduced new plant and animal species into fragile ecosystems, but were unable to solve problems of overgrazing on the drought-ravaged Navajo and Papago reservations. On a cultural level, the programs backfired by ignoring Native explanations and ecological methods, resulting in increased Indian economic dependence. Since then, tribes have had to deal with overgrazing and erosion, invasive noxious plants, reclamation, and improper land use. Given past experience, tribes are beginning to weigh the relative utility of leasing lands to non-Indians against developing their own operations which might be more sensitive to sustainable agricultural alternatives.

> *"Land, its loss, location, and resource wealth or poverty, . . . all define the modern environmental debates."*

In the early twentieth century, some reservations contained extensive forests that made them attractive targets for exploitation. To protect these forests government officials outlawed Indian burning as a means of environmental management—clearing forest underbrush to reduce the potential for destructive crown fires while improving game animal habitat and useful vegetal materials. Government-managed timber sales brought some economic development and prosperity to the Yurok, Karuk, Hupa, and Klamath of California and Oregon; to Western Apaches in Arizona; and to Chippewas and Menominees in Minnesota and Wisconsin. But gross mismanagement of sustained yield programs led to reckless clear-cutting, erosion, and the loss of forest habitats on all these reservations. In the Black Hills of South

Dakota and near Taos Pueblo's sacred Blue Lake, lumbering operations in national forests threatened sacred sites. The process continues today as the Bureau of Land Management chain-clears piñon-juniper forests in Nevada to improve the grazing potential of the land for white permit holders, destroying traditional Western Shoshone resources and gathering areas without Indian consent.

Hunting and Fishing Rights

Modern hunting, gathering, and fishing rights based on nineteenth-century treaties have created a number of problems between Indians, sportsmen, and state and federal governments. In the early twentieth century, under pressure from commercial and sports fishermen, state and federal officials limited Indian off-reservation hunting and fishing. These regulations hit Native fishermen in the Northwest particularly hard. They were competing with a growing number of commercial operations and losing Native fishing sites to dams. In the 1960s, Indian activists staged "fish-ins" to publicize the situation, and tribes took their case to court. In *United States v. State of Washington* (1974), Judge George Boldt reaffirmed the rights of Northwest tribes to harvest fish under provisions of the 1854 Treaty of Medicine Creek, without interference by the State of Washington. The *Boldt* decision restored a measure of Indian control over their environment and natural resource use. Today, these tribes have built a world-class fishery management system,

> *"Tribes are beginning to weigh the relative utility of leasing lands to non-Indians against developing their own operations."*

allowing them a sizable subsistence and small commercial catch. Likewise, the Mescalero Apaches, Pyramid Lake Paiutes, Wind River Shoshones, and Arapahos have developed scientific and culturally sensitive programs for managing their faunal resources.

Across the country, hunting and fishing rights continue to stir public debate. In Wisconsin, ugly confrontations between whites and Chippewas over off-reservation hunting and spearfishing continue even after court decisions quantified Indian treaty rights at 50 percent of the annual harvest—a level Indians have never approached. On the Uintah-Ouray Reservation in Utah, Northern Utes and terminated mixed-blooded people fight over reservation hunting, fishing, and use privileges. White sportsmen and environmentalists question Native rights to kill bald eagles, bowhead whales, Florida panthers, or other endangered species guaranteed under the National Environmental Policy Act of 1969 and the American Indian Religious Freedom Act of 1978—both of which have environmental consequences by protecting Native cultural and religious practices. The acts have safeguarded and allowed Indian access to sacred non-reservation areas and resources, and injected a level of legal tolerance to Native religious practices that revolve around resource use.

121

Chapter 3

Water

Since the majority of Indian reservations are in the arid West, it is understandable that water has been a central environmental issue. By 1900, whites actively competed with Indians for this scarce resource. At Fort Belknap Indian Reservation in Montana, white settlers diverted water from the Milk River. When ordered to stop, they argued that the Indians had not made prior appropriation use. In 1908 the Supreme Court ruled in *Winters v. United States* that in establishing reservations, Congress implied and reserved the priority water rights necessary for present and future use. Encouraged by the *Winters* decision, the Indian Bureau used Indian funds to construct elaborate irrigation systems to protect Indian water and improve the agricultural potential of tribal and allotted holdings. Irrigation promised to change the landscape and increase Indian self-sufficiency, but the systems suffered from poor construction, improper use and maintenance, and often ended up in the hands of white settlers who bought up the best Indian lands.

Twentieth-century reclamation, irrigation, and big dam projects have had unforeseen consequences for Indians and their lands. As part of the Newlands Project in 1905, the government dammed and diverted the Truckee River for white irrigation. The Lahontan trout, the Pyramid Paiutes' chief source of subsistence, became extinct, and the diversion of water nearly killed Pyramid Lake. During the New Deal, the Civilian Conservation Corps and Indian Emergency Conservation Works program completed numerous, if not always successful, water and erosion control projects on western reservations. Since the 1930s, dams on the Columbia River and its tributaries have impeded the migration of salmon and other anadromous species, flooded sacred sites and Indian fisheries like Celilo Falls, and ruined upstream spawning grounds. On the Missouri River, the Pick-Sloan Plan for damming and flood control proved disastrous for Indians of the Standing Rock, Cheyenne River, Crow Creek, and Fort Berthold reservations. They watched the waters cover rich agricultural lands, villages, and sacred sites in the name of progress. Similar things happened in the 1960s and 1970s with Senecas and the Kinzua Dam, and Eastern Cherokees and the Tellico Dam.

Today, these dams raise important environmental issues of water flow through places like the Hualapai and Havasupai reservations in the Grand Canyon, of aquatic species preservation and Indian fishing rights, and the ownership and sale of water. While the *Winters* Doctrine assured Indian water rights, it never quantified those rights. The issue of how much water tribes can legitimately use and sell has become critical in the arid West, especially for tribes in states member to the Colorado River Compact. The pending

> *"Hunting, gathering, and fishing rights . . . have created a number of problems between Indians, sportsmen, and state and federal governments."*

122

completion of the Central Utah and Central Arizona projects promises a massive redistribution of water in the arid West and a test of Indian water rights. Future water marketing by Shoshones, Utes, Paiutes, Navajos, Tohono O'odhams, and other groups raises critical economic and environmental issues for Indian peoples and the entire region.

Pollution

In addition to water, the mineral wealth of some modern western Indian reservations has proved both a blessing and a curse. Beginning as early as 1900 with the discovery of oil on Osage land, non-renewable resource development to ease reservation economic dependency has unleashed the most environmentally destructive forms of exploitation, threatening tribal land, water, air, and health. Government mismanagement has compounded these problems. Coal and uranium mining on the Navajo Reservation has destroyed large areas of land, polluted water and air, and caused untold long-term health problems. The 273-mile-long Black Mesa coal-slurry pipeline sucks 1.4 billion gallons of water every year out of the arid region, lowering the water table and literally undermining Hopi water sources. Coal from Black Mesa fires the Navajo Generating Station near Page, Arizona, casting a haze over the Grand Canyon and Four Corners region. Despite the efforts of the Council of Energy Resource Tribes to balance use and protection of Native resources, mining, oil, and gas exploration scars thousands of acres of Indian land. In Alaska, the Alaska Native Claims Settlement Act (1971) and the subsequent North Slope energy boom with its drilling sites, pipelines, and access roads has transformed the landscape, threatening migratory mammals and waterfowl and contributing to changes in Native Alaskan land use and ownership patterns.

> *"Governments and industries are looking at reservations as potential disposal sites for solid, hazardous, and nuclear wastes."*

Off-site pollution is a major problem for Native Americans. When tankers like the Exxon *Valdez* spill their cargoes of crude oil, they pollute thousands of miles of coastline destroying both Native and white resources. Pollutants from mining and processing plants migrate into reservation air and water. Cyanide heap-leach mining in Montana is polluting water on the Fort Belknap Reservation. Radioactive pollution and toxic waste from the Hanford nuclear weapons plant threatens all tribes who depend on the Columbia River salmon for their livelihood. The Mdewakanton Sioux of Prairie Island, Minnesota, fear the health impacts of a nuclear power plant built on the edge of their small reservation, while Western Shoshones protest the use of their land as a nuclear test site. Industrial waste dumps surround the St. Regis Indian Reservation, fouling the St. Lawrence River. Poorly treated urban waste and agricultural effluent threatens nearby reservation environments. Today, groups like the Standing Rock

Sioux and Northern Cheyenne are beginning to enforce federal laws protecting their land, water, and air from such pollution.

Governments and industries are looking at reservations as potential disposal sites for solid, hazardous, and nuclear wastes. In 1990 the Pine Ridge Sioux rejected proposals by subsidiaries of O&G Industries to build a landfill, but the neighboring Rosebud Sioux council approved a 5,700-acre facility, "big enough to take care of all the waste in the United States." Under the proposal, they would receive one dollar per ton of trash, an economic bonanza for the depressed reservation unless, as some Sioux and environmental critics warn, the dump becomes a toxic nightmare. The pressure for some type of economic development and employment on underdeveloped and resource-poor reservations has led the Campo of California to agree to a 600-acre landfill, and the Kaibab-Paiutes of Arizona and Kaw of Oklahoma to accept hazardous waste incinerators. Presently, the Mescalero Apaches, Skull Valley Goshutes, and others are debating the location of nuclear waste storage facilities on their lands. Their decisions may pose long-term environmental problems that could outweigh the short-term benefits.

At Odds with Environmentalists

In recent years, tribal development and land use has put some Indians at odds with environmentalists. This fascinating turn of events emerges as modern Indians begin placing needs over older cultural regulatory patterns, shattering white stereotypes of Indians as "the original conservationists." Early environmentalists found inspiration in Native American actions and attitudes. Those who followed perpetuated many of the grosser stereotypes of Indians as beings who left no mark on the land, essentially denying them their humanity, culture, history, and modernity. In the 1960s and 1970s, Indians became symbols for the counterculture and conservation movements—Iron Eyes Cody shedding a tear in television ads as he looked over a polluted landscape; an apocryphal speech attributed to Chief Seattle became the litany of true believers. The issue continues to be hotly debated. Indians were never ecologists—something that refers to a highly abstract and systematic science—but they were careful students of their functional environments, bound by material and cultural needs and constraints, striving for maximum sustained yield, not maximum production. They possessed an elaborate land ethic based on use, reciprocity, and balance. Those attitudes persist today and contribute to the debate within and between Indian communities, corporations, environmentalists, and governments about the future of Indian peoples and environments.

Native Americans Have the Right to Restrict the Development of Tribal Resources

by Gail Small

About the author: *Gail Small is a member of the Northern Cheyenne tribe and Director of Native Action, a nonprofit organization in Lame Deer, Montana. She graduated from the University of Oregon School of Law in 1982.*

My tribe, the Northern Cheyenne, lives on 500,000 acres of beautiful ponderosa pine country in southeastern Montana. Our reservation has tremendous cultural significance for us. Two years after the Cheyenne defeated Custer at the Battle of Little Bighorn [in 1876], they were taken as prisoners of war in reprisal, and marched to Indian Territory in what is now Oklahoma. Tribal oral tradition states that the Cheyenne were quickly dying there of malaria and other diseases, and agreed that they would rather die fighting to return to their beloved northland than die of the white man's diseases, as his prisoners.

The Cheyenne told the U.S. government agent that they were leaving for their homeland, and asked him to let them get a short distance from the fort before bloodying the ground. Only a few hundred Cheyenne survived this walk north. Our reservation thus represents the blood and tears of our grandparents, who willingly gave their lives so that we might live here.

The Threat from Coal Mines

The Cheyenne now find our reservation being surrounded by the largest coal stripmines in this country, and the threat that the mines will encroach on our own land is ever-present. I have been involved in the fight to protect our reservation and southeastern Montana from coal mining since the 1970s, when I was in high school. It was then that the Cheyenne learned the horrifying news that

From Gail Small, "War Stories," *Amicus Journal*, Spring 1994. Reprinted with permission.

the Bureau of Indian Affairs had leased over half our reservation for stripmining, at the paltry rate of 17 cents per ton, with no environmental safeguards included in the leases.

Every resource of our small tribe was committed to the battle against those leases. The enormity of our situation frightened and angered us. I was one of several young Cheyenne sent by the tribe to investigate coal mines in Navaho country and Wyoming; at one point, twenty of us had our picture taken standing inside a huge coal shovel, to demonstrate the size of the

> *"Our reservation has tremendous cultural significance for us."*

industrial operation that coal mining would bring to our land. After college, I served on the tribal committee charged with voiding the leases—the only member with a college degree. We were fortunate to find a capable young attorney with a passion for Indians and for justice, but it took almost fifteen years of anxiety and sacrifices by the people before the Northern Cheyenne convinced Congress to void the coal leases.

Today, however, Cheyenne coal has become still more valuable. There are no coal mines on my reservation yet, and no coal leases have been signed. But every year, the tribe debates again whether we can afford to continue refusing the offers of the coal companies. And every year the mines on nearby land come closer. Current plans call for opening up the Powder River Country (our best hunting grounds) by building a railroad directly along the Tongue River (our major water source). Our most traditional village, the Birney community, is directly across the river from the site of the proposed railroad and the five new coal mines.

The Northern Cheyenne are not the only Indians who face such problems. Tribes across the country find their lands aggressively sought after for their energy resources and as dumping grounds for America's waste. Indian tribes own over a third of the low-sulfur coal west of the Mississippi, as much as half of the privately owned uranium in the country, and sizable reserves of oil, natural gas, and oil shale. The instability and depletion of world energy supplies—along with the 1990 Clean Air Act Amendments, which favor low-sulfur coal—have increased the pressure for these reserves. Promises of overnight wealth to impoverished tribes serve to divide and conquer the people, as federal agencies, energy corporations, and private speculators seek to dump nuclear waste or get rich off Indian land.

Sovereignty and Trusteeship

By necessity, then, Indian tribes are major players in the environmental justice movement. Their legal situation, however, is unique. It derives from their status as the indigenous peoples and the original landlords of this country.

Indian reservations represent an American legal quid pro quo: in return for relinquishing claim to thousands of acres of their aboriginal lands, the tribes reserved for themselves homelands and various other rights in the treaties they negotiated with the United States. The premise of the Reserved Rights Doctrine is that the treaties were not a grant of rights to the Indians, but rather a reservation of rights they already possessed. Many past judicial decisions have complicated what is now known as tribal sovereignty, but the tribal right of self-government has been repeatedly affirmed by the U.S. Supreme Court, and the tribes' jurisdiction over their homelands remains substantially intact.

Another factor complicating tribal sovereignty is the unique trust relationship between the federal government, specifically Congress, and the Indian tribes. The federal government, as trustee, asserts plenary power over Indian tribes (under the legal rhetoric that we need protecting). In general, federal laws apply on reservations, although tribal governments have the inherent right to establish tribal environmental laws that are stronger than the federal statutes. Because the trust relationship preempts jurisdiction by the states, it has served to safeguard Indian rights and resources and preserve Indian self-government. The trust relationship also requires that any action by the federal government, or its agencies, affecting Indian property or rights be consistent with the most exacting fiduciary standards.

> "Indians believe in the spiritual nature of the environment."

As self-governing entities, tribes have the legal authority for environmental regulation and enforcement of tribal environmental laws; they also have the proprietary and police powers for environmental protection. Why, then, is it so difficult for Indian tribes to protect their environments? One reason is that, as the Northern Cheyenne found when we fought the coal leases in court during the 1970s and 1980s, it is extremely difficult for Indian tribes to sue our federal trustee for breach of trust.

Another reason, which cannot be underestimated, is that no significant federal assistance has ever been provided to develop the tribal government infrastructure necessary for environmental protection. In fact, fiduciary standards or no, only a dime of every dollar appropriated by Congress for Indians ever reaches the reservations. Most of the monies are eaten by the massive bureaucracy of the Bureau of Indian Affairs. (And yet, when it is a question of the study and development of coal mines, uranium mines, and nuclear waste dumps on reservations, federal funds always appear.)

My tribe experienced this problem in 1977, when, seeing the coal mines growing larger and coming closer, our tribal leaders decided to protect our air quality. They petitioned the U.S. Environmental Protection Agency (EPA) for the right to designate our air quality as Class I, among the cleanest in the country, and to apply the most stringent air-quality standards. The Northern Cheyenne tribe was the first government entity to take this step—but we had to lead the EPA by the hand for more than ten years before it acknowledged that we were a government, with the right to funding and enforcement authority under the Clean Air Act. The Northern Cheyenne are still fighting this battle. We were eventually forced to settle with the coal companies in a lawsuit we had brought over some nearby power plants, simply to get the funds to establish air quality monitoring stations on the reservation.

A Need for Funds

As tribes begin to draft and enact their own environmental laws, the need for government infrastructure is becoming more desperate. Tribal environmental protection agencies must be adequately funded and staffed to implement these laws, tribal courts to enforce them. And the monies should go directly to the tribes, not to the various intermediary organizations that claim to provide technical assistance.

This means that it is not enough for our federal trustee simply to amend environmental laws by acknowledging tribal governments for "substantially the same treatment as a state," a step that is now becoming more common. Without adequate funding, the laws will remain law on paper only. At a series of Tribal Issues Workgroups held by EPA's Office of Environmental Equity throughout 1993, tribal delegates informed EPA that it has never fully implemented either the spirit or the letter of the law. Indeed, some tribes declared the phrase "treatment as a state" offensive, considering the long-standing funding inequities.

The funding question is made still more urgent by the general poverty of the tribes. The Northern Cheyenne have refused extravagant offers from the coal companies, while directing every resource we have to the legal battles against coal mining on nearby land. The people have foregone indoor plumbing, roads, and schools for the environmental integrity of this region. It is no small sacrifice. The elderly man who lives next door to my office must use an outhouse, and as I write it is 20 degrees below zero. And our tribe is now fighting the coal boom towns in order to secure a high school of our own for our 400 high-school-aged students, but the boom towns have far more money.

Many younger Cheyenne regard EPA's failure to fund tribal environmental protection as institutional racism. We have also seen this attitude in the white environmental organizations, which failed to respond to our calls for help in fighting mining in the region—even though the mines are destroying pristine wilderness on

> *"Whenever the destructive forces threatening Indian reservations prevail, the real loser is the American public."*

federal lands. It was my idea to make these requests, and when they went unanswered, our Tribal President told me that I was young and naive, and that I had to learn to strategize under the assumption that we have few allies. And indeed, it has been my experience that Americans would rather fight for the rainforest than join the battle being waged in their own backyards.

Opposing Views

Perhaps this is true partly because opposing world views separate our understanding of the environment from that of other Americans. Indians believe in the spiritual nature of the environment, something that cannot be quantified and cannot be preserved through "mitigation" of environmentally harmful development. As an elder of my tribe has said, "There is no word in our language for mitigation. We cannot even understand the concept."

The federal agencies charged with helping us protect our environment cannot do so unless they understand this interdependence of environment, culture, and religion in the tribal way of life. When I worked as a tribal sociologist some years ago, I once took a draft tribal water code to the five villages of my reservation for public input. I found that protection of the water spirits was a preeminent concern throughout the reservation, and that the spirits varied depending on whether the water source was a river, lake, or spring. I reported back to the attorneys who had been contracted by the U.S. government to draw up the code, and they laughed at my findings.

But it was no laughing matter a few years later, when an elderly Cheyenne man with a rifle held off an ARCO drilling team that had planned to lay lines of dynamite across his spring—an archaic practice no longer used in most drilling operations outside Indian reservations. "Today is a good day to die," he said, holding his old hunting rifle before him. I represented him in tribal court the next morning, seeking a restraining order against ARCO. And I cried with him as he told me how the water spirits sometimes came out and danced at this spring.

Eventually, we saved the spring. But whenever the destructive forces threatening Indian reservations prevail, the real loser is the American public; for what is at stake is the last remaining indigenous knowledge of the spiritual and curative powers of this country's environment. And as I write, the coal fight is beginning again on my reservation, as it has every year for the past three decades. Another coal contract is before the Council, the coal company is promising to make every Cheyenne a millionaire, and some are arguing that we must cut off the toe to save the body—that we should lease a small part of the reservation, because we need the white man's money in order to give our children a way out of poverty.

Like many Cheyenne, I feel as if I have already lived a lifetime fighting strip-mining. We live with fear, anger, and urgency. And we long for a better life for our tribe.

Native Americans Should Use Their Resources More Efficiently

by Terry L. Anderson

About the author: *Terry L. Anderson is the executive director of the Political Economy Research Center in Bozeman, Montana, and a professor of economics at Montana State University.*

Hollywood images and romantic environmentalism would have us see American Indians as so in harmony with nature they left no mark on it. A Sierra Club book about forestry claims, "For many thousands of years, most of the indigenous nations on this continent practiced a philosophy of protection first and use second of the forest." According to former Secretary of the Interior Stewart Udall, "The Indians were, in truth, the pioneer ecologists of this country." Calling for an environmental ethic patterned after that of Native Americans, Sen. John H. Chafee (R-R.I.) quoted words allegedly spoken by 19th-century Indian Chief Seattle: "Man did not weave the web of life. He is merely a strand of it."

A Myth, Not Reality

This image of a Native American environmental ethic, however appealing, is more myth than reality. The actual history of Native American resource use does not always mesh with the spiritual environmental ethos attributed to them. By focusing on myth instead of reality, environmentalists patronize American Indians and neglect the lessons of their rich institutional heritage encouraging resource conservation.

The impression that American Indians were guided by a unique environmental ethic often can be traced to the speech widely attributed to Chief Seattle in 1854. But Chief Seattle never said those oft-quoted words: They were written by Ted Perry, a scriptwriter, who acknowledged paraphrasing a translation of the speech for a movie about pollution. According to historian Paul Wilson,

From Terry L. Anderson, "Dances with Myths," *Reason*, February 1997. Reprinted with permission of the publisher.

Perry's version added "a good deal more, particularly modern ecological imagery." For example, Perry, not Chief Seattle, wrote that "every part of the Earth is sacred to my people." (Perry, by the way, has tried unsuccessfully to get the truth out.)

The speech reflects what many environmentalists want to hear, not what Chief Seattle said. The poignant and romantic image created by the speech obscures the fact, fully acknowledged by historians, that American Indians transformed the North American landscape. Sometimes these changes were beneficial, at other times harmful. But they were almost always a rational response to abundance or scarcity.

For example, where land was abundant, it made sense to farm extensively and move on. Indians would commonly clear land for farming by cutting and burning forests. After clearing, they would farm the fields extensively until they depleted soil fertility; then the Indians would clear new lands and start the process again. From New England to the Southwest, wherever Indian populations were dense and farming was intense, deforestation was common. Indeed, the mysterious departure of the Anasazi from the canyons of southeastern Utah in the 13th century may have been due to their having depleted the wood supplies they used for fuel.

Slaughtering Game

Similarly, where game was plentiful, Indians used only the choicest cuts and left the rest. When the buffalo hunting tribes on the Great Plains herded hundreds of animals over cliffs in the 18th and early 19th centuries, tons of meat were left to rot or to be eaten by scavengers—hardly a result consistent with the environmental ethic attributed to Indians. Samuel Hearne, a fur trader near Hudson's Bay, recorded in his journal in the 1770s that the Chipewayan Indians would slaughter large numbers of caribou and musk ox, eat only a few tongues, and leave the rest to rot.

Indians also manipulated the land to improve hunting. Upland wooded areas from east to west were burned to remove the undergrowth and increase forage for deer, elk, and bison. Indeed, because of this burning, it's possible that fewer "old growth" forests existed in the Pacific Northwest when the first Europeans arrived than exist today. In some cases, however, the improvements sought by burning were short term, because anthropogenic fire altered the succession of forests. In the Southeast, for example, oak and hickory forests with a higher carrying capacity for

"American Indians transformed the North American landscape."

deer were displaced by fire-resistant longleaf pine that support only limited wildlife. Biologist Charles Kay concludes that "Native Americans were the ultimate keystone species, and their removal has completely altered ecosystems, not only in the Intermountain West but throughout North America."

Generally the demand for meat, hides, and furs by relatively small, dispersed populations of Indians put little pressure on wildlife. But in some cases game populations were overharvested or even driven to extinction. Anthropologist Paul Martin believes that the extinction of the mammoth, mastodon, ground sloth, and the saber-toothed cat directly or indirectly resulted from the "prehistoric overkill" by exceptionally competent hunters.

> *"American Indian tribes produced and sustained abundant wealth because they had clear property rights to land, fishing and hunting territories, and personal property."*

Historian Louis S. Warren drives the final nail in the coffin of the "living in harmony with nature" myth: "[T]o claim that Indians lived without affecting nature is akin to saying that they lived without touching anything, that they were a people without history. Indians often manipulated their local environments, and while they usually had far less impact on their environments than European colonists would, the idea of 'preserving' land in some kind of wilderness state would have struck them as impractical and absurd. More often than not, Indians profoundly shaped the ecosystems around them."

Of course, shaping doesn't have to mean despoiling. Whether this shaping encouraged conservation depended, for Indians as for humans everywhere, on the incentives created by the extant system of property rights. The historical American Indians did not practice a sort of environmental communism in tune with the Earth; yesterday, as today, they recognized property rights.

Today we refer to "Indian nations," but this term mostly reflects the U.S. government's desire to have another government with which to negotiate. In fact, Indian tribes were mainly language groups made up of relatively independent bands with little centralized control except at specific times when they might gather for ceremonies, hunts, or wars. And after the horse allowed small bands to efficiently hunt buffalo, even that level of centralization diminished.

Indian Property Rights

Just because Indians lacked modern concepts of government doesn't mean they lacked rules. American Indian tribes produced and sustained abundant wealth because they had clear property rights to land, fishing and hunting territories, and personal property. Pre-Columbian Indian history is replete with examples of property rights conditioning humans' relations with the natural environment.

Where land was scarce and making it productive required investments, private ownership by family units was common. Families among the Mahican Indians in the Northeast possessed hereditary rights to use well-defined tracts of garden land along the rivers. Europeans recognized this ownership, and deeds of white settlers indicate that they usually approached lineage leaders to purchase this land. Before European contact, other Indian tribes recognized Mahican ownership of these lands by not trespassing.

In the Southeast and the Southwest, private ownership of land was also common. "The Creek town is typical of the economic and social life of the populous tribes of the Southeast," writes historian Angie Debo. "[E]ach family gathered the produce of its own plot and placed it in its own storehouse. Each also contributed voluntarily to a public store which was kept in a large building in the field and was used under the direction of the town chief for public needs." The Havasupai and Hopi also recognized private ownership of farmland as long as it remained in use. Clans identified their fields with boundary stones at each corner with their symbols painted on them.

> *"Indians . . . built their societies around institutions that encouraged good human and natural resource stewardship."*

Fruit and nut trees that required long-term investment and care were privately owned and even inherited. In one case a Northern Paiute Indian reflected that his father "paid a horse for a certain piñon-nut range," suggesting that the property rights were valuable and could be traded. Among Indians in California, families owned piñon, mesquite, screw-bean trees, and a few wild-seed patches, with ownership marked by lines of rocks along the boundaries. Though owners would sometimes allow others to gather food during times of abundance, trespass was not tolerated. John Muir, founder of the Sierra Club, even reports that the owner of a piñon tree killed a white man for felling his tree.

Wildlife Conservation

Throughout North America, Indians dependent on hunting and fishing had well-defined territories within which they practiced wildlife conservation. Hunting groups among the Montagnais-Naskapi of Quebec between Hudson Bay and the Gulf of St. Lawrence recognized family and clan hunting areas, particularly for beaver when it became an important trade item. Quoting Indian informants, anthropologists Frank Speck and Wendell Hadlock report that, for New Brunswick, "It was an established 'rule that when a hunter worked a territory no other would knowingly or willfully encroach upon the region for several generations.' Some of the men held districts which had been hunted by their fathers, and presumably their grandfathers." They even had a colloquial term that translates to "my hunting ground." The Algonkian Indians from the Atlantic to the Great Lakes also had family hunting territories that passed from generation to generation. In these tracts, families sustained harvestable game populations by deliberate rotation systems. The Paiute Indians of the Owens Valley in California hunted together in groups with well-defined territories bounded by mountains, ridges, and streams. Distinct Apache bands had their own hunting grounds and seldom encroached on other territories.

In the Pacific Northwest, Indians had well-defined rights to spawning streams. To capture salmon returning from the ocean to spawn in freshwater streams, they placed fish wheels, weirs, and other fixed appliances at falls or shoals where the fish were naturally channeled. The Indians' technology was so efficient they could have depleted salmon stocks, but they realized the importance of allowing some of the spawning fish to escape upstream.

Relying on salmon as their main source of food, then, the coastal Tlingit and Haida Indians established clan rights to fishing locations where salmon congregated on their journey to spawning beds. (They also had rights to bear and goat hunting areas, berry and root patches, hot springs, sea otter grounds, seal and sea lion rocks, shellfish beds, cedar stands, and even trade routes.) The management units could exclude other clans or houses from their fishing territories. Management decisions were generally made by the yitsati, or "keeper of the house," who had the power to make and enforce decisions regarding harvest levels, escapement, fishing seasons, and harvest methods.

Indian salmon fishing rights stand in sharp contrast to the white man's law that supplanted them. When Europeans arrived on the Columbia River, they ignored Indian rights and simply placed their nets at the mouths of rivers, leaving no fish to spawn. To counter the overfishing, nets were outlawed at the beginning of the 20th century and ever since, fishermen have been encouraged to chase salmon around the open ocean in expensive boats equipped with sophisticated gear. The result is what economic historian Robert Higgs has called the "legally induced technical regress in the Washington salmon fishery."

The Benefits of Private Ownership

Private ownership encouraged investment and production in personal property as well. The tepee of the Plains Indians, for example, was owned by the woman who might spend weeks or months collecting, scraping, tanning, and sewing together eight to 20 buffalo hides for the completed shelter. Time spent chipping arrowheads, constructing bows and arrows, and weaving baskets was rewarded with private ownership of the completed capital equipment.

The horse was the most vivid example of the benefits of private ownership to the American Indian. Acquired by Plains Indians in the latter half of the 18th century, the horse offered them a life of abundance. With the horse they could follow the vast buffalo herds and ride into the herd to harvest as many animals as they wanted. The horse became one of the Indian's most important sources of wealth. In Canada in the early 1800s, a buffalo horse cost more than 10 guns—a price far higher than any other tribal possession. A turn-of-the-century account of a wealthy Blackfoot man describes it as a "fine sight to see one of those big men among the Blackfeet, who has two or three lodges, five or six wives, twenty or thirty children, and fifty to a hundred horses; for his trade amounts to upward of $2,000 a year." Converting this amount to current dollars, such a man had an annual income of approximately $500,000.

Just as private ownership encouraged resource conservation, positive rewards encouraged investment in human and physical capital. In the case of rabbit hunts, which required leadership skills and nets for catching the rabbits, the leader and owner of the net garnered a larger share of the catch.

For hunting larger game with bow and arrow, not only did the archer have to spend hours chipping arrowheads, making arrows, and constructing his bow, he had to perfect his shooting and riding skills. The proficient hunter was rewarded for his investment with the buffalo's skin and the choicest cuts of meat. To establish his claim on an animal, the archer marked his arrows with distinctive symbols. Those without horses or without riding and shooting skills assisted in the butchering and thereby earned a right to lower cuts. The Omaha tribe developed an elaborate nomenclature to describe rewards for those who killed and butchered buffalo.

The Importance of Incentives

In sum, faced with the reality of scarcity, Indians understood the importance of incentives and built their societies around institutions that encouraged good human and natural resource stewardship. Though ethics and spiritual values may have inculcated a respect for nature, more than mysticism encouraged conservation of scarce resources. Rather, an elaborate set of social institutions that today would be called private property rights discouraged irresponsible behavior and rewarded stewardship. As historian Louis Warren puts it, "Among other things, Indian history is a tale of constant innovation and change. . . . If there is a single, characteristic Indian experience of the environment, perhaps it is the ability to change lifeways in radical fashion to maintain culture and identity."

Unfortunately, this historic innovation and adaptation have been lost today in a morass of bureaucratic controls emanating from Washington. Throughout Indian reservations, especially in the West, Indians control abundant natural resource and environmental amenities that could be better managed if tribes would return to their rich heritage of positive rewards for good stewardship instead of relying on romantic world views promoted by non-Indian environmentalists.

Wildlife management on Indian reservations offers a distinct contrast between lessons lost and lessons learned from the history of Indian culture and institutions. In many respects, Indians on reservations have tremendous resources. Relying on treaties signed in the 19th century, courts have granted Indians sovereign rights to fish and wildlife, both on and off reservations. Indians have rights to half the harvestable salmon and steelhead in the Pacific Northwest. They may use gillnets not available to non-Indian fishers in the Great Lakes. They may hunt walruses and polar bears without regulation by the state of Alaska. In Wisconsin,

> *"Modern reservations are often a wildlife 'commons' where ownership is only established by killing animals."*

135

they have special hunting privileges on public lands, including an 85-day deer season and the right to hunt from vehicles.

When Killing Establishes Ownership

On most reservations, however, wildlife managers have lost sight of the value of the sort of private property institutions Indians used to rely on. Modern reservations are often a wildlife "commons" where ownership is only established by killing animals. Often, that policy results in the decimation of wildlife populations. Indian gillnetting for salmon on the West Coast has wiped out major runs of salmon on the Klamath/Trinity river system. An Alaska Fish and Game Department report documented one case of 214 caribou carcasses left to rot and "counted 24 caribou left whole—there was a snow machine track to each one. . . . Most had been there a considerable time."

On most western reservations, big game species are almost nonexistent despite excellent potential habitat. On the Crow Reservation in Montana, for example, very few big game animals such as deer and elk remain. According to a tribal wildlife official, non-Indians are not allowed to hunt on the reservation, but tribal members can hunt all year without limits. The few big game animals there are wander in from outside; they are not managed on a sustainable basis.

Outdoor writer Ted Williams describes what happens when wildlife belongs to everyone until it is harvested: "Over the past 25 years Shoshones and Arapahoes, equipped with snowmobiles, ATV's and high-powered rifles, have virtually wiped out elk, deer, moose and bighorns on the 2.2 million-acre Wind River Reservation in Wyoming. Repeated motions for modest self-regulation emanating from within the reservation have been defeated by vote of the tribal leaders. . . . [I]n one confined area 31 dead elk were found. In another, a retired Indian game warden mowed down an entire herd of 14. Meat piled up at local dumps. Antlers were exported to the Orient where antlers and horns are ground to a power and hawked as an aphrodisiac."

Sustainable Management

The White Mountain Apache of east-central Arizona, by contrast, have shown what can happen in Indian country if you pay attention to incentives. This tribe is managing its trophy elk population and other wildlife opportunities on a sustainable basis—and making a profit. The Fort Apache Reservation covers 1.6 million acres—diverse habitat ranging from oak chaparral at lower elevations to mixed coniferous forests at the heights. This habitat supports about 12,000 free-ranging elk.

To get some idea of the success elk hunters enjoy, consider the reservation's track record. From 1977 to 1995, nontribal hunters have bagged 90 bull elk that made either Boone and Crockett or Safari Club record books. In comparison, this is about the same number of record elk taken from the entire state of Montana since record keeping began in 1932. Since 1980, nontribal hunters have enjoyed a 90 to 95 percent success rate. The average score for antlers has been 366 Boone and Crockett points. Such scores are the equivalent of a foursome averaging three under par for a round of golf.

The White Mountain Apaches have a large resource base, prime habitat and, according to reservation biologists, an elk herd whose genetics are ideal for producing trophy elk. But entrepreneurship and incentives have played a pivotal role on Fort Apache.

Before 1977, elk hunting on the reservation was better than on nearby national forest lands, but nowhere near its quality today. At that time, the state of Arizona issued about 700 nontribal hunting licenses, priced at $150 each, for hunting on the reservation. The state permits were required in addition to a tribal license, but the tribe received none of the revenue collected by the state. Each license entitled the bearer to shoot a bull elk regardless of size. Typical of state agencies, this policy maximized the number of hunter opportunities rather than the value of the hunt.

> *"Property rights are an integral part of American Indians' heritage."*

Fortunately for both the tribe and the elk, tribal leaders decided that they could capitalize on the market for trophy elk. In 1977, tribal Chairman Ronnie Lupe, with the backing of the 11-member tribal council, informed the state that the tribe would allow elk hunting without a state permit and would control all hunting and fishing on the reservation. The state opposed this but eventually acquiesced after a federal court decision.

The tribe's first order of business was to reduce the hunting pressure on immature bulls by ending the general elk hunt and replacing it with the trophy elk hunt. Elk hunting permits were reduced dramatically from 700 under state management to 30, and the price per permit was increased from $150 to $1,500. Revenue from the sale of these reservation permits went to the tribe's general fund.

The trophy elk hunting program blossomed. Mature bulls as a percentage of all bulls increased to 73 percent, and the number of record-book elk taken increased from three in the final six years of state management to eight per season. In addition to promoting trophy elk production, the tribe also designed a fine hunting experience, free from the crowded conditions on public lands.

The tribe tapped into the mother lode of hunter demand. In 1995, revenue from trophy elk hunting totaled well over $850,000. Sixty-six hunters paid $12,000 each for a seven-day trophy hunt. A special auction for four additional openings was also held, with an average winning bid of $24,000 and a high bid of $30,000. In spite of the $12,000 price tag, there is a five-year waiting list of hunters.

Other Opportunities

Less-expensive hunting opportunities exist too. These offer a way to maintain the proper bull-to-cow ratio in the herd and to manage other wildlife species.

For example, the tribe periodically issues 100 antlerless permits priced at $300 each, which have a hunter success rate of 80 percent. The tribe also offers hunting permits for bear ($150), javelina ($75), and wild turkey ($750). It costs $50 per season or $5.00 per day to hunt quail, squirrel, and cottontail rabbits.

In addition to hunting, the tribe manages other resources for amenity values and collects fees. While most reservation lakes and streams are open to bait fishing, certain select waters are restricted to flies and lures. Fish species include native Apache cutthroat, brown, brook, and rainbow trout, and some Arctic grayling. Yearly fishing permits are priced at $80, summer permits at $50, and day permits at $5.00. There is even a rent-a-lake program which allows Cyclone and Hurricane lakes to be rented for $300 a day with a three-day minimum. Fishing rights have proved lucrative, generating $600,000 in revenue in 1995.

When revenue from other services such as camping, boating, river rafting, and photographic safaris are added, amenity-based recreation enterprises generated nearly $2 million in 1995. This is comparable to the tribe's logging operation, casino, and ski resort as an important source of revenue and jobs. Entrepreneurship and management institutions that conserve wildlife have benefited both the White Mountain Apache and the wildlife on the reservation.

Wildlife Management Through Property Rights

American Indian history shows that calls for spiritual awakenings aren't enough for the environment; you need workable institutions that provide positive incentives for good stewardship. Because American Indians adapted their institutions to resource constraints, they were able to sustain life, often in hostile environments. Property rights are an integral part of American Indians' heritage. Refocusing on these institutions, as the White Mountain Apache have done, offers the best way for Native Americans to manage their resources on a sustainable, profitable basis.

Non-Indians also would do well to stop promulgating myths about the Indians as a solution to modern environmental problems. Devolution of authority and responsibility offers the best hope for resource conservation. Rather than shunning property rights solutions for mythical spiritual ones, we should embrace them, as did our Indian predecessors on this continent.

Indians Should Oppose the Storage of Nuclear Waste on Reservations

by Grace Thorpe

About the author: *Grace Thorpe, the daughter of Olympic athlete Jim Thorpe, is the president of the National Environmental Coalition of Native Americans, an activist organization devoted to keeping nuclear waste off Indian lands. In addition, she is on the board of directors for the Nuclear Information and Resource Service, serves on the Greenpeace American Indian Advisory Committee, and is a health commissioner and tribal court judge for the Sac and Fox Indian Nation.*

The Great Spirit instructed us that, as Native people, we have a consecrated bond with our Mother Earth. We have a sacred obligation to our fellow creatures that live upon it. For this reason it is both painful and disturbing that the United States government and the nuclear power industry seem intent on forever ruining some of the little land we have remaining. The nuclear waste issue is causing American Indians to make serious, possibly even genocidal, decisions concerning the environment and the future of our peoples.

I was a corporal, stationed in New Guinea, at the end of World War II when the first atomic bomb was dropped on Hiroshima. The so-called "nuclear-age" has passed in the beat of a heart. As impossible as it seems, 1995 marked the fiftieth anniversary of that first blast. The question of what to do with the waste produced from the commercial and military reactors involved in weapons manufacture and the generation of nuclear energy has stumped the minds of the most brilliant physicists and scientists since "Little Boy" was detonated above Japan on August 6, 1945. *No* safe method has yet been found for the disposal of such waste, the most lethal poison known in the history of humanity. It remains an orphan of the nuclear age.

In rich areas, people have the leisure time to organize an easy access to media

From Grace Thorpe, "Our Homes Are Not Dumps: Creating Nuclear-Free Zones," a speech delivered at the North American Native Workshop on Environmental Justice, ILLIF School of Theology, Denver, Colorado, March 17, 1995. Reprinted with permission.

139

and elected representatives. For this reason, *the nuclear industry is talking about locating disposal sites in poor regions.* Indians are being deluged by requests. Devastation due to nuclear energy, however, is nothing new to Indian peoples.

Dangerous Levels of Radiation

Between 1950 and 1980, approximately 15,000 persons worked in uranium mines. One-fourth of these were Indian. Many of these mines were located on lands belonging to the Navajos and the Pueblos. In 1993, Dr. Louise Abel of the Indian Health Service disclosed that, of the 600 miners tested who had worked underground for more than a year, only 5 qualified for payments under the Radiation Exposure Act of 1990. By 1994, only 155 uranium miners and millers or their families had been awarded compensation, less than half the claims filed at that time. Radiation from tailings piles, the debris left after the uranium is extracted, has leached into groundwater that feeds Indian homes, farms, and ranches. High concentrations of radon gas continually seep out of the piles and are breathed by Natives in the area. Background levels of radiation are at dangerous levels. Thus Indians living near the mines face the same health risks as those working underground.

In 1973 and 1974, two nuclear power reactors commenced operation at Prairie Island, Minnesota, only a few hundred yards from the homes, businesses, and child care center of

> *"Devastation due to nuclear energy . . . is nothing new to Indian peoples."*

the Prairie Island Mdewankanton Sioux. The facility was on the site of the ancient Indian village and burial mound, dating back at least 2,000 years. On October 2, 1979, *a 27-minute release of radiation from the plants* forced evacuation of the facility, *but the tribe was not notified* until several days later. By 1989, *radioactive tritium* was detected in the *drinking water*, forcing the Mdewankanton to dig an 800-foot-deep well and water tower, completed in 1993. Prairie Island residents *are exposed to six times the cancer risk* deemed acceptable by the Minnesota Department of Health.

Nuclear Waste Disposal Sites

By 1986, the problem of nuclear waste disposal had become acute. The U.S. Department of Energy began to explore the possibility of locating a permanent nuclear repository in Minnesota's basalt and granite hardrock deposits. Among the sites considered was the White Earth Reservation in the northwestern part of the state. The Anishiaabe who live there took the government's interest seriously enough to commission a study of the potential impact. The Minnesota legislature responded by passing the Radioactive Waste Management Act, stating that no such facility could be located within the state without the express authorization of the legislature.

The following year, however, Congress voted to locate the permanent repository at Yucca Mountain, about 100 miles northwest of Las Vegas, Nevada, on land belonging to the Western Shoshone. Plans called for the opening of the facility in 2010. The Nuclear Waste Policy Act set in motion a nationwide search for a community that would accept a temporary site until Yucca Mountain came online. *Indian tribes again were specifically targeted.*

One by one, tribes who considered accepting the so-called Monitored Retrievable Storage (MRS) facility on tribal land decided against it. As of 1995, of the 17 tribes who began discussions and study, only three remain: the Mescalero Apache of New Mexico, the Goshutes in Utah, and the Fort McDermitt Reservation in Nevada (which houses both Paiutes and Western Shoshones). In addition, Pojoaque Pueblo in New Mexico announced in March 1995 that it was considering locating the MRS on tribal lands. This move, however, was an overt power play to persuade the New Mexico legislature to halt a bill that would expand gambling in the state to the detriment of the Pojoaque's own gambling inter-

> *"We should also not believe that the problem [of nuclear waste storage] is limited to the United States."*

ests. According to Pojoaque Governor Jacob Viarrial, *"If the public does not want his tribe to store the waste, they should put pressure on the lawmakers to put a halt to the expansion of gaming off reservations."*

The National Environmental Coalition of Native Americans (NECONA) was formed in 1993 in Las Vegas to lobby against the MRS or any nuclear waste disposal on Indian lands and to encourage Native Nations to declare themselves Nuclear Free Zones instead. As the number of tribes considering the MRS dwindled, pressure on Washington mounted. NECONA persuaded U.S. Senator Jeff Bingaman of New Mexico, who had been one of the moving forces behind the Radiation Exposure Compensation Act for uranium miners, to oppose the MRS on the energy and the appropriations committees. As a result, Congress withheld funding for the program.

With the federal government out of the MRS-construction business, but with the problem of waste disposal still unresolved, utilities began to get desperate. Dozens of plants would be forced to shut down or find alternative sources of fuel unless a temporary storage site were located in the near future. Thirty-three utilities, accounting for 94 reactors, began seeking a location. Led by Northern States Power (NSP), the consortium approached Minnesota about locating a facility adjacent to the NSP plant at Prairie Island. Although the plant supplies 15% of the state's electricity, *"not a single kilowatt reaches the Mdewankanton community it borders."*

The Prairie Island Sioux had applied for a Phase I MRS grant, which provided DOE [Department of Energy] funds for initial feasibility studies. According to tribal officials, however, the application was tactical. The intent was to use the government's own money to prove that neither an MRS nor a nuclear power plant should be located at Prairie Island. One study showed that the cancer risk would be 23 times greater than the state standard. At the time of the NSP initiative, a survey showed that 91.6 percent of the tribe opposed construction of the MRS. The tribe fought the NSP proposal before the legislature and won. *They subsequently declared the Prairie Island Reservation a Nuclear Free Zone.*

The Mescalero Apaches

Meanwhile, NSP has signed an agreement with the Mescalero Apache to move ahead with development of an MRS in New Mexico. Under the terms of the agreement, the tribe was to seek two 20-year licenses to store up to 40,000 metric tons of spent nuclear fuel. Total revenues over the 40-year life of the facility, estimated at $2.3 billion, would bring as much as $250 million in benefits to the tribe. The tribal council believed that it could proceed with the program by its own authority; it was confident enough of victory to put the issue to tribal members in the form of a public referendum. According, however, to a Native newspaper, *The Circle*, opponents of the storage facility considered the Mescalero tribal government, headed by Chairman Wendall Chino, "dictatorial, and likely to conduct a campaign of intimidation and vote fraud if a referendum takes place."

The Mescalero don't need this nuclear waste. They have a five-star resort, a casino, two ski lifts, forestry resources, and a sawmill.

The referendum took place January 31, 1995. The Mescaleros voted down the MRS by a vote of 490 to 362. Shortly after the vote, however, a petition began circulating, calling for a new election. According to Fred Peso, the vice chairman, "A group of grass-roots people presented the petition to the tribal council." Peso blamed "outside interference from environmentalists and other anti-tribal groups" for the defeat of the proposal. In reality, Wendell Chino's powerful political machine was behind the petition. The tribal government controls jobs, housing, schools, and the court system. One of the organizers of the petition drive, Fred Kaydahzinne, is director of the federally subsidized tribal housing program. As Rufina Marie Laws, one of the referendum's opponents, stated, "It was real hard for people to turn him down." Petition organizers gathered more than 700 signatures calling for a new vote. When a second ballot was held on March 9, 1995, the measure passed 593 to 372.

There is a great deal of uncertainty as to what will happen now at Mescalero. Opponents of the MRS could seek yet another referendum. They have stated that they will appeal the second vote to the tribal court, but they are not optimistic. The state of New Mexico has prohibited transport of spent nuclear fuel on state highways in an attempt to derail the proposal. Vice Chairman Peso has announced that the tribe will proceed with licensing applications and technological studies. Officials of NSP have announced that they will move ahead with plans for the project. Contracts are being finalized, and licensing is anticipated to be concluded by December 1996. [The Mescaleros suspended negotiations in April 1996.]

If the Mescaleros withdraw, there are the Skull Valley Goshutes in Utah and the tribes at Fort McDermitt standing right behind them. Both reservations are isolated, and unemployment is a problem on both. At the moment, Fort McDermitt seems to be out of the running because it straddles the Nevada state line. The law says that the MRS and the permanent site cannot be in the same state, but that could change. The Goshutes already have waste incinerators, nerve gas plants, and a bombing range bordering their lands. There is a feeling of indifference about the MRS among the few people who live on the reservation. They have signed

> *"The utilities are using our names and our trust lands to bypass environmental regulations.* **The issue is not sovereignty. . . . The issue is environmental racism."**

an accord with Richard Stallings, a federal negotiator charged with locating a temporary storage site, to provide a framework for further talks, and the University of Utah has agreed to undertake a feasibility study with the utilities.

We should also not believe that the problem is limited to the United States. First Nations in Canada are facing the issue. An article in the free trade agreement between Canada and the United States prohibits Canada from preventing nuclear waste coming into the country. The Meadow Lake Cree in Saskatchewan are in discussion with the Atomic Energy of Canada Ltd. (AECL), a corporation of the Canadian government, concerning becoming a permanent repository. According to recent reports, they have also held negotiations with the Mescalero to become the storage site for wastes temporarily housed at the proposed Arizona facility. Meanwhile, AECL continues to market nuclear technology throughout the Americas. The situation in Mexico is terrible. They have very little environmental regulation.

Environmental Racism

Tribal officials at Mescalero and other reservations that have considered the MRS contend that the issue is one of sovereignty. They use the issue of sovereignty against the environment. It is a very tough tightrope to walk. How can you say to a tribe, "Hey, you shouldn't be doing this; you should be protecting the earth?" Then they would turn around and reply, "Hey, we can do as we please. This is Indian sovereignty." In one sense, they would be right. Allowing utilities to build MRS facilities on our lands, however, is not truly an expression of sovereignty. Those supporting such sites are selling our sovereignty. The utilities are using our names and our trust lands to bypass environmental regulations. *The issue is not sovereignty.* The issue is Mother Earth's preservation and survival. *The issue is environmental racism.* The purpose of NECONA is to invite tribes to express their sovereign national rights in a more creative way in favor of our Mother, by joining the growing number of tribal governments that are choosing to declare their lands Nuclear Free Zones. Fred Peso at Mescalero has declared, *"It is ironic that the state continues to fight our tribe (over the MRS) when New Mexico has enjoyed the benefits of nuclear projects since 1945."* The real irony is that after years of trying to destroy it, the United States is promoting Indian national sovereignty—just so they can dump their waste on Native land.

The DOE and the utilities have said that it is natural that we, as Native peoples, should accept radioactive waste on our lands. They have convinced some of our traditionalists that as keepers of the land they must accept it. As Russell Means has said, however, "We have always had our false prophets." The government and the nuclear power industry attempt to flatter us about our abilities as "earth stewards." Yet as I declared to the National Congress of American Indians in 1993, *"It is a perversion of our beliefs and an insult to our intelligence to say that we are 'natural stewards' of these wastes."* The real intent of the government and the utilities is to rid themselves of this extremely hazardous garbage on Indian lands so they are free to generate more of it.

The Dangers of Nuclear Waste

Our traditional spiritual leaders have warned us for hundreds of years about taking resources from the earth. They have warned that the earth will become unbalanced and be destroyed. In one of the stories the Navajos have about their origins, they were warned about the dangers of uranium. The People "emerged from the third world into the fourth and present world and were given a choice. They were told to choose between two yellow powders. One was yellow dust from the rocks, and the other was corn pollen. The [People] chose corn pollen, and the gods nodded in assent. They also issued a warning. Having chosen the corn pollen, the Navajos were to leave the yellow dust in the ground. If it was ever removed, it would bring evil."

Wherever there are uranium mines, wherever there are nuclear power plants, and wherever our people have been downwind on nuclear tests, the cancer rate goes up. Among the Western Shoshone in Nevada as a result of nuclear testing, many of the people now have thyroid cancer. They are dying a younger death. They have leukemia, which was unheard of in earlier times. Pollution and toxic waste from the Hanford nuclear weapons facility threatens all Native peoples who depend on the Columbia River salmon for their existence. A few years ago, a vial of nuclear material the size of a human finger was lost on the road from Los Angeles to Sacramento. An SOS went out to the media about this little silver vial: "If you find it, don't pick it up. Alert us immediately. If you pick it up and put it in your pocket for two days, you'll get sick. If you keep it a week, it can kill you. If you breathe a 100th of a grain of salt, it can cause lung cancer."

Now those who visited all these horrors upon us want us to accept their nuclear waste, too. Darelynn Lehto, the vice president of the Prairie Island Mdewankanton, testified before the Minnesota State Senate during the fight against MRS there, *"It is the worst kind of environmental racism to force our tribe to live with the dangers of nuclear waste simply because no one else is willing to do so."* Why do we tolerate it? How long can we tolerate it? What kind of society permits the manufacture of products that cannot be safely disposed? NECONA is currently lobbying Congress for a bill that will say simply, "Nothing is to be manufactured, used, or reproduced in the United States that cannot be safely disposed of." Is that too simple a thing for a legislator to understand? Probably it is, but it makes sense, doesn't it?

Spent nuclear fuel is permeated with plutonium, the principal ingredient in atomic weapons. Plutonium has a half life of 24,360 years. Significant amounts would therefore remain active for more than 50,000 years. The so-called permanent repository proposed for Yucca Mountain is designed to hold canisters containing nuclear waste for only 10,000 years. The steel containers holding the material would disintegrate long before the radioactivity had decayed.

No Permanent Repository

Yucca Mountain, however, is nowhere near on its way to becoming the permanent repository. It was originally to have begun receiving waste in 1998, but near-unanimous opposition in Nevada slowed the process. In 1992, an earthquake measuring 5.6 on the Richter scale struck the area, raising additional questions as to the site's viability. Most recently, scientists at the Los Alamos National Laboratory in New Mexico raised the possibility that wastes buried at the Nevada location could explode after the steel container canisters dissolve, setting off a nuclear chain reaction.

These factors make the targeted date of 2010—when Yucca Mountain currently is estimated to be accepting shipments of waste—look improbable. Mescalero tribal officials, in obtaining their tribe's permission, emphasized that their proposed facility was strictly temporary and that *"at no time would the tribe take possession of the fuel."* What will happen, however, if Yucca Mountain *does not* come online as projected? What if no permanent storage site is available at the end of the MRS's 40 years of *"temporary"* storage? New Mexico Attorney General Tom Udall has raised similar questions. He fears that the state "may ultimately have to pick up the pieces." Indians suspect we know who will be left holding the bag.

The debate over nuclear waste has already done serious damage to harmonious relationships among our people. Why must we go through this divisive agony again?

> *"The United States is promoting Indian national sovereignty—just so they can dump their waste on Native land."*

As a mother and a grandmother, I am concerned about the survival of our people just as Mother Earth is concerned about the survival of her children. There is currently a moratorium on construction of nuclear power plants in the United States. There is also current legislation, however, that would allow new building if arrangements are made for the waste. Is this the legacy that we want to leave for our children and for our Mother Earth? The Iroquois say that in making any decision one should consider the impact for seven generations to come. As Thom Fassett, who is Iroquois, reminds us, taking such a view on these issues often makes us "feel we are alone, rolling a stone up a hill. It keeps rolling back down on us." That may be the only way, however, for us to live up to our sacred duty to the land and to all of creation.

Storing Nuclear Waste on Reservation Land Can Benefit Native Americans

by The Skull Valley Goshute Tribe Executive Committee

About the authors: *The Skull Valley Band of Goshute is a small tribe of about 120 Indians who have an 18,000-acre reservation in Tooele County, Utah.*

Editor's note: The Skull Valley Goshute Tribe received two grants from the Department of Energy in the early 1990s to study the feasibility of building a monitored retrieval storage (MRS) facility for spent nuclear fuel rods. The spent fuel would be stored for up to forty years in the MRS facility, after which it would be transferred to a permanent facility planned to be built in Yucca Mountain in Nevada. When the Goshutes and the Mescalero Apaches of New Mexico indicated interest in the third stage of the study—which included a $2.8 million grant—the government shut down the project.

Truth is like a turtle crawling slowly over the sands of time, spreading her message to all who will listen. Rumor flies on the wings of a dove, spreading poison on smiles that glisten
                                                                    —author unknown

Approximately 80 miles Southwest of Salt Lake City, Utah, is located the Skull Valley Goshute Reservation. These 18,000 acres of low foothills and desert sagebrush are all that remains of an area which once stretched from the Wasatch Front into Wells, Nevada. Today, the small village on the Reservation has less than twenty families.

Defense Cutbacks

The current Reservation employers are the Tekoi Rocket Test facility and the Pony Express Station (the Tribal Store). Hercules Aerospace tests rocket engines for America's strategic defense systems on the Reservation. With the cut-

From The Skull Valley Goshute Tribe Executive Committee, "Taa-Pai Phase IIA Report: A Comparison of Utah Waste Facilities to the Taa-Pai Industrial Park," 1993. Reprinted by permission.

backs in defense, Hercules may no longer continue to test rocket engines. The Tribe is uncertain whether or not an agreement will be reached to renew the lease of the Tribal-owned Tekoi facility in 1995. [Hercules Aerospace was sold to Alliant Technology and the lease was renewed until 1998.]

Like our neighbors in Dugway, Tooele, Magna, Brigham City and nation-wide, we are affected by the loss of defense jobs. For too long we have been economically dependent on the arms race. Quite unlike corporate America, whose main motive in the arms race was greed, we have depended on the testing of rocket engines for economic survival.

Some of our members will be affected by the loss of jobs at the Tooele Army Depot. Other members will be affected by the loss of jobs if the Tekoi Rocket Test Facility is shut down. Hercules, which has laid off close to half of its work force, has also reduced security jobs on the Reservation.

The uncertainty in the defense sector of the national economy has forced change. The Tribe decided to find alternatives to Hercules Aerospace and the testing of rocket engines. The Pony Express Station (the Tribal Store), Dugway Proving Grounds and the Tooele Army Depot all combined account for the majority of Tribal employment.

Business Proposals and Scams

We have reviewed so many businesses. It seemed that every businessman who had ever failed at anything or simply wanted the Tribe to take the financial risk on some very speculative venture approached us. In this capacity we learned a great deal about the waste industries. We have been approached to be the site for municipal solid waste sludge from New York and New Jersey. Others wanted an experimental hazardous waste incinerator to be funded by the Tribe. Others wanted the Reservation to be the site for a rock salt dump, a by-product of a mining plant. Another "deal" was for the Tribe to fund one-half of the purchase of a lumber/hardware store in return for an individual to manage the project on behalf of himself and the Tribe. Probably the silliest business project was a defunct defense contractor who wanted the Tribe to purchase his business if he relocated on the Reservation.

> *"The charges of 'environmental racism' and the need to 'protect' and 'save' us smacks of patronism."*

There were others. The businessmen who had been criminally convicted and had creditors and/or banks chasing them wanted us to be their salvation and reward for the numerous years of dishonesty and failure.

When we first saw the M.R.S. [monitored retrieval storage] proposal we thought it was a scam, just like all of the numerous other get-rich-quick schemes and scams we'd encountered. After careful investigation we concluded that there is no conspiracy between the nuclear energy industry and the Department of Energy. There is gross, if not criminal, mismanagement of the defense nuclear waste sites around the country. And there is a potential breach of contract looming between the Department of Energy and the nuclear energy industry.

We have continued to solicit businesses to come onto the Reservation. Since some of these negotiations are ongoing and therefore confidential, suffice it to say that large Fortune 500 companies have contacted the Tribe about locating in Utah.

The charges of "environmental racism" and the need to "protect" and "save" us smack of patronism. This attitude implies we are not intelligent enough to make our own business and environmental decisions.

Doing Business with the Government

Unlike corporate executives who try to manage utility industries and have at best forty years of experience, we have a long history of business deals with the U.S. Government. First time, shame on them. Second time, shame on us. We clearly understand the frustration of corporate executives who need to make long-term business decisions with a partner that changes the deal *after* it has been signed and acted upon. The utility companies, like the Indian community, have the continual misfortune of new U.S. Government administrations who *will* change policy which will affect their long-term business decisions.

It is not that this ubiquitous Government can't be trusted. It is simply that when a new administration comes to power, the new administrators change the policies of the old administrators. This creates an atmosphere of uncertainty and doubt. Utility companies and Tribes like to plan for longer than four years. We need to learn patience. Four years is a very short period of time. It can take longer than four years to build power plants to generate electricity or locate a suitable business for a Reservation.

> **"A temporary storage facility for spent fuel rods is not a 'nuclear waste dump.'"**

Because of the commonality of interests in long-term planning and the credibility which exists with business partners we can trust, we have decided to apply for a Phase IIB grant to study the environmental and social consequences of building a temporary storage facility for spent nuclear fuel rods to world-class standards on the Taa-Pai Industrial Park within the boundaries of the Skull Valley Goshute Reservation.

The Skull Valley Goshute Taa-Pai Industrial Park currently has two businesses: the Tekoi Rocket Test Facility and the Pony Express Station. If negotiations are successful, the credibility of the partners checks out and the numbers make sense, other businesses will be located in Skull Valley.

Media Hype and Hysteria

Having thoroughly examined the storage of nuclear fuel rods in other countries, we know this project is much safer than many industrial projects we have examined and more dangerous than others. The hysteria which surrounds the words "nuclear" and "radiation" will clearly make the world's most expensive storage facility unpopular with certain people and organizations who have this altruistic need to "save" us. We know that informed decisions which are in the best interests of our people and are made with their consent will not always be popular with *everyone*. Leadership is not a popularity contest.

Having studied the issue and understanding it, we are thankful for the media hype and hysteria. If it was not for the media misinformation and hysteria, the dollar value of this industrial project would be considerably less. Let's be serious for a moment and realize that the nerve gas incinerator and dump out at the Tooele South Area is at least 1,000 times more dangerous than this temporary storage facility could ever hope to be.

> *"We are clearly convinced that the M.R.S. can be a safe industrial project."*

A temporary storage facility for spent fuel rods is not a "nuclear waste dump." Each fuel rod assembly costs over $750,000.00. A new Congress might again decide reprocessing [rather than storing] is in the nation's best interest. The price of uranium might increase. The nation's repository at Yucca Mountain or elsewhere might be completed. Twenty years is a long time. Forty years is even longer. These casks which cost over $500,000 per cask are built to last hundreds of years and safely contain all of the radiation.

The decision to go into Phase IIB is not a decision to build an unsafe facility. Tooele County and the State of Utah stand to potentially benefit considerably from this project. They also assume the risks from transportation accidents and site accidents. Because this project is well over $1.5 billion in steel and concrete and creates over 500 permanent jobs, we will insist that only Utah companies to the fullest extent possible provide the material and employment.

Safety First

From the interim spent fuel storage facilities we toured in Japan, France, Britain, Sweden and on-site storage facilities in this country, we are clearly convinced that the M.R.S. can be a safe industrial project. However, like all decisions, this is a choice. We also understand that this is America. Our workplace will be as safe as we make it. All of us who work in blue-collar industries are aware of someone who at one time or another was injured on the job—some permanently, others were down for a while. The real behaviors which exist in the American workplace are not always the best. The 1984 Wilbern Mine disaster [a mine-shaft fire that killed several miners] with the quick tragedy being inflicted upon Carbon County families reminds us of just how dangerous the Utah workplace really can become. Each year thousands of Utahns and hundreds of thousands of Americans are injured in the workplace. Every industry is as safe or as dangerous as the people who operate it.

The future and safety of the Tribal members, especially the children, are involved in the safety of this facility. We will not tolerate anything less than the best labor and/or technology on the planet for this industrial project. If anyone has a problem with this policy, we suggest they provide their shoddy materials, bad manners and/or poor labor habits to someone else.

In Phase IIB we will further study the site-specific environmental effects and best designs for this project. Under the 1982 Nuclear Waste Policy Act and the 1987 Amendments, we reserve the right to cancel this project at any time if we deem it in the best interest of the Tribe.

Nuclear Waste Storage Sites Are Not Dangerous

by Miller Hudson

About the author: *Miller Hudson is a Denver public relations consultant.*

Editor's note: The Mescalero Apaches in New Mexico received two grants worth $300,000 in the early 1990s from the Department of Energy to study the feasibility of building a temporary storage facility for spent nuclear fuel rods on their reservation. When the tribe indicated its willingness to continue the feasibility study, the federal government ended the program. In 1994 the Mescaleros negotiated directly with a consortium of nuclear utility companies to develop a monitored retrieval storage (MRS) facility for spent nuclear fuel on the reservation. The tribe suspended the negotiation with the consortium in 1996.

A small Apache tribe in New Mexico is currently concluding negotiations with 33 nuclear utilities for the joint construction and operation of a centralized spent fuel storage facility. [The negotiations were suspended by the tribe in 1996.] There's no getting around it—that's a bizarre development, isn't it? You don't have to know much about public policy to suspect this wasn't the original plan. So, how did it happen, and is it a good idea?

Fear

It's hard to know where to start in providing an answer to these questions. The roots of nuclear waste policy failure in this country probably extend back a half century or more—and the list of villains is long—government secrecy at the outset of the atomic age, shoddy science education in our schools, arrogance and elitism in the nuclear industry and an ignorant and alarmist media, to name just a few. The accepted, "normal" reaction to all things nuclear in America is to be afraid.

I acquired this insight from a persistent reporter—one among dozens I've

From Miller Hudson, "Fuel Storage," a speech delivered to the American Nuclear Society, Washington, D.C., November 17, 1994. Reprinted with permission.

dealt with as project spokesman for the Mescaleros' Spent Fuel Storage Initiative. He kept badgering me with a single question, "Why aren't you scared of this stuff?" All the assurances in the world about engineering safeguards wouldn't shut him up. Eventually, after I decided he wasn't trying to "slit our throats" with a negative story, I asked him why he expected me to be frightened. Actually a science writer, he told me he had never interviewed a supporter of a nuclear project who hadn't had some personal familiarity with the technology or the science.

> *"A great business opportunity existed with very little associated risk."*

I acknowledged to him that my father worked for the Atomic Energy Commission and that I had grown up in nuclear towns like Idaho Falls, Oak Ridge and Los Alamos. I was still in grade school when my father first took my brother and I out to look at a spent fuel pool and the nifty blue glow in the water. That's not to say I don't appreciate the risks involved. My father died ten years ago at 59— even he suspected his illness was occupationally related, but he harbored no bitterness about it. He recognized that there had been a carelessness, even recklessness, in the early years of the atomic age when risks were not fully understood. Nonetheless, he retained his faith in the benefits that would eventually accrue to society from the application of nuclear technology. He was a scientist and an optimist.

The Future Needs Nuclear Energy

I suppose I carry some of those attitudes with me. Though the near-term prospects for nuclear power in this country are dismal, I can't imagine we will continue to rely on coal-fired generation fifty or a hundred years from now. Unfortunately, when the time comes to convert from fossil fuels, it appears we will have to purchase the requisite technology and expertise from the Japanese or the European community. Nuclear power in America is terminal. I strongly suspect that there is virtually no public constituency for the expansion of nuclear power. . . .

As David Guston and Kenneth Keniston point out in the November 1994 issue of *Technology Review,*

> Popular support for science has waned. The almost unqualified public enthusiasm that characterized the immediate postwar period has given way to a far more nuanced view of science and technology. Attitudes have been negatively influenced by conspicuous technological failures—Chernobyl, Bhopal, the Challenger—which raise concerns about science by the reverse application of the logic that predicts technological benefits from scientific triumphs.

Into this breach have rushed the apostles of what Irving Langmuir, the Nobel Laureate, identified forty years ago as "pathological science" or "the science of things that aren't so."

153

In collusion with tabloid journalism, catastrophists of every stripe allege that virtually every aspect of modern life is contributing to disease and death—despite objective data which demonstrates increasing life expectancies and improved public health. Nasty public debates erupt over purported health effects that always seem to reside at the limits of detectability. The public is then further confused when scientific opinion concedes its inability to prove a null hypothesis. At the same time we ignore the ravages of alcohol, auto accidents and domestic abuse because we think we understand their origins—and they "happen" to everyone.

Apathy and Ignorance

It wouldn't be fair to conclude my remarks without mentioning the role of public apathy and individual ignorance. I was reminded of this when a voter told an "exit" pollster that he had just voted Republican for the first time because he was tired of Washington "fooling around with his Medicare."

Americans are similarly schizophrenic about things nuclear. They love "warp drive" on Star Trek—they even tell pollsters they expect to see more nuclear plants in the next century—but they don't want any built next year, or the year after, or anywhere near them. In a utility survey that asked customers for their preference among a hydro-electric dam, a coal-fired plant and a nuclear generating station as a source of expanded capacity—one respondent wrote back and said, "I don't want any of them. I just want electricity like you get out of the wall." If this country is to enjoy a secure energy future, there is a huge, huge public education process which needs to be launched. . . .

> "[Antinuclear activists] seem to believe the Apaches should . . . [freeze] their social development and tribal culture."

While some public opposition to spent fuel storage grows out of legitimate and reasonable concerns about health and safety—concerns that can usually be calmed with full and accurate information—there also exists a vocal, politically sophisticated anti-nuclear community whose antipathy to nuclear power is visceral, emotional and often religious in character. These individuals sincerely believe that nuclear technology represents a disrespectful tampering with the fundamental, divine laws of the universe. Nuclear power plants and the wastes they produce symbolize a sacrilegious "pact with the devil" that will inevitably lead to some form of horrific retribution visited upon arrogant humans.

Oddly enough this attitude is portrayed by the media as "liberal" or "left" in nature, when it is actually a kind of "know nothing" conservatism that advocates a return to the seventeenth century with vaccines. Philosophically, it is premised on the fallacy of a romantic, "lost" agrarian past free of the strains and stresses of modern life. The media would have us believe this delusion represents an authentic environmental ethic. Nothing could be further from the truth. To the contrary, it constitutes a recipe for ecological disaster and widespread social insecurity. What's worse, they're winning the public debate!

The Preferred Solution

One of my favorite writers on contemporary politics is Lewis Lapham, the editor of *Harper's* magazine. I treasure each issue for Lapham's "notebook" column. In June 1994 he wrote about Washington and observed that

> Congress warily avoids solutions to "real problems" because solutions invariably mean that somebody has to lose something or give up something; solutions imply change, and change is unacceptable because change translates into resentment, and resentment loses votes.

This analysis says all that needs to be said about spent fuel storage. Gridlock is the preferred political solution.

While I served in the Colorado legislature I used to joke that whenever a member received five letters—I'm talking about *real* letters now, not the form letters which are becoming far too prevalent as PR [public relations] firms attempt to influence Congress and statehouses by creating the illusion of grassroots involvement—but five genuine letters on a particular issue, then the legislator began to worry whether a revolution was underway back in the district. For better or worse, that's how politicians react—it can even be argued that that's what they should be doing—representing the folks back home, even when "the folks" are ignorant and self-destructive.

What it means is that we get "squeaky wheel" government and non-solutions. The creation of the nuclear waste negotiator's office is a typical example. Utilities bellyached about DOE's [Department of Energy's] failure to produce an MRS [monitored retrieval storage], so Congress created a negotiator to nose around for a "voluntary host" community. No one really expected the office to succeed, and they were horrified when it flushed out willing applicants. Governors were authorized to veto participation, which they did—unanimously, leaving sovereign Indian nations as the only active participants in the federal program. The anti-nuclear community promptly charged "environmental racism" and everyone dove under the bed—Congress, DOE and the negotiator—eventually killing the grant program.

> *"Stories that eventually reach the public appear in a skewed and perverse light that confuses rather than clarifies the issue at dispute."*

It was assumed that would be the end of the matter. But they underestimated the perseverance and toughness of the Mescalero Apache Tribal Council. In a community that can avoid the disruption of its internal political dialogue by outsiders and where voters actually have confidence in their leaders, it was possible to reach the conclusion that a great business opportunity existed with very little associated risk. The Mescaleros are pursuing that business opportunity, without government help, in the form of a joint venture agreement with 33 nuclear utilities.

Racist Paternalism

Now, you would think Washington should be ecstatic—that Congress would be organizing a ticker-tape parade for the Mescaleros. Think again! The Mescaleros have pursued their involvement in both the federal MRS process and now their own private fuel storage initiative, against a background of nearly constant muttering and grumbling about "this Indian thing." Antinuclear activists, whose self-professed goal is to shut down all nuclear plants as quickly as possible, are nearly apoplectic. Wrapping themselves in the righteous mantle of environmental "guardians," they practice a racist paternalism which would substitute their "better," non-Indian judgment for that of the Mescaleros themselves. They seem to believe the Apaches should reside in a living history museum that freezes their social development and tribal culture in a nineteenth-century time warp—even if this residency must be enforced against their will. The twenty-first century apparently is to be reserved for everyone but Indians.

> *"The spent fuel storage solution the tribe offers is a truly win-win opportunity."*

These frauds, and they are frauds, are aided and abetted in this behavior by a mutant form of journalism that claims it has an obligation to report "both sides" of every controversy. Let me assure you that nothing has frustrated me more than my encounters with these self-proclaimed, "balanced" journalists. They subscribe to a very peculiar definition of what composes "both sides" of an issue.

If a member of the Mescalero Tribal Council carefully explains why he or she believes spent fuel storage will be a safe business and then goes on to outline the economic benefits that are expected to improve the lives of tribal children as a consequence of the project, opponents are not asked to contradict these points—to provide evidence that the facility will be unsafe, or to argue that jobs and money will not, in fact, strengthen the economic condition of the tribe. Instead, they are encouraged to offer unsupported and scurrilous slanders alleging chicanery, intimidation or corruption.

Thus, the stories that eventually reach the public appear in a skewed and perverse light that confuses rather than clarifies the issue at dispute. This is all transpiring in a political arena with no real constituency for nuclear power—or its wastes. The Mescaleros have persisted out of self-interest and concern for the prosperity of generations not yet born. The spent fuel storage solution the tribe offers is a truly win-win opportunity for the Mescaleros and the nuclear industry, but let me assure you that success is a long way off and the alliance fragile. Incoming fire is heavy and will remain so!

Chapter 4

Should Indian Sovereignty Be Restricted?

Indian Sovereignty: An Overview

by Robert Bryce

About the author: *Robert Bryce is a freelance writer.*

During an April 1994 meeting with more than 500 American Indian leaders at the White House, President Bill Clinton vowed to "honor and respect tribal sovereignty." His statement brought prolonged applause from the tribal leaders.

The president, however, cannot prevent individual states and local governments from challenging sovereignty, and tribes continue to skirmish with state and local jurisdictions on matters ranging from taxation and environmental issues to fishing rights and gambling.

Sovereignty Issues

Like semi-independent island nations, 545 federally recognized tribes compete for jobs, money, and business opportunities. Each tribe has its own goals and objectives, which often clash with the jurisdictions around them.

In 1993, the Oklahoma Tax Commission lost a decision in the U.S. Supreme Court over levying taxes on members of the Sac and Fox tribe who live on tribal lands. The state wanted to collect income taxes and vehicle taxes from tribal members, but the high court disagreed.

"There has always been tension between state and tribal authorities on sovereignty issues," says John Echohawk, director of the Native American Rights Fund, a Colorado-based group that provides legal services to tribes. He says that as tribes push for gambling and environmental rights, sovereignty becomes more contentious. Despite the current battles, Mr. Echohawk sees hope for the future. "We are seeing more negotiated settlements of jurisdictional issues and more building of tribal-state relations." He says states and tribes are beginning to realize that they must coexist.

Since 1979, when the Seminole tribe in Florida opened a bingo hall, gambling has become big business in Indian country. In 1993, tribal-owned casinos took in some $6 billion, and state governments are eager to get a piece of the action.

From Robert Bryce, "U.S. Indians Fight for Sovereignty," *Christian Science Monitor*, November 7, 1994. Reprinted by permission of the author.

The state of Texas won a decision in the U.S. Court of Appeals in 1994 that prevents the Tigua tribe from expanding their casino operation near El Paso. Gov. Ann Richards has called such casino-gambling operations a "cheesy way" to make money. The Tiguas say they will appeal the ruling. [The U.S. Supreme Court refused to hear the case, so the court of appeals ruling stands.] . . .

Some states have found it easier to cooperate rather than fight. In Connecticut, where slot machines at the Foxwoods Casino on the Mashantucket Pequot reservation are taking in over $1 million a day, the state is profiting handsomely. In 1993, Gov. Lowell Weicker signed an agreement with the tribe that guarantees the state will not allow non-Indians to run slot-machine operations.

> *"Tribes continue to skirmish with state and local jurisdictions on matters ranging from taxation and environmental issues to fishing rights and gambling."*

Doug Twait, commissioner of corporate affairs for the Mille Lacs Band of the Chippewa tribe in Minnesota, calls sovereignty the tribes' "greatest asset." He points out that almost a third of Indians live in poverty and that tribes must exercise their sovereignty if they are to reduce their dependence on the federal government and develop self-sustaining economies.

Mr. Twait said Grand Casino Mille Lacs provides about $1 million a month in revenue to the tribe, which it has used to build two new schools and a clinic. However, proposals pending in the state legislature could allow slot-machine gambling in bars. [The measures did not pass.] The Mille Lacs tribe and other Minnesota tribes are fighting the proposal because it will reduce their profits. "In the eyes of tribal leaders, this is part of the same historical pattern," Twait said. "Anytime Indian tribes have had access to resources, whether it's timber, water, wildlife, land, or now gambling, the white culture has always sought to take it away."

Hazardous Waste Disposal

The storage of hazardous wastes is also an issue. In Mississippi, Choctaw tribal leaders continue to negotiate on a hazardous waste dump. In New Mexico, the Mescalero Apache tribe has plans for a nuclear waste storage facility. Both projects have garnered widespread opposition from state and local authorities as well as environmental groups.

Fred Peso, vice president of the Mescaleros, says he doesn't look at the project as a test of sovereignty, but as "a private business enterprise."

Hunting and Fishing Rights

Hunting and fishing rights have also been a focal point of state-tribal disputes. In Minnesota, the Mille Lacs tribe continues to fight for the right to extend tribal hunting and fishing rights onto three million acres of non-reservation land. A federal court has given the tribe initial approval for the expansion. A final decision won't be rendered until 1996. [The court upheld the ruling in January 1997.]

Scott Strand of the Minnesota Attorney General's office said the Mille Lacs gave up their right to hunt and fish in a treaty they signed with the government in 1855.

In Montana, anti-Indian groups have called for an end to all Indian sovereignty rights. However, treaties with Indian tribes are protected by the U.S. Constitution, which calls treaties "the supreme law of the land." Because of that, Indian-law experts don't see any diminution of tribal rights in the offing.

Indians Should Not Seek Complete Sovereignty

by Fergus M. Bordewich

About the author: *Fergus M. Bordewich, the author of* Killing the White Man's Indian: Reinventing Native Americans at the End of the Twentieth Century, *traveled for many years among Indian reservations during his childhood in the 1950s and 1960s.*

Superficially, the May 1994 Albuquerque "Listening Conference," as it was rather self-consciously billed by its sponsors, the Departments of Justice and the Interior, provided a spectacle of enlightened official concern. Three members of President Bill Clinton's cabinet—Attorney General Janet Reno, Secretary of the Interior Bruce Babbitt, and Secretary of Housing and Urban Development Henry Cisneros—along with Commissioner of Indian Affairs Ada Deer sat side by side in a stylishly appointed meeting room at the Albuquerque Conference Center, cocking the ear of government both literally and symbolically to the oratory of a hundred or so assembled tribal leaders who had been invited to express their concerns. The conference differed from similar periodic gatherings that take place mostly in Washington only in the lofty credentials of the satraps on the dais, who were determined to show the depth of the new Democratic administration's interest in Indian problems.

For two days, the procession of tribal leaders recited the incantatory formulas of the sovereignty movement. "Sovereignty is a non-negotiable item," Wendell Chino of the Mescalero Apaches, the longest-serving tribal chairman in the country, declared. He then demanded that President Clinton issue an executive order "so that the whole U.S. knows that we are governments." A spokesman for the Sisseton-Wahpeton Sioux called for Indian affairs to be transferred to the State Department because "the Department of the Interior deals with wildlife, and State deals with governments." Appropriations to tribes, it was asserted by others, should be treated as foreign aid. State and federal courts were called upon to recognize Indian "national" courts for the "extradition" of convicted criminals. The establishment of gambling casinos was described repeatedly as "a fundamental sovereign right," while several speakers called upon the federal government to create an official Indians-only game of chance that would give tribes a permanent competitive edge in the gambling industry. Others demanded the complete ouster of state governments from regulatory oversight and all other aspects of tribal affairs. "Since tribes are governments," Joanne Jones of the Wisconsin Winnebago Tribe said with breathtaking logic, "their activities are thus self-regulating."

The Contradictions of Tribal Sovereignty

There was a monotony to all this after a while, as the dialogue took on the strange, stylized quality that it always does at such affairs, as if Indians and officials had been forever frozen like figures in a Babylonian frieze, facing each other in postures of complaint and defensiveness, rage and guilt, as if it were impossible to consider Indians as anything but beleaguered victims and government as anything but the culpable heir to an unbroken history of deceit and repression. Not a soul spoke about the need to protect the civil rights of individual Indians from their own governments or those of non-Indian residents of "sovereign" reservations. No one spoke of the need to ensure a free press, free speech, and separation of powers. No one spoke of the futility of attracting investment to remote reservations without resources, trained workers, transportation, or nearby markets, or asked how Indian tribes might fit into the larger national and world economies. No one spoke of the bloated and expanding tribal bureaucracies or the inherent contradiction in proclaiming "national sovereignty" while relying on federal and state appropriations or about the urgency of finding common cause between tribes and their non-Indian neighbors. No one mentioned the catastrophic effects of alcoholism on Indian economies, governments, and families, or showed even the slightest grasp of the social consequences that may ensue from widespread tribally run gambling. Nor did anyone even hint at the long-term political implications that may one day result from the fact that, by any traditional measurement of ethnicity, Native Americans are rapidly becoming less "Indian" by the decade.

> *"By any traditional measurement of ethnicity, Native Americans are rapidly becoming less 'Indian' by the decade."*

A Potential Disaster

Behind the boilerplate rhetoric of tribal sovereignty, modern Indians are still difficult to see clearly. . . . For the most part, their concerns still come to us like distant voices distorted by the lingering effects of guilt, arrogance, and wishful thinking. For much of American history, the national discourse about Indians has seemed like a kind of intellectual solipsism, a closed dialogue among popular fantasies about a people who are simultaneously "savage," "noble," and "pathetic" and who are forever said to be on the brink of vanishing from the earth. As a result, even the best-intentioned efforts to create a place for Indians in American society have sometimes proved disastrous to the very people they were intended to help.

In an age when guilt and romantic fantasy masquerade as politics, tribal sovereignty seems like a panacea for the wounds of the past. However, like so many other hopeful policies that have gone before, along with the obvious benefits it brings tribes, the drive toward sovereign autonomy is freighted with the seeds of potential disaster. Profound questions that bear upon the very nature of the United States itself hovered glaringly unasked in the mauve conference room at Albuquerque: What are the limits of federal powers? How can tribalism be squared with the legal and moral dictates of equal protection under the law? What is the role of the states in Indian Country and of the tribes in the constitutional democracy? What is the scope of tribal regulatory powers? What is the civil jurisdiction of tribal courts? How can the United States support tribal regimes that reject fundamental aspects of American democracy? What does it mean to be a citizen of a state and yet to be immune from its laws? What is the basis for asserting that reservation Indians shall have representation in state government but without taxation? On the other hand,

> *"Even the best-intentioned efforts to create a place for Indians in American society have sometimes proved disastrous."*

what is the basis for asserting that non-Indian residents of Indian Country shall not be represented in tribal government yet be subject to tribal law, courts, and taxation? How can we, as Americans, tolerate double standards?

A Dying World

There is nothing abstract about such concerns in Glencross, South Dakota. Once, 150 people lived there. There was a railroad station, two schools, three lumberyards, two feed companies. Trucks used to line up twenty deep alongside the grain elevators. "The elevators were right over here, but they're gone now," Steve Aberle is saying in his softly modulated, lawyerly voice. His compact frame and pale, finely boned features accentuate the impression of a man who values efficiency and control; in his business suit and tie, he seems almost spectral amid the desolation. "There was a real nice Catholic church. It's abandoned now. All around here there were dozens of houses. Over there"—pointing to a squat peak-roofed building—"that was a school. And here was the café. They sold up and moved to Texas." Aberle's clapboard house is one of the last three still occupied in Glencross. He likes the emptiness; in his spare time, he plants trees. "It's a good place for my kids. They can raise their own livestock. They get to see how things grow."

It is also an eerie place. Buffalo grass has reconquered the unpaved streets. Perfectly aligned tree belts mark the boundaries of farms that no longer exist. The decaying buildings seem too recent, too familiar to be ruins; there is an unsettling sense of witnessing the end of one's own world. How fast it all happened! In the span of a single lifetime a town was born, flourished, shriveled, and died, a monument to the demise, or at least to the ambiguous transformation, of the American West. Nothing breaks the silence, not even the B-1 bomber that streaks soundlessly high over the coppery green prairie toward some destination in another world.

> *"The adventurous emigrants [who settled former Indian land] . . . were also the victims . . . of the disappearing and now magically reappearing reservation."*

Glencross suffered no special, violent fate. The Great Plains are filled with failed communities like this, which seem to drift like derelict ships upon the rolling hills, sinking before your eyes. Trail City has shrunk from a population of 350 to 30, Firesteel to a single general store; Landeau has disappeared completely. The entire region is hemorrhaging jobs and people. In Dewey County, the only labor market that is expanding is the bureaucracy of the Cheyenne River Sioux Tribe. Six of the neighboring counties have lost half their population since 1930. Fifty of Nebraska's fifty-two Plains counties have lost population, thirty-eight of North Dakota's forty-one, twenty-two of Oklahoma's twenty-three. Entire towns have lost their doctors, banks, and schools. Dreamers speak seriously of returning vast tracts to the buffalo. From a certain angle of vision, Sioux demands for the restoration of the reservation to its original nineteenth-century limits are simply an anticlimax.

Every morning, Aberle drives to the storefront office that he shares with his father across the street from Pepsi's Café in Timber Lake, nine miles west of Glencross. The glory days when Indians pledged their allegiance here, as if Timber Lake were some capital city of the prairie, are long past. But there is nonetheless a certain suggestion of steadiness in the cottonwood-lined streets of frame cottages, Quonset huts, and trailers. Timber Lake is one of the lucky places: the presence of the Dewey County offices will keep it alive, along with the jobs at the rural electric co-op, the central school, the cheese factory. Even so, one hundred of the six hundred people who lived here a decade ago have moved away to places with better prospects and more hope.

Cultural Blending

The people of Timber Lake—the mechanics, the teachers, the co-op clerks, the men who work at the grain elevator, the retired farmers—are the human fruit of allotment, the flesh-and-blood culmination of the cultural blending that Senator Henry L. Dawes so idealistically envisioned a century ago. [Dawes believed that the reservation system resulted in racial segregation, and that Indians must adopt white ways in order to survive.] "Everyone here has got some relatives who are Indian, or a brother or a sister married to an Indian," says Aberle. There is the white nurse who just married a Sioux, and a few houses down from her the quarter-Indian school aide who married a white man; down the block lives Timber Lake's former mayor, who is married to a one-eighth Indian, and beyond him a farmer married to another one-eighth Indian.

Aberle is one of the offspring of the Senator's dream, too. His paternal grandparents were ethnic Germans who fled Russia eighty years ago, family tradition holds, to escape some kind of now only vaguely remembered persecution. His father married a Ducheneaux, the descendant of a prominent clan of French trappers and traders who had intermarried with the Sioux and become powers in the tribe. Steve Aberle, who was born in 1960, is thus one-eighth Sioux; he is a voting member of the tribe and served for two and a half years as chairman of the tribal police commission. "Probably I associate myself more with the Indian quantum because people make more of it. But I don't deny that I'm Russian-German or that I'm part French."

Second-Class Citizenship

There is little support in Timber Lake for the kind of blanket sovereignty that the Cheyenne River Sioux tribal leaders in Eagle Butte now claim. Although Aberle is himself a tribe member, he shares the resentment of non-Indians who feel themselves slipping toward a kind of second-class citizenship within reservation boundaries. "It would be better to be in a situation where everybody works together and deals with people as people, but it's hard to do that when people know they pay taxes but are excluded from benefits and services. My grandparents were outcasts in Russia. The United States government told them that they would be full citizens if they moved out here. Now I see people being told that they can't even take part in a government that wants to regulate them. Something is inherently wrong when you can't be a citizen where you live because of your race. It just doesn't fit with the traditional notion of being a U.S. citizen. At some point, there has to be a collision between the notion of tribal sovereignty and the notion of being United States citizens. The people who settled here never had any idea that they would be living on an Indian reservation. The land was given to them fair and square by the government. These people have been here almost one hundred years themselves now. Then the rules were changed in midstream. Anytime you have a group not represented in the political process, they will be discriminated against. It's going to hurt these communities. People start looking for jobs else-

> *"The achievement of a sovereignty that drives away taxpayers, consumers, and enterprise may be at best but a Pyrrhic victory."*

where. You lose a business here, a business there. There's going to be more and more friction. People don't want to see their kids growing up feeling victimized by the Indians.". . .

A New Political World

The Lakotas were the victims of nineteenth-century social engineering that decimated their reservation. But the adventurous emigrants from Oslo and Odessa were also the victims of a terrible historical prank, the trick of the disappearing and now magically reappearing reservation. Their grandchildren are today discovering themselves in a strange new political world that was not of their making, hungry for protection and obliged to learn the new and difficult language of tribal power. It is a rhetoric that, reasonably enough, demands for tribes a degree of self-government that is taken for granted by other Americans; it also asks non-Indians to live under tribal taxation, police, and courts of sometimes dubious reliability. Moreover, the achievement of a sovereignty that drives away taxpayers, consumers, and enterprise may be at best but a Pyrrhic victory over withered communities that beg for cooperation and innovation if they are to survive at all.

> *"[The ideology of sovereignty] seems to presuppose that cultural purity ought to, or even can, be preserved."*

On a deeper plane, the ideology of sovereignty seems to presume that racial separateness is a positive good, as if Indian bloodlines, economies, and histories were not already inextricably enmeshed with those of white, Hispanic, black, and Asian Americans; it seems to presuppose that cultural purity ought to, or even can, be preserved. With little debate outside the parochial circles of Indian affairs, a generation of policymaking has jettisoned the long-standing American ideal of racial unity as a positive good and replaced it with a doctrine that, seen from a more critical angle, seems disturbingly like an idealized form of segregation, a fact apparently invisible in an era that has made a secular religion of passionate ethnicity. As Arthur Schlesinger has written in *The Disuniting of America:*

> Instead of a transformative nation with an identity all its own, America increasingly sees itself in this new light as a preservative of diverse alien identities. Instead of a nation composed of individuals making their own unhampered choices, America increasingly sees itself as composed of groups more or less ineradicable in their ethnic character.

The belief that Indians are somehow fundamentally different from other Americans, however romantically the idea may be expressed in terms of native "tradition" or magical notions of affinity for the earth, implies a failure of basic American values, for it leads inexorably toward moral acceptance of political entities defined on the basis of racial exclusion. Although the concept of tribal sovereignty has parallels in other ideologies of racial and ethnic separatism, it is potentially far more subversive, for Indian tribes, unlike the nation's other minorities, possess both land and governments of their own and have at least the potential to transform not only their hopes and creativity but also their biases into political power in a way that others never can. It should, moreover, be obvious to anyone that legitimizing segregation for Indians will set a precedent for its potential imposition upon black, Asian, and Hispanic Americans.

The Disappearing Indian

Such critical concerns will surely be further exacerbated in the years to come as Indian identity becomes increasingly ambiguous. Virtually all Indians, whether they acknowledge it or not, are moving along a continuum of biological fusion with other American populations. "A point will be reached—perhaps not too far in the future—when it will no longer make sense to define American Indians in generic terms, only as tribal members or as people of Indian ancestry or ethnicity," Russell Thornton, a Cherokee anthropologist based at the University of California at Berkeley and a specialist in native demographics, has written. Statistically, according to Thornton, Indians are marrying outside their ethnic group at a faster rate than any other Americans. Most Indians are already married to non-Indians, and by the late twenty-first century only a minuscule percentage of Native Americans will have one-half or more Indian blood. It is plain that the principle, or the pretense, that blood should be a central defining fact of being Indian will soon become untenable.

How much blending can occur before Indians finally cease to be Indians? Unfortunately, the implications of this dramatic demographic trend remain virtually unexamined. The question is sure to loom ever larger in the coming generations, as the United States increasingly finds itself in "government-to-government" relationships with "Indian tribes" that are, in fact, becoming less ethnically Indian by the decade. Within two or three generations, the nation will possess hundreds of semi-independent "tribes" whose native heritage consists mainly of autonomous governments and special privileges that are denied to other Americans.

In the meantime, relations between Indian tribes and both the federal and state governments are likely to become more complicated. Increasing control over their sources of revenue will enable more and more tribes—primarily those with marketable natural resources, well-run tribal industries, and proximity to big cities—to achieve some degree of practical autonomy. However, without enlightened leadership and an educated and self-confident electorate,

> *"How much blending can occur before Indians finally cease to be Indians?"*

not to mention the collaboration of the federal government, political sovereignty is only a pipe dream. "There's no such thing as being half sovereign any more than there is being half pregnant," says Ramon Roubideaux [a member of the Rosebud Sioux Tribe, who has probably litigated more civil rights cases than any other lawyer in South Dakota over the last half century]. "We are only sovereign insofar as the U.S. allows us to be. Sovereignty can only be preserved as long as you have the force to protect it, not just brute force, but political force, too. So unless you have an army, you'd better get used to that. Indians who think differently are just kidding themselves.". . .

Integration

History was . . . not only a story of wars, removals, and death but also one of calculated compromises and deliberately chosen risks and of both Indian communities and individuals continually remaking themselves in order to survive. To see change as failure, as some kind of cultural corruption, is to condemn Indians to solitary confinement in a prison of myth that whites invented for them in the first place. In the course of the past five centuries, Indian life has been utterly transformed by the impact of European horses and firearms, by imported diseases and modern medicine, by missionary zeal and Christian morality, by iron cookware, sheepherding, pickup trucks, rodeos and schools, by rum and welfare offices, and by elections, alphabets, and Jeffersonian idealism as well as by MTV, *Dallas,* and *The Simpsons* and by the rich mingling of native bloodlines with those of Europe, Africa, and the Hispanic Southwest. In many ways, the Indian revolution of the 1990s is itself a form of adaptation, as Indians, freed from the lockstep stewardship of Washington, search out new ways to live in the modern world.

> *"To see change as failure . . . is to condemn Indians to solitary confinement in a prison of myth that whites invented for them in the first place."*

"Our lives have been transmuted, changed forever," Rayna Green, who is of mixed Cherokee extraction and director of the Native American Program at the Museum of American History, said in a speech at the New York Public Library in 1993. "We live in a world where everything is mutable and fragile. But we are here, and we are not going to go away. Indians look around at the malls and stores of America, and say, 'None of this is ever going to be ours.' But none of it is going to go away either. This is still our home. We are all here willy-nilly together. Somehow we must face the consequences of history and live with it. We don't need only to remember the tragedy, but to also remember the gift, to live in this place, to know it gave us birth, to feel the responsibility we have for it. We have to sit down and figure out how to not hurt each other any more."

Self-determination gives Indian tribes the ability to manage the speed and style of integration, but not the power to stop it, at least for long. Integration may well mean the eventual diminishing of conventional notions of "tribal identity," but it must also bring many new individual opportunities along with membership in the larger human community. Those tribes that succumb to the impulse to exclude and to segregate, to build walls against the outside world, are likely to pay a high price. "People and their cultures perish in isolation, but they are born or reborn in contact with other men and women, with man and woman of another culture, another creed, another race," the Mexican author Carlos Fuentes has written. Indians will continue to survive as people, although they will surely be much less recognizable as the white man's idea of "Indians" as time goes on. Tribes, too, will survive, if anything as stronger and more problematic entities than they have been for many generations. The question is whether they will attempt to survive as islands isolated from the American mainstream or as vital communities that recognize a commonality of interest and destiny with other Americans.

Indian Sovereign Immunity Should Be Restricted

by James M. Johnson

About the author: *James M. Johnson is an attorney in private practice in Olympia, Washington. He has represented private landowners and commercial and sportfishing interests in Washington, Minnesota, and California against Indian claims of extended fishing rights. He is also a former senior assistant attorney general for Washington and the former head of the state's Special Litigation Division.*

It is often claimed that tribes are like separate or even foreign nations over which state or federal courts may not exercise jurisdiction. It is even claimed this status is conferred by treaties with the United States. Neither is historically accurate.

Recognized Tribes

As an important prefatory note, the number of "tribes" in the United States, as "recognized" by the list prepared by the present Assistant Secretary of Interior for Indian Affairs, Ada Deer, has climbed to over five hundred, which she characterizes as entitled to:

> [T]he same privileges, *immunities*, responsibilities and obligations as other Indian tribes under the same or similar circumstances including the right, subject to general principles of Federal Indian law, to exercise the same inherent and delegated authorities available to other tribes.

. . . Two important points should be noted. The list of "tribes" has been growing—in part based on BIA [Bureau of Indian Affairs] determinations to add to the list of their constituencies. Also, those "tribes" now include entities not historically recognized as "tribes," at least through treaties.

Indeed, most of the tribes as currently listed by the BIA are "non-treaty"; the United States government never entered into treaties recognizing such entities. There are a total of 367 ratified treaties entered into between 1778 (Delaware)

From James M. Johnson's testimony in *Tribal Sovereign Immunity: Hearing Before the Committee on Indian Affairs, U.S. Senate*, 104th Cong., 2nd sess., September 24, 1996.

and 1868, when the last with the Nez Perce was entered. Of that number, numerous were entered into with the same tribe or tribes. In that number are not counted the treaties entered into by the Confederacy. The oft-quoted provision that Indian lands would be held in common and not be part of states "so long as grass shall grow and water run" were found only in these Confederacy treaties, which also guaranteed slavery—not in any treaty between the United States and tribes.

Dependent Nations

Second, the treaties themselves generally recognized and specified that any tribal sovereignty was reduced (to control over their own members) as the tribes all became the "dependent nations" of which Chief Justice John Marshall spoke.

Francis Paul Prucha notes in *American Indian Treaties* (1994) that the assumption that the Indian tribes were not independent sovereigns was reflected in the treaties through "some such phrases as the following":

> [T]he said Indian nations do acknowledge themselves and all their tribes to be under the protection of the United States . . . (or later) admitted that they resided within the territorial limits of the United States (and) acknowledged its supremacy.

From pre-revolutionary times, the Indians were not treated as equivalent to foreign sovereign nations. Under the Articles of Confederation, Article VI provided for foreign treaties, and Article IX provided for Congress to regulate trade and manage all Indian affairs and other domestic matters.

Even during the Revolutionary War, Indian affairs were treated as a domestic and military matter, not as foreign or diplomatic questions. The Treaty of Paris (1783) recognized the transfer of sovereignty from Great Britain to the Colonies to western lands reaching to the Mississippi. The tribes were not mentioned, though they had largely sided with the British in the war.

> *"The treaties themselves generally recognized and specified that any tribal sovereignty was reduced (to control over their own members)."*

Later major additions of land to the United States were made by treaties with other nations, e.g., the Louisiana Purchase from France, the Treaty of Guadalupe Hidalgo from Mexico, Alaska through the Treaty of Cession from Russia. In some of these areas treaties were made with Indian tribes. In Alaska and California, they were not.

In 1871, Congress passed an Act providing that:

> [H]ereafter no Indian nation or tribe within the territory of the United States shall be acknowledged or recognized as an independent nation, tribe, or power with whom the United States may contract by treaty.

The Supreme Court jurisprudence from early on distinguished Indian tribes from such foreign "nations."

Chief Justice John Marshall had written *Johnson v. McIntosh* in 1823 speaking of the tribes' rights to sovereignty as "necessarily diminished" in concluding the Indians could not even convey lands.

Marshall's *Cherokee Nation v. Georgia* (1831), expressly held the Cherokee were not a "foreign state" and so not entitled to sue the State of Georgia for diversity jurisdiction purposes under Article III, Sec. 2. He referred to them as:

> [D]omestic dependent nations (whose) relation to the United States resembles that of a ward to his guardian (and) so completely under the sovereignty and dominion of the United States that any attempt to acquire their lands or to form a political connection with them, would be considered by all as an invasion of our territory and an act of hostility.

Even these notions of limited sovereignty found in some of these early decisions were later referred to as "platonic notions of Indian sovereignty" by the Supreme Court in decisions in the twentieth century: "Modern cases thus tend to avoid reliance on platonic notions of Indian sovereignty and to look instead to the applicable treaties and statutes. . . ."

Tribal Sovereignty

Those treaty provisions, as noted above (citing Prucha), assumed, and often expressly provided, that the tribes were not fully "sovereign." *South Dakota v. Bourland* (1993) refers to modern "reality after *Montana* [*v. United States* (1981)], tribal sovereignty over non-members cannot survive without expressed Congressional delegation and is therefore *not* inherent." (Emphasis in original.)

Under the United States Constitution, of course, there are only two sovereigns: the United States and the states which formed that Union. Authority over Indian affairs is vested in Congress as one of its Article I, Section 8 powers through the Indian Commerce Clause.

No Express Prohibition

Unlike the XI Amendment providing for the states' immunity from suit in federal courts, there is no such express prohibition with respect to the tribes. Indeed, historically both in statute and treaty, there has frequently been specific provision for such actions against tribes.

As noted in the original *Handbook of Federal Indian Law*, by Felix S. Cohen (1942):

> [T]here are a number of statutes which authorize suits against Indian tribes . . . (some) authorized suits against Indian Tribes and allowed, in effect the execution of judgment upon the tribal funds in the United States treasury.

(He then refers to previous chapter, sections 1 and 3, which include numerous such statutes.) As only one example: a general provision for Court of Claims jurisdiction over "all claims for property of citizens . . . taken or destroyed by Indians belonging to any band, Tribe, or nation" he refers to as "an outgrowth of the collective responsibility imposed by early statutes and treaties for the torts of their members." That, and the accompanying text and footnotes, recounts an extensive list of cases brought against tribes under such authorizations by Congress.

In a later section Cohen further noted Congress' historical practice of passing Acts authorizing suit which were specific to a tribe or tribes: "Congress has from time to time authorized various other suits against Indian Tribes by private citizens." Examples follow. The quoted example

> *"The general authorization in Acts of Congress allowing tribes to bring suit or the United States to sue on their behalf must be made reciprocal."*

allowed judgments to be paid either from funds in the United States treasury for the tribe or from any annuities.

Many of the statutes Cohen discussed are no longer in effect. They do give a more realistic idea of the historic practice which included an evolution from a treaty-period practice of providing for paying claims directly from tribal funds held by the United States to allowing suit in courts.

This moderate approach protected tribal assets, allowing recovery up to the amount of funds the United States provides the tribes.

Notwithstanding that the treaties limited such payments, generally to twenty years, today the United States still provides millions to the tribes. Thus it is an added source of friction that persons harmed by tribes feel (correctly) their own tax dollars fund the problem source, where the actions are by tribal agents or employees.

Additionally, many tribes are in the casino gambling business. The millions thus derived add to federal funding, making them relatively wealthy, taking away the major historic argument for shielding tribes by immunity: the fear that tribes would be impoverished.

Immunity Must Be Waived

The general authorization in Acts of Congress allowing tribes to bring suit or the United States to sue on their behalf must be made reciprocal. Tribes of today should be viewed as responsible for their acts and fully subject to suit. This will also allow full consideration and resolution by the same court of counterclaim and cross-claims when tribes bring suit.

Justice Harry Blackmun stated in *Puyallup Tribe v. Department of Game* (1977):

> I entertain doubts . . . about the continuing vitality in this day of the doctrine of tribal immunity. . . . I am of the view that the doctrine may well merit reexamination in an appropriate case.

An ironic postscript to this comment is that after it was written, on remand, the Puyallup tribe asserted its immunity and refused to further participate in that case. Having litigated three times to the United States Supreme Court, the tribe took the benefits of those issues on which it had prevailed, but left the Court rather than accept the burdens and responsibilities (which could be enforced only against individual members).

As previously noted, this practice continues to the present. It is time it be ended by Congress' adoption of a waiver of immunity for all tribes.

States Should Be Allowed to Tax Tribal Revenues

by Lyn Nofziger

About the author: *Lyn Nofziger is a Republican strategist and adviser.*

It may be time for their fellow Americans to quit feeling sorry for Native Americans.

Thanks to Congress and the national penchant for gambling, Indian tribes and bands are raking in big bucks these days in untaxed and sometimes illegal dollars.

The money largely comes from Indian-owned gaming casinos that gross between $4 billion and $5 billion tax-free annually.

At last count, there were 231 tax-free casinos run by 200 tribes and sub-tribes some with fewer than a hundred members—on reservations in 29 states. The nation's biggest casino in terms of take is not in Las Vegas or Atlantic City; it's in Connecticut, where the Mashantucket-Pequot tribe's Foxwoods Casino rakes in more than $800 million per year. There are fewer than 500 members of the tribe.

The Indian Gaming Regulatory Act

All this has come about because of a 1988 law called The Indian Gaming Regulatory Act.

The act, laden with loopholes, largely ignores state laws that affect non-Indian gaming, as well as the rights of surrounding communities. It requires any state that permits any form of gaming to negotiate "in good faith" with any of the 557 federally recognized tribes that want to offer similar games.

It is, in fact, an open door for any tribe to open a casino on its reservation. It has led New York Gov. George Pataki to worry publicly about "the proliferation of casinos and entertainment complexes that pay no property taxes, no sales taxes and no income taxes."

Because of the unique relationship between Indians and government, both state and federal, opportunities for corruption and illegal activities abound. A

From Lyn Nofziger, "Indian Gaming's End Run Around Taxes," *San Diego Union-Tribune*, September 8, 1996. Reprinted by permission of the author.

Government Accounting Office report warns that casinos are in danger of being used for money-laundering purposes. The danger is enhanced by the fact that Indian gaming does not fall under the Bank Secrecy Act of 1970 and therefore is not required to disclose its record-keeping and currency transactions.

Additionally, in California, Attorney General Dan Lungren charges that more than 12,000 slot machines and other gaming devices are being operated illegally by at least 20 Indian casinos. Both Lungren and Gov. Pete Wilson argue that, contrary to the law, the devices are being operated without the benefit of a signed agreement between the governor and the tribes.

> *"Though Indian casinos and business ventures pay no taxes, they benefit from state and local services, including roads, fire and police protection."*

A federal court of appeals ruling in 1996 supports their claim, saying that the devices are illegal on Indian lands unless there is a tribal-state compact and that the machines are legal elsewhere in the state.

So far, neither condition has been met.

Regardless, Indian gaming has strong congressional support, including that of Arizona Sen. John McCain, whose state has the nation's third-largest Indian population, behind only Oklahoma and California. McCain, chairman of the Senate Committee on Indian Affairs, has told the National Governors Association that he views it as "intransigent in discussions on amendments to the IGRA" and that he remains committed to the rights of Indian tribes "to conduct gaming."

The governors are urging amendments that would force Indians to follow the same state gambling laws that non-Indian establishments must follow.

A Valuable Benefit?

The value of the casinos to the states in which they operate is hotly debated.

Proponents point to increased jobs within the Indian community as well as contributions from casino profits to charities and reservation infrastructures. A friendly article in the *San Diego Union-Tribune* says three casinos in San Diego County attract 15,000 gamblers daily and gross more than $300 million a year. It asserts that the casinos have created more than 5,000 jobs, with an annual payroll of $22 million.

One tribe plans to build a $30 million retail and entertainment center on reservation land with its profits. This is not unusual. Many tribes have opened commercial businesses on reservation land near their casinos. These, too, pay no taxes and thus undercut existing businesses.

Some tribes use casino profits to buy land that is put in "trust" and thus becomes a part of the reservation and pays no property taxes. Commercial ventures placed on trust lands also pay no taxes.

On the surface, the fact that casinos have brought new prosperity to many Indian tribes is something to cheer about. But there is a downside, too.

Take, for instance, the retail and entertainment center.

Because it will pay no taxes, it will underprice merchants in the area, eating not only into the profits but also into state and county tax revenues derived from those merchants. A report by the Wisconsin Policy Research Institute found that many businesses adjacent to casinos are significantly hurt by neighboring tax-free, Indian-owned businesses.

In California and other states with state-run lotteries, there also are indications that Indian gaming is diverting large amounts from the lotteries. This means reduced state revenues, which, along with the casinos' negative effect on small business, is almost certain to bring about higher taxes at both state and local levels.

Though Indian casinos and business ventures pay no taxes, they benefit from state and local services, including roads, fire and police protection.

Additionally, casinos and business ventures built on reservation land are not subject to zoning and building codes or other restrictions that apply off the reservation.

Studies also show that the casinos add substantially to the financial burdens of states and nearby localities, not only because of increased crime, but also because of added burdens placed on water, and sewer and traffic systems. Regarding crime, Minnesota is a typical example. There, between 1988 and 1994, counties with casinos had twice as much crime as counties without casinos.

Indian leaders are aware of the increasing opposition to the growth of their tax-free casinos and have adopted a common tactic to fight it; they have hired expensive lobbyists and are contributing heavily to political parties.

In California, the 18-member Cabazon band of Mission Indians has given more than $600,000 in campaign contributions. Between 1994 and 1995, political contributions from Indian groups in the state totaled nearly $2.5 million.

Finally, despite their multibillion-dollar gaming income, Indians still have their hands as deeply as ever in the federal trough. In fact, the 1997 budget request by the Bureau of Indian Affairs, arguably the worst-run federal agency, is $211 million higher than it was for 1996.

Indian Sovereign Immunity Must Not Be Restricted

by Susan M. Williams

About the author: *Susan M. Williams is a lawyer in private practice in Albuquerque, New Mexico. She has represented Indian tribal governments throughout the country on issues of tribal sovereign immunity.*

> *Editor's note: The following viewpoint is taken from the author's written testimony before the U.S. Senate Committee on Indian Affairs on September 26, 1996.*

My testimony, in sum, is that it is essential that Congress not legislate a sweeping waiver of tribal sovereign immunity specially to protect non-Indians and non-members owning or using land within Indian reservations. Both law and public policy suggest this conclusion. First, several dangers exist in legislating a broad waiver of tribal sovereign immunity. A broad waiver of this nature may result in serious, unintended impacts. It would undermine the historic common-law right and federal policy granting Indian tribes autonomy and self-determination as sovereigns, and it would expose the limited financial and economic resources of modern-day tribal governments to unfettered litigation and ultimate depletion. Second, a broad waiver of tribal immunity from suit simply is not necessary to protect non-Indians and non-members. The federal government and tribal governments already afford substantial legal protections to the interests of non-tribal entities and individuals on reservation lands. Tribal governments are dealing with non-tribal entities and individuals with increased frequency in the civil regulatory, commercial, and environmental contexts. As proactive measures and of their own volition, tribes have initiated programs and policies designed to solicit input and participation of non-tribal members. This has resulted in more effective administration, enforcement, and adjudication of tribal laws and regulations. For these reasons, it is essential that Congress refrain from legislating a broad waiver of tribal sovereign immunity.

From Susan M. Williams's testimony in *Tribal Sovereign Immunity: Hearing Before the Committee on Indian Affairs, U.S. Senate*, 104th Cong., 2nd sess., September 24, 1996.

[The U.S. Supreme Court has long] recognized that Indian nations possess "the common-law immunity from suit traditionally enjoyed by sovereign powers." The basis of this immunity has been expressed as an inherent aspect of tribal sovereign powers predating the United States Constitution and as consistent with federal policy in preserving the existence of tribal autonomy. The United States thus must tread lightly in this area as the important federal interest in tribal self-determination is at stake. Indian tribes, however, are not cloaked with an absolute, unqualified immunity from suit. Like other sovereign powers of Indian tribes, tribal immunity may be waived by congressional act. Courts also have recognized exceptions to tribal immunity from suit. In fact, tribal sovereign immunity is similar, but not identical, to that enjoyed by the federal government, state governments, or other foreign sovereigns.

> *"Tribal immunity from suit is essential to preserve tribes' autonomous political existence and tribal assets."*

Origin and Scope of the Doctrine

As a general matter, the doctrine of sovereign immunity has been supported on the theory that official actions of government must be protected from undue interference. As a practical and policy matter, the doctrine has been deemed necessary to protect public treasuries from depletion by unfettered litigation. Thus, the common law doctrine of immunity from suit remains viable, not only for tribal governments but also for the state and federal governments.

The Supreme Court applied the common law immunity doctrine to Indian tribes for the first time in 1940. The Court has viewed the common law sovereign immunity possessed by tribes as "a necessary corollary to Indian sovereignty and self-governance." Courts have recognized that tribal immunity from suit is essential to preserve tribes' autonomous political existence and tribal assets, as well as to promote the federal policies of tribal self-determination, economic development, and cultural autonomy. From a policy standpoint, tribal immunity from suit advances the federal policy of assuring that Indian nations remain viable cultural and political entities.

Current-day jurisprudence does not regard the scope of tribal sovereign immunity from suit, however, as identical to that of other sovereigns. Indian nations are subject to broad federal control and definition. Consequently, tribes are characterized as "quasi-sovereigns," and as such, tribal immunity from suit "is not congruent with that which the Federal Government, or the states, enjoy," according to the U.S. Supreme Court. Thus, the scope of tribal sovereign immunity from suit is *not* unlimited and is subject to a number of exceptions or waivers by the United States and tribes themselves.

Tribes and tribal agencies and officials are subject to suit under various exceptions to tribal sovereign immunity recognized in the courts. For example, courts have applied the age-old doctrine established by *Ex parte Young* in the tribal context. This doctrine works as an exception to the general rule of sovereign immunity from suit and is applied to federal and state governments. At its core, the *Ex parte Young* doctrine permits suits for prospective injunctive or declarative relief to require governmental officials to comply with the law. It is based on the notion that an action against individual government officials engaging in unauthorized or illegal conduct is not an action against the sovereign government itself. Thus, in the tribal context, a litigant may seek injunctive or declaratory relief against individual tribal officials who allegedly have acted outside the scope of their authority. This exception to tribal sovereign immunity has been broadly construed, permitting, for example, developers or individuals to obtain adjudications of the validity of various tribal laws and actions. Thus, although the *Ex parte Young* doctrine was intended to waive state immunity to vindicate violations of federal law by state officials, the doctrine has been extended to act by tribal officials in derogation of tribal or federal law.

> *"Tribal sovereign immunity may be waived by either acts of Congress or acts of the tribes."*

Tribal sovereign immunity has been limited by various court decisions establishing other exceptions to tribal immunity from suit. For instance, where particularly egregious allegations of personal restraint and deprivation of personal rights were raised, the Tenth Circuit distinguished the *Santa Clara Pueblo v. Martinez* case and permitted a claim for damages for constitutional violations of personal and property rights against a tribe. In addition, an exception based upon the equitable recoupment doctrine has been recognized in the Tenth Circuit. These trends are disturbing as the power of the United States to waive tribal sovereignty rests in Congress, not the courts, and that power must be exercised judiciously.

Tribal sovereign immunity may be waived by either acts of Congress or acts of the tribes. Although Congress has power to waive a tribe's common law immunity from suit, Congress, appropriately, only sparingly has exercised this power. Only a few instances can be cited where Congress has waived tribal immunity from suit.

In addition, tribes may waive sovereign immunity from suit voluntarily. The Supreme Court ruled that tribal waivers of sovereign immunity must be "unequivocally expressed." Courts have found tribal waivers of immunity from suit in a variety of circumstances. For instance, courts have held that an Indian tribe's contract providing for resolution of disputes by arbitration and making the arbitration agreement enforceable in any court having jurisdiction creates a right to sue, and thus constitutes a waiver of the tribe's sovereign immunity. Most courts also have held as a general rule that the presence of "sue and be sued" clauses in corporate charters established under the Indian Reorganization

Act (IRA) constitute a waiver of sovereign immunity.

In the commercial context, increased economic development involving non-tribal entities have resulted in tribal governments voluntarily waiving tribal immunity and providing protections to non-Indians' and non-members' interests as necessary. For example, in its gaming compact with the State of Arizona, the Yavapai-Apache Nation agreed to establish procedures for the disposition of tort claims arising from alleged injuries to patrons of its gaming establishment. Under the gaming compact, it was agreed that the procedures may be analogous to the remedial system available for similar claims arising against the State. Pursuant thereto, the Yavapai-Apache Nation adopted comprehensive tort remedies procedures, wherein the Nation waives the sovereign immunity of the gaming establishment and/or the Nation for the express purpose of allowing patrons to bring tort claims against the Nation and/or the gaming establishment in the Nation's tribal court.

These are but some examples of circumstances in which tribal immunity from suit has been limited. Given this discussion, it is clear that tribes are not cloaked by an impermeable shield of sovereign immunity from suit. The courts appear to be finding exceptions and waivers by tribes of tribal sovereign immunity with increasing frequency. Thus, a sweeping waiver of tribal sovereign immunity is unnecessary and will undermine tribes' entitlement as sovereigns to common law immunity from suit afforded other sovereigns. As with any sovereign, tribal governments must retain their autonomy and ability to protect their treasuries from attack and to subject themselves to government on a case-by-case basis.

Protecting the Interests of Non-Indians

A broad waiver of tribal sovereign immunity from suit is unnecessary because the federal government and tribal governments already are providing protections to non-Indians and non-members within the boundaries of reservations. Existing federal oversight protects the interests of reservation residents without destroying tribal autonomy.

Congress ensures the protection of non-Indians and non-members by requiring federal approval of certain tribal laws and ordinances governing a variety of civil regulatory areas. While it is arguable that Congress oversteps the "guardian" role of the United States over tribes and effectively usurps tribal governments through this type of legislation, it is certainly

> *"Increased economic development involving non-tribal entities has resulted in tribal governments voluntarily waiving tribal immunity."*

less harmful than legislating broad waivers of tribal immunity from suit in these areas. Thus, where tribes exercise regulatory jurisdiction in these areas, the involvement and oversight of the federal government already protects the interests of non-Indians and non-members.

For instance, tribes are allowed to enact their own liquor laws within the limitations set by a federal jurisdiction statute. While Congress has set forth the requirements of the tribal ordinances and maintained a federal certification and oversight role, actual regulation of the liquor sales remains vested in the tribes within their jurisdictional boundaries. Several tribes have enacted liquor ordinances under these procedures. Significantly, a recent federal court decision upheld a tribal ordinance that authorized the Cheyenne River Sioux Tribe to regulate liquor sales in non-Indian communities, on lands held in fee by non-Indians within the reservation. Other examples include federal agency involvement in forestry and agriculture.

> *"A sweeping waiver of tribal sovereign immunity . . . will undermine tribes' entitlement as sovereigns to common law immunity from suit afforded other sovereigns."*

In addition, Congress has authorized federal agencies to assist tribes in developing tribal ordinances and regulations related to the particular agency's areas of concern. For example, the Indian Energy Resources Act authorized the secretaries of interior and energy to provide assistance to Indian tribes in the development, administration, implementation, and enforcement of tribal laws and regulations governing the development of energy resources on Indian reservations. The Indian Gaming Regulatory Act authorizes the chairman of the National Indian Gaming Commission, a federal agency, to approve tribal gaming ordinances and resolutions. The interests of all reservation citizens is taken into account by the federal agency's evaluating tribal undertakings in these areas.

Tribal Environmental Regulations

In the area of environmental protection, Congress has acknowledged that tribal governments, like state governments, have the authority to regulate environmental matters. This authority, however, is subject to federal agency oversight. The Environmental Protection Agency ("EPA") is authorized to approve certain tribal environmental codes as part of federal government programs. Specific EPA authority is found in the Clean Water Act and the Safe Drinking Water Act.

Under the "primacy" provision of the Safe Drinking Water Act, tribes are provided the opportunity to assume principal responsibility for the enforcement of drinking water supply regulations within the jurisdictional boundaries of the tribe. To attain primacy status, a tribe must have drinking water regulations at least as strict as EPA's and establish an independent agency within the tribal government that has the power to enforce tribal regulations. Increasing numbers of tribes are undertaking principal responsibility, with the assistance of the EPA, for protecting sources used for drinking water under the federal enabling legislation.

Tribes also are undertaking environmental regulation under the Clean Water Act. Congress has permitted tribes to be "treated as states" for purposes of this legislation. As such, tribes can obtain funds necessary to pursue the planning required for protecting water resources vital to the tribes. Section 106 of the Clean Water Act allows for development of a surface water management program, and section 104 provides for water quality management. Once a tribe's water quality standards have been approved by the EPA, the tribe also is treated as a state for purposes of the certification process under section 401 of the CWA. The section 401 certification process requires the technical review of pending permit applications to determine their impacts on water quality standards, and most tribal law-making bodies avoid becoming directly involved in carrying out this kind of technical review process. Another statutory requirement is that tribes, like states, adopting their own water quality standards must conduct a public review of their standards at least every three years. These burdensome administrative procedures ensure the input and protection of the interests of affected non-Indians and non-members.

Despite the strict statutory burdens of undertaking tribal environmental regulation, many tribes are establishing the necessary administrative and adjudicatory procedures and expertise in order to protect the resources that are vital to the welfare and future of their tribe. For example, tribal governments have developed extensive solid and hazardous waste regulations, particularly in response to the Eight Circuit's 1989 decision in *Blue Legs v. U.S. Bureau of Indian Affairs*, which held that tribal governments are responsible for managing solid waste disposal on reservations and may be held liable for failing to meet this responsibility. The Campo Band of Mission Indians, for example, has established compre-

> *"The authority of tribal governments to exercise tribal jurisdiction over non-Indians has been one of the most disputed issues in Indian affairs."*

hensive tribal regulatory and enforcement mechanisms for regulating solid waste on the reservation. In many of these tribal ordinances, tribes provide a waiver of their sovereign immunity from suit for purposes of appeal of administrative decisions by tribal agencies. The Lummi Water and Sewer Ordinance is an example.

Tribal Economic Development

The interests of non-Indians and non-members are protected to the extent required by federal law or the terms of commercial transactions. The federal government, for instance, is inextricably involved in tribal housing development. The Department of Housing and Urban Development ("HUD") has requirements for tribal housing authorities receiving HUD funds. For example, the Indian Housing Loan Guaranty Program allows HUD to guarantee loans for the purchase, construction, or rehabilitation of family dwellings on restricted lands and in Indian areas. In order for an individual Indian borrower or an Indian Housing Authority to participate in the program, the tribal government must enact both eviction and foreclosure procedures to protect borrowers, lenders, and HUD, in the event of a default. Here, too, tribal housing ordinances often contain a waiver of tribal sovereign immunity from suit to enforce individual rights under these ordinances.

In the commercial context, tribes have a built-in incentive to waive their immunity from suit or otherwise protect non-Indians. Interested parties will not be interested in conducting business on Indian reservations without an ability to seek redress for grievances. Tribes, thus, will choose to waive immunity or take other similar steps to consummate a business deal. Clearly, no intervention is necessary in this context.

Non-Indian Participation in Tribal Government

The authority of tribal governments to exercise tribal jurisdiction over non-Indians has been one of the most disputed issues in Indian affairs during the modern era. In 1978, the Supreme Court held in *Oliphant v. Suquamish Indian Tribe* that tribes could not prosecute and convict non-Indians unless authorized to do so by Congress. In 1990, the Supreme Court extended the *Oliphant* ruling to non-member Indians; Congress later reinstated tribal authority over non-member Indians. In 1996, controversies relating to tribal authority to exercise civil jurisdiction and regulatory authority over non-Indians and non-members residing within reservation boundaries persist. In certain civil contexts, particularly taxation and land use, tribal authority over non-Indians and non-members has been upheld.

Tribal authority to regulate non-Indians on non-tribal trust land within reservation boundaries is subject to certain rules under federal law. In *Montana v. United States* (1981), the Supreme Court enumerated the rule for establishing tribal jurisdiction over non-Indians in this context. First, "[a] tribe may regulate, through taxation, licensing, or other means, the activities of non-members who enter consensual relationships with the tribe or its members, through commercial dealing, contracts, leases, or other arrangements." Second, "[a] tribe may also retain inherent power to exercise civil authority over the conduct of non-Indians on fee lands within its reservation when that conduct threatens or has some direct effect on the political integrity, the economic security, or the health or welfare of the tribe." Under the "tribal welfare" test, lower courts have upheld broad tribal civil powers over non-Indians on non-Indian land in a tribal zoning ordinance, a tribal health and safety ordinance, and tribal regulation of non-Indian lands bordering tribal trust property. With regard to water use, the courts have upheld federal and tribal control to the exclusion of state control over water use by non-Indians on an Indian reservation.

Tribal Programs Involving Non-Indians

Many tribes have responded to the civil regulatory concerns involving non-Indians as well as tribal members by adopting extensive legal codes and restructuring tribal government capable of adjudicating Indian and non-Indian civil disputes in their own courts and administering their increased regulatory responsibilities. This makes tribal governments more accessible and "user-friendly" to tribal members and non–tribal members alike.

For example, the Zuni Pueblo has adopted extensive legal codes, including the Zuni Business Code which controls and regulates the activities of non-Zunis and non-residents of the Reservation in their commercial dealing with the Zuni Reservation and the people living thereon. The Zuni Business Code establishes procedures and requirements consistent with federal laws and regulations governing the conduct of business on the Zuni Reservation.

In addition, because tribes have civil regulatory authority and jurisdiction over non-Indians and non-members, tribal governments are developing initiatives to increase the participation of non tribal members in the government. For example, the Navajo Nation has established a five-member Navajo Tax Commission, two of whom may be non-Indians and non-members. Particularly important to note here, also, is that Navajo law permits an adjudication of a refund action in tribal court in specific instances for certain taxes. Thus, reservation citizens have direct access to both regulatory and judicial relief.

Another example of tribal initiatives to involve non-Indians includes the six-member Board of Commissioners of the Wind River Housing Authority, established by the Shoshone Indian Tribe and the Arapahoe Indian Tribe, which requires that two members of the Board be non-members. In addition, the Zuni Pueblo has established the Zuni Tribal Enterprise Board of Directors, and the five-member Board may be comprised of "[a]ny person, Zuni or non-Zuni, resident or non-resident," who shows a willingness to further the purposes of the Tribe.

> *"Tribal governments are developing initiatives to increase the participation of non-tribal members in the government."*

A particularly good example of tribal agency activities directly involving non-Indians is the Lummi Tribal Sewer and Water District Ordinance. The Lummi Ordinance involves the participation of non-Indians and non-members by permitting the election of two of the five members of the Sewer and Water Board from the entire community within the boundaries of the Lummi Tribal Sewer and Water District. The candidates and electors for these open positions consist of all persons residing within the District. In addition, the rules and procedures for voting and conducting the election are developed by a committee, which includes a non-Indian appointed by the Sewer and Water Board. Clearly, Lummi's regulation and administration of its water and sewer ordinance seeks to protect the interests of non-Indians and non-members within its reservation boundaries.

With increasing frequency, courts are interpreting federal laws and tribal laws, conduct, and contracts as waivers of sovereign immunity and creating exceptions to tribal immunity. In addition, tribes, themselves, are waiving their immunity from suit in appropriate circumstances. Moreover, federal law already provides a great deal of oversight of tribal affairs, even while acknowledging the fundamental importance of supporting tribal self-governance autonomy. In this context, Congress should remain very cautious in the area of tribal sovereign immunity from suit and refrain from legislating a sweeping waiver of tribal immunity.

States Should Not Be Allowed to Tax Indian Casino Revenues

by Franklin Ducheneaux

About the author: *Franklin Ducheneaux is a private consultant whose clients include the Minnesota Indian Gaming Association. He was the counsel to the U.S. Senate Committee on Indian Affairs from 1973 to 1990.*

The field of Indian gaming has been plagued by misperceptions, distortions and outright lies which many of us in the Indian community believe border on economic racism. . . .

Let me first lay to rest one of the biggest myths created by this atmosphere of distortion and lies. Despite what Donald Trump and his high-priced lawyer state in their judicial attack on Indian people, IGRA [the Indian Gaming Regulatory Act] did not—I repeat—*did not* authorize Indian tribes to engage in gaming free of state regulations.

Indian Tribes Are Sovereign Governments

To the contrary, the enactment of the IGRA was a lesson in the exercise of the raw political and economic power of the non-Indian gaming industry to destroy the sovereign, governmental rights of Indian tribes. The concept that is missed or ignored is that Indian tribes are governments with sovereign powers of self-government. These powers are inherent and not derived from the states or the United States. In New Mexico, the Pueblo tribes had forms of government and were exercising sovereign powers of self-government long before the Europeans landed on the shores of this continent.

The power of Indian tribes to regulate conduct and affairs on their lands, including the power to engage in or license and regulate gaming, are derived from those inherent powers. The 1987 Supreme Court decision in the *California v. Cabazon Band of Mission Indians* case was a clear recognition of the rights of

From Franklin Ducheneaux's testimony in *Implementation of Indian Gaming Regulatory Act: Oversight Hearing Before the Subcommittee on Native American Affairs of the Committee on Natural Resources, House of Representatives*, 103rd Cong., 1st sess., June 7, 1993, Serial no. 103–17, Part II.

Indian tribes to regulate gaming on their lands free of state laws where the state permitted those activities in their own jurisdictions.

The 1988 IGRA is a legislative litany of the destruction of many of those rights. The Indian tribes opposed enactment of IGRA and reluctantly accepted it as a part of an overall compromise which the enemies of Indian tribes, who pushed so hard for the compromise, now want to abandon.

I repeat, IGRA was an instrument of destruction of tribal rights, not a law conferring rights.

Indians and Taxes

Now I would like to turn to the myth of Indian immunity from taxation. This is another myth growing out of the atmosphere of misperceptions, distortions and lies about Indian gaming. The myth, repeated blindly by the press, is that Indians and Indian tribes don't pay taxes on revenues derived from gaming and, therefore, have an unfair economic advantage over poor Mr. Trump and the other gambling barons of Nevada and New Jersey. This is either false or a gross distortion of fact. I will briefly respond in three ways.

First, just as they have assumed their responsibility to fight in this nation's wars in numbers far beyond their relative population levels, individual Indians also share in the obligation to pay federal income taxes. Indians pay all the federal taxes non-Indians pay except in one small area. They do not pay taxes on income which they directly derive from property which is held in trust for them by the United States. This exception has no relevance in the area of Indian gaming.

It is true that, because of the sovereign status of tribes and because of federal laws interpreting that status, individual Indians living and working on Indian lands are not liable for the payment of most state or local governmental taxes. But it is equally true, but most often not reported, that few of the state and local government programs funded by those taxes are made available to Indians on the reservations. In those cases where the state or local governments do have a presence on the reservations, it is often not for the benefit of, or welcomed by, the Indians.

"It is racist to say that [Indian tribes] should have to pay taxes on their revenues while other sovereign or government entities do not have to do so."

Second, Indian gaming has, in fact, generated new tax revenues for the federal government, and for state and local governments. In generating employment opportunities for Indians, Indian gaming has had a double impact on taxation. It has taken these Indians and their families off of the welfare rolls, easing that burden on the non-Indian taxpayers. It has also given these Indian families an income for the first time which, as I have noted, is subject to federal taxes and even, in some cases, to state taxes.

But it has done more than that. It has created jobs for non-Indians, on and off the reservations. These people clearly pay both federal and state income taxes. It has sparked the non-Indian economies in both the local areas and in the state as a whole. New sales, excise and property taxes are generated. Indian gaming has drawn customers from outside the state in question and even, in some cases, from outside the country which is a fresh addition to the economy of that state and the local areas. Indian gaming is a tax-plus for almost all involved and affected.

Economic Racism

Finally and most importantly, we must address and lay to rest the argument that Indian tribes do not pay taxes. Mr. Trump and his allies attack Indian gaming on the grounds that Indian tribes which derive revenues from gaming activities do not pay federal, state and local taxes and, therefore, this is unfair to the New Jersey and Nevada gambling palaces.

The enemies of Indian tribes, capitalizing on the general lack of knowledge among the American public about the status of Indian tribes, attempt to equate tribes and their gaming enterprises with the commercial, for-profit cash-cows of Mr. Trump and his fellow barons of gambling. This constitutes economic racism in the minds of Indian people.

Indian tribes are governments with governmental responsibilities to their citizens. After the theft of their most valuable lands and resources and after decades of benign and, sometimes, not-so-benign neglect, they almost uniformly lack a tax base to support their governmental needs. They have had to rely upon the inadequate largess of federal appropriations to carry out their operations and programs.

A few—a minority—of tribes have found in gaming a means to not only provide jobs and economic activity on their reservations, but a source of badly needed governmental revenue, a substitute for a tax base. Indian tribes are governments and do not and should not have to pay taxes on their governmental revenues to any other government. In fact, the IRS made a finding in the 1960's that Indian tribes, as governments, are not taxable entities.

And why should they be? Does the state of New Jersey pay federal income taxes on the revenue it derives from its state lottery? Do the majority of other states that operate state lotteries or other state gaming enterprises pay taxes on their revenues? Of course not, nor should they.

Do Alaska and the other oil states pay federal taxes on their share of lease revenues from federal oil leases? Of course not.

Do state, county, or municipal governments which operate government-owned liquor stores or other commercial enterprises pay taxes to each other and to the federal government on their net receipts from these commercial activities? Of course not.

Indian tribes are governments. It is racist to say that they should have to pay taxes on their revenues while other sovereign or government entities do not have to do so. This charge against Indian tribes is specious and racist.

States Cannot
Tax Indian Nations

by Ray Halbritter

About the author: *Ray Halbritter represents the Oneida Indian Nation for the American Indian Program.*

History shows that ever since the first Europeans came to North America, Indian people have been confronted with one challenge after another. Often, the challenge has been simple survival, as people and as sovereign nations. And just as we meet and conquer one challenge, another arises.

There's an old Indian joke about the race to the moon being started because white men believed there was Indian land there. I have often said that Indian people never have anything for very long before the white man tries to take it away. That is the situation confronting us today.

The problem is that after 200 years of neglect by the federal government, some Indian nations have seized the initiative and have begun using their sovereign rights and power to create economic development opportunities for their people. The success of these efforts, particularly those based on gaming enterprises, have caused other governments to look hungrily at what they see as large, untapped sources of revenue for their strained and often poorly administered government budgets. So, it now seems as if attention from federal authorities may be just as bad as neglect.

Until recently, the federal and state governments have never utilized taxation as a means of dealing with Native Americans for one simple reason: no success. As a result of past policies, many of our people have been living in abject poverty. We have had no revenue that could be taxed.

Economic Prosperity

Today, for the first time, however, a handful of Indian nations are enjoying a small measure of economic prosperity. We are putting people to work and beginning to secure the future for the generations to come. A recent study commissioned by the International Game Technology Company showed that un-

From Ray Halbritter, "Indian Economic Futures: Governance and Taxation," a speech delivered at Cornell University, Ithaca, N.Y., November 13, 1996. Reprinted with permission.

employment on Indian reservations has been reduced by as much as 40 percent since gaming was introduced on our lands. Many nations, the Oneida Indian Nation included, are using the revenues from these enterprises to rejuvenate our nations, to revitalize cultures, traditions and languages almost lost to decades of drives to assimilate Indian people into white society. We are providing health care, educational opportunities, decent housing and other social services that are enabling some Indian people to enjoy a better quality of life than they have had for the past 200 years.

We have been able to do all of this mostly because Indian nations, during the past thirty years, have been successful in reacquiring lands unlawfully taken from them in prior centuries. Having regained possession of our territories, tribes are reasserting their inherent sovereign powers, including the right to conduct and regulate commercial activities on our lands.

> *"Some Indian nations . . . have begun using their sovereign rights and power to create economic development opportunities for their people."*

Having said all this, reviewing some of the positive news from Indian nations today, let me remind everyone that this is not the full story. It is important to remember that only a small percentage of Indian nations have achieved tangible improvement in their economic welfare over the past twenty years. The vast majority of tribes still find their members living in conditions of poverty. Statistics show that almost 32 percent of Indian people live in poverty. That compares to 13 percent of the general population in the United States. Nearly 15 percent of Indian people are unemployed. Our people still suffer from higher rates of liver disease, diabetes, alcoholism, suicide, homicide and accidental death, all signs of a society in stress, a culture endangered and a species nearly extinct. Sometimes it seems as if society is more concerned about spending dollars to save eagles from extinction than it is about saving indigenous peoples.

The highly visible success a very few Indian nations have been able to achieve has distorted the picture of what life is like for the vast majority of Indian people. Even in cases like that of my nation, where the quality of life of our members is better today than it has been in two centuries, three years of modest prosperity cannot undo 200 years of discrimination and poverty.

Reduced to simple terms, this is what today's clash between Indian nations and other governments is all about, our struggle, their greed. Federal, state and local governments have inflated views of the revenues being generated by Indian gaming enterprises. They also severely underestimate the need that still exists on Indian reservations and the cost of recovery from 200 years of poverty and neglect. Nor do they fully comprehend the economic benefits that Indian gaming bestows on surrounding communities. Finally, they do not understand, or often respect, the meaning of Indian nation sovereignty.

The sovereignty of Indian nations is the key to all of this. It is what enables Indian nations to engage in economic development initiatives, such as gaming enterprises. It is what prevents other governments from being able to tap into the revenues of those enterprises through taxation. . . . It never hurts to remind ourselves occasionally of what sovereignty means for Indian nations. Indian people have fought long, hard and bitterly to preserve and protect that sovereignty since the first Europeans landed here. The fight continues today and it is hard to see when, if ever, it will end. . . .

The Oneida Nation Today

Today, the Oneida Nation, like most Indian nations, continues to function as a sovereign government exercising jurisdiction over a territory with historically recognized boundaries. Our nation prescribes laws and ordinances which are legally binding within our territory. These are basic principles of sovereignty.

We maintain our own police force and provide numerous governmental and social welfare services, such as housing, medical care and educational programs. We are proud that the territory our nation occupies today consists exclusively of our ancestral homeland, that the Oneida Nation has never been conquered by the United States (we have always been allies, fighting alongside of the United States in every war in which this country has been engaged), that the Oneida Nation has never been displaced to a distant "reservation," and that our nation's lands have never been held "in trust" by the United States.

We have used our sovereignty to empower ourselves in a way that cannot be denied, and in a way that allows us to do things for our people that we have been unable to do for centuries. Ours is a real, practical sovereignty that has renewed the self-esteem of our people and brought back hope to our nation. We have created a new standard for judging leadership in Native American communities. Leaders must be judged by their actions, not their rhetoric. The old saw holds true, actions speak louder than words.

And while some of our actions have been controversial, there are those who believe that gaming is not the way to lift an Indian nation up and out of poverty, we believe the debate ends when one looks upon the once muddy thirty-two acres of the territory that has always been in Oneida hands and the once potholed road on it and sees the wonderful buildings, services and new opportunities we can now provide for our people.

> *"This is what today's clash between Indian nations and other governments is all about, our struggle, their greed."*

Since 1991, we have created over fifty programs and services for our members. The first building we built with our profits as a nation was a council house, a spiritual and governmental meeting place where we can now conduct our ceremonies on a regular basis. We have since built a cook house, a health services center, a cultural center and museum, a recreational center, a swimming pool, a bath house, a children's play-ground, a gymnasium, and a lacrosse box. We have established scholarship programs, medical, dental and optical services, job training and legal assistance programs, Oneida language and song classes, mental health and substance abuse programs, elder meals programs and a day care center for our children.

We have established a police force, paved our roads, built a septic system, consecrated a burial ground, opened a youth center and built housing for our people. With the opening of our casino, Turning Stone, in 1993, we have become one of the major economic powers in Central New York and one of the region's largest employers.

In the short run, we will build more housing, complete construction of an Elder and Child Care Center, launch more enterprises and expand existing programs. In the future, we will be limited only by our imaginations.

We are not dependent upon the federal government, the state government, the counties, towns or cities, churches, charities, or any other entity. I believe that such empowerment is more than just a statement of sovereignty, it is sovereignty. We have established that sovereignty without waiting for or depending on other people to define what that term means.

The Consequences of Success

Our very success, and that of other Indian nations, at exercising our sovereignty to bring to an end the centuries of poverty and despair in which Indian people have been trapped is what is driving other governments to consider breaking the covenant chain. They are greedily eyeing what they think are huge pots of money and contemplating infringing on our sovereignty with measures that would force us to serve as revenue agents and tax collectors for other governments.

In 1995, for example, legislation was introduced in Congress that called for the imposition of a 35 percent corporate income tax on the net revenues earned by an Indian nation from gaming activities. This was the first time the United States has ever sought to extend its income tax to Indian governments. [The legislation did not pass.]

In addition, another piece of legislation was introduced that would have tied the trust status of Indian land to an Indian nation's willingness to pay state and local taxes. This is a clear violation of federal policy and Native American sovereignty. [The bill did not pass.]

"A tax on an Indian nation violates tribal sovereignty."

In New York, the state has sought to apply its cigarette and fuel excise tax rules to Indian reservations. This action would force Indian nations and Native American sole proprietors to become tax collectors for the state. In Louisiana, the governor has formed a task force for the purpose of finding ways to tax Native American gaming profits and revenues generated by Indian tribes from other commercial activities. Other states are entertaining similar proposals and are closely watching the efforts of other state governments to extract revenue from Native Americans.

Although all of these threatened tax initiatives are different in some respects, they each have [these] things in common.

One, they are unlawful.

Two, all of them would have adverse economic consequences for both Indian people and for the non-Indians in surrounding communities. . . .

The Illegality of Proposed Tax Initiatives

The reasons why federal and state efforts to force Indian nations into serving as revenue agents and/or tax collectors for other governments are illegal are numerous. They include the following:

One. A tax on an Indian nation violates tribal sovereignty. As already discussed, Indian tribes are sovereign nations, recognized as such by the United States. They are governmental entities, exercising many of the same sovereign powers and possessing many of the same governmental responsibilities as the United States and state governments. Trying to impose taxes on Indian nations is as ridiculous as the United States trying to tax the income of Canada, of New York State

> *"Trying to impose taxes on Indian nations is as ridiculous as the United States trying to tax the income of Canada."*

or Ithaca. The same sovereign rights enjoyed by state governments preclude the United States from taxing the commercial activities of Indian nations.

Two. Taxing Indian nations would violate the U.S. Constitution. Specifically, it would constitute discrimination against Native Americans and therefore would violate the Equal Protection Clause. In addition, such an action would constitute an unlawful taking of property without compensation in violation of the Fifth Amendment. And finally, it would be a violation of Congress' fiduciary obligations to Indian nations.

In other words, not only would a tax on Indian nations violate the principle of sovereignty embodied in international law, it could not be reconciled with the supreme law of the United States.

Three. Taxes on Indian nations would abrogate numerous treaties.

Four. The taxation proposals are based on false definitions. For example, the proposed tax on Indian gaming that was introduced in Congress in 1995 would have treated tribal governments as "charities" and subjected their gaming revenues to the "unrelated business income tax." Needless to say, Indian tribes are not charitable organizations.

Five. Many of the tax proposals are racist. In order to comply with New York State's new cigarette and gasoline excise tax rules, a Native American retailer would be required to determine which of his or her customers are Indian since, under the state's rules, Native American customers would not be subject to cigarette and fuel excise taxes. In other words, a Native American retailer would be required to make racial classifications, a difficult, if not impossible, task that also could be discriminatory.

The Negative Economic Consequences of Tax Proposals

In addition to the illegality inherent in any proposal to force Indian nations into serving as revenue agents and/or tax collectors for other governments, there are several economic reasons why such efforts are bad ideas.

First, the federal and state governments will be required to return to Indian nations whatever they take away. One must never forget that the main reason Indian governments operate business enterprises is to finance government services and fulfill governmental responsibilities. For example, as I already told you, the Oneida Nation uses our revenues to finance our police department, provide subsidized housing, maintain a health clinic, fund tuition subsidy and scholarship programs, and underwrite numerous other governmental services. If the United States or the New York government impairs our ability to provide these services, then our members will make increasing demands on the social services of those governments. And I can assure you, the Oneida Nation is currently providing those services far more efficiently and on a more cost-effective basis than either the federal or the state government could.

Second, taxes on Indian nations could cause them to breach contracts and lending agreements. Many Indian nations have incurred extensive commercial debt obligations in order to finance governmental and commercial enterprises. The ability of those nations to honor their loan commitments and repay their debts are based on the assumption that their revenues will not be impaired by illegal federal or state tax initiatives. If, however, the United States or any state feels compelled to unlawfully tax tribal revenues, then some Indian nations would be forced to default on their loan obligations.

Third, taxing Indian nations undermines the goal of tribal self-sufficiency and is inconsistent with the goal of making tribes less dependent on federal and state assistance. The irony of these tax proposals is that they are appearing at a time when Congress is drastically reducing federal grants made to Indian tribes. Not content with reducing the financial aid Indian nations need to subsidize critical governmental projects, the federal and state governments also want to bleed them from

> *"Taxing Indian nations will, in many instances, result in a net revenue loss for the federal and state governments."*

the other end through taxation.

Fourth, taxing Indian nations will, in many instances, result in a net revenue loss for the federal and state governments. The loss could start with the closure of many tribal businesses. As a result, the employees of those businesses could make claims against federal and state governments for unemployment compensation. In addition, the non-Indian employees of those Native American enterprises would cease paying income taxes until they found other employment. Also, in some instances, Indian nations could find lawful means of avoiding the tax.

> *"Indian nations are no different from any other sovereign government."*

Let me tell you a little story that will illustrate this point. A few years ago, a state senator in Oklahoma was asked his opinion about a judicial ruling imposing the state cigarette excise tax on the retail operations of Indian tribes. He said, "Why, this simply means that the Indians will start making their own cigarettes." The Oklahoma Tax Department later reached the same conclusion and decided to negotiate a tax compact.

Fifth, local economics could be adversely affected by taxes on Indian nations. A tax on tribal income could, in many instances, cause significant damage to local economies that have been boosted by the construction and operation of Indian enterprises. Taxing Indian nations and their commercial operations could force tribes to lay off workers, suspend services and reduce investment in infrastructure and other business enterprises, resulting in a contraction in the local economy and an overall reduction in tax revenues. . . .

Changing the Environment

What do we do with all of [the] federal and state taxation efforts that are looming on the horizon? Because, unfortunately, I do not think they will go away. In fact, I expect that proposals to tax Indian nations and tribal enterprises will only increase in the years to come. History has taught us that the white man is, if nothing else, persistent in his efforts to subjugate Native Americans and "keep them on the reservation." So, how do we, as sovereign Indian nations, meet this new challenge?

First and foremost, we must educate federal and state political leaders about our status as sovereign governments. We must teach them that we have the same governmental responsibilities that they do. We are obligated to provide police protection, health care, education, housing, and so on. In general, we have responsibility, just as do other governments, for ensuring the safety and well-being of our people.

Some people will say, "But you run businesses and, therefore, you should be taxed as corporations." The difference is that the revenues from business enterprises operated by Indian nations go to finance government operations. This is no different from any other government which sponsors gaming, such as lotteries, keno and off-track betting, to raise revenue for government programs.

The Oneida Nation owns and operates an RV park and charges for its use. Oneida County owns and operates municipal golf courses and assesses an admission fee for those who wish to use the facilities. Other local governments own and maintain recreational facilities that serve a dual purpose: providing a government service and generating additional revenue.

In essence, Indian nations are no different from any other sovereign government. Unfortunately, this is a fact that has been lost on many political leaders.

Second, we should enlist the help of our friends. Many non-Indian businesses depend quite heavily on the contracts they have with tribal governments and enterprises. Their representatives in Congress need to hear their concerns and understand the economic ramifications of the decisions those members of Congress intend to make.

Finally, we must insist that the state and federal governments deal with us on a government-to-government basis. Differences between independent sovereigns cannot be resolved in the court system of either party. Both sides must honor each party's sovereignty and must acknowledge and honor existing treaty obligations. Such an approach can serve as the foundation for new treaties for the purpose of resolving differences concerning taxes and other issues.

In the final analysis, federal and state proposals to tax Indian nations and tribal business enterprises are a form of unlawful tribute, the effort of one sovereign to compel a payment from another. Jesus Christ urged his followers to render unto Caesar that which is Caesar's. But our territories, our governmental revenues and our tribal enterprises do not belong to Caesar. They belong to us. In order for us to pay tribute to the State of New York or the federal government, we would first be required to deny our sovereign existence. That we will not do.

Bibliography

Books

Edward F. Anderson	*Peyote: The Divine Cactus*. Tucson: University of Arizona Press, 1996.
Terry L. Anderson	*Sovereign Nations or Reservations? Dian Economies: An Economic History of American Indians*. San Francisco: Pacific Research Institute for Public Policy, 1995.
Thomas Biolsi and Larry J. Zimmerman, eds.	*Indians and Anthropologists: Vine Deloria Jr. and the Critique of Anthropology*. Tucson: University of Arizona Press, 1997.
Fergus M. Bordewich	*Killing the White Man's Indian: Reinventing Native Americans at the End of the Twentieth Century*. New York: Doubleday, 1996.
Ward Churchill	*Indians Are Us? Culture and Genocide in Native North America*. Monroe, ME: Common Courage Press, 1994.
Ward Churchill	*A Little Matter of Genocide: Holocaust and Denial in the Americas, 1492 to the Present*. San Francisco: City Lights Books, 1997.
Vine Deloria Jr.	*Red Earth, White Lies: Native Americans and the Myth of Scientific Fact*. New York: Scribner's, 1995.
Richard Drinnon	*Facing West: The Metaphysics of Indian-Hating and Empire-Building*. Norman: University of Oklahoma Press, 1997.
Donald Lee Fixico, ed.	*Rethinking American Indian History: Analysis, Methodology, and Historiography*. Albuquerque: University of New Mexico Press, 1997.
Dan McGovern	*The Campo Indian War: The Fight for Gold in California's Garbage*. Norman: University of Oklahoma Press, 1995.
Donald Mitchell and David Rubenson	*Native American Affairs and the Department of Defense*. Santa Monica, CA: Rand Corporation, 1996.
Joane Nagel	*American Indian Ethnic Renewal: Red Power and the Resurgence of Identity and Culture*. Oxford: Oxford University Press, 1996.

National Indian Gaming Association	*Speaking the Truth About Indian Gaming.* Washington, DC: National Indian Gaming Association, 1993.
Francis Paul Prucha	*American Indian Treaties: The History of a Political Anomaly.* Berkeley: University of California Press, 1997.
William Norman Thompson	*Legalized Gambling: A Reference Handbook.* Santa Barbara, CA: ABC-CLIO, 1994.
Jace Weaver, ed.	*Defending Mother Earth: Native American Perspectives on Environmental Issues.* Maryknoll, NY: Orbis Books, 1996.
Rick Whaley with Walter Bresette	*Walleye Warriors: An Effective Alliance Against Racism and for the Earth.* Philadelphia: New Society Publishers, 1994.

Periodicals

American Enterprise	"The Indian Romance," September/October 1995.
American Indian Quarterly	Special issue on Native American Graves Protection and Repatriation Act, Spring 1996. Available from University of Nebraska Press, PO Box 880484, Lincoln, NE 68588-0484.
James Brooke	"What's in a Name? An Affront, Say Some Tribes," *New York Times,* November 17, 1996.
Ben Nighthorse Campbell	"The Foxwoods Myth," *New York Times,* March 29, 1995.
Ward Churchill	"Subterfuge and Self-Determination," *Z Magazine,* May 1997.
Mary H. Cooper	"Native Americans' Future," *CQ Researcher,* July 12, 1996. Available from 1414 22nd St. NW, Washington, DC 20037.
Miriam Davidson	"Hopis Balk at Blackjack, Dance to Different Drum," *Christian Science Monitor,* April 19, 1995.
Walter Echo-Hawk	"Native Worship in American Prisons," *Cultural Survival Quarterly,* Winter 1996.
Jesse Emspak	"Repatriation Battles," *Progressive,* July 1995.
Monique Fordham	"Within the Iron Houses: The Struggle for Native American Religious Freedom in American Prisons," *Social Justice,* Spring/Summer 1993.
Suzan Shown Harjo	"Now and Then: Native Peoples in the United States," *Dissent,* Summer 1996.
Richard G. Hill	"The Future of Indian Gaming," *Cultural Survival Quarterly,* Winter 1994.
Leslie Alan Horvitz	"Indians and Anthropologists Are Battling Over Old Bones," *Insight,* November 18, 1996. Available from 3600 New York Ave. NE, Washington, DC 20002.
Miller Hudson	"MRS on Indian Lands? Congress Shuffles Feet," *Forum for Applied Research and Public Policy,* Winter 1995.

Bibliography

George Johnson   "Indian Tribe's Creationists Thwart Archeologists," *New York Times,* October 22, 1996.

Tom Kavanagh   "Laid to Rest at Last," *Common Boundary,* September/October 1994. Available from 5272 River Rd., Suite 650, Bethesda, MD 20816.

Michael D. Lemonick   "Bones of Contention," *Time,* October 14, 1996.

Oren R. Lyons   "Law, Principle, and Reality," *New York University Review of Law and Social Change,* vol. XX, no. 2, 1993.

Oren R. Lyons and John C. Mohawk   "Sovereignty and Common Sense," *Cultural Survival Quarterly,* Winter 1994.

Kallen Martin   "Indians Not Taxed," *Native Americas,* Summer 1996.

Jeannie McCabe   "Sweat-Lodge Miracle," *Fate,* March 1997. Available from PO Box 64383, St. Paul, MN 55164-0383.

Janet McGowan   "What's in a Name?" *Cultural Survival Quarterly,* Winter 1995.

John Mohawk   "Taxation and Indian Country," *Native Americas,* Summer 1996.

Ron Pazola   "Sacred: What Native Americans Believe," *U.S. Catholic,* February 1994.

Brenda Peterson   "The Power Animals' Dance," *New Age Journal,* Sourcebook, 1996.

Andy Rooney   "Angry Smoke Signals," *Liberal Opinion,* February 24, 1997. Available from PO Box 468, Vinton, IA 52349.

Christopher Shaw   "A Theft of Spirit?" *New Age Journal,* July/August 1995.

Paul Shukovsky   "Sincerely Yours," *Common Cause Magazine,* Fall 1995.

Jeffrey Sipe   "State Sues over Wronged Sioux," *Insight,* January 22, 1996.

William Thompson and Diana R. Dever   "A Sovereignty Check on Indian Gaming (Part II): The Downside of the Sovereignty Equation," *Indian Gaming Magazine,* May 1994. Available from 15825 Shady Grove Rd., Suite 130, Rockville, MD 20850.

Marchell J. Wesaw   "Finders Keepers?" *Cultural Survival Quarterly,* Winter 1995.

David E. Wilkins   "Convoluted Essence," *Native Americas,* Spring 1997.

David E. Wilkins   "Indian Treaty Rights: Sacred Entitlements or Temporary Privileges?" *American-Indian Culture and Research Journal,* vol. 20, no. 1, 1996. Available from UCLA-American Indian Studies Center Publications, 3220 Campbell Hall, Box 951548, Los Angeles, CA 90095-1548.

Organizations to Contact

The editors have compiled the following list of organizations concerned with the issues debated in this book. The descriptions are derived from materials provided by the organizations. All have publications or information available for interested readers. The list was compiled on the date of publication of the present volume; names, addresses, phone and fax numbers, and e-mail/Internet addresses may change. Be aware that many organizations take several weeks or longer to respond to inquiries, so allow as much time as possible.

American Civil Liberties Union (ACLU)
125 Broad St.
New York, NY 10004-2400
(212) 944-9800
fax: (212) 869-9065
Internet: http://www.aclu.org

The ACLU is a national organization that works to defend the civil rights guaranteed by the U.S. Constitution. Its members believe that it is essential to be informed of one's rights in order to be able to exercise them. The ACLU publishes and distributes policy statements, pamphlets, the semiannual newsletter *Civil Liberties Alert,* and several books, including *The Rights of the Indians and Tribes: The Basic ACLU Guide to Indian and Tribal Rights.*

Midwest SOARRING (Save Our Ancestors' Remains & Resources Indigenous Network Group)
312 S. Oak Park Ave.
Oak Park, IL 60302
(708) 383-6773
e-mail: soarring@juno.com
Internet: http://www.usd.edu/anth/soarring.htm

Midwest SOARRING works to facilitate the repatriation of Native American ancestral remains and burial goods; to preserve the burial, cultural, and sacred sites throughout the Midwest; and to protect the natural environment. The organization publishes the seasonal newsletter *Wings* and maintains a website.

National Tribal Environmental Council (NTEC)
2221 Rio Grande NW
Albuquerque, NM 87104
(505) 242-2175
fax: (505) 242-2654

The National Tribal Environmental Council is dedicated to assisting tribes in the protection and preservation of the reservation environment. The mission of the NTEC is to enhance each tribe's ability to protect, preserve, and promote the wise management of air, land, and water for the benefit of current and future generations. It provides several services, including national advocacy, a resource clearinghouse and reference library, and workshops on specific environmental issues. It also publishes the periodic newsletter *Tribal Vision.*

Native American Rights Fund
1506 Broadway
Boulder, CO 80302
(303) 447-8760
Internet: http://www.narf.org/

The Native American Rights Fund is a legal organization that works to defend and promote the legal rights of the Indian people. It strives to ensure that national and state governments live up to their legal obligation; assists tribes in negotiating with individuals, companies, and governmental agencies; and helps draft and promote legislation favorable to Native Americans. The fund publishes the *Annual Report,* periodic legal reviews, and current press releases, all of which are available through their website.

Political Economy Research Center (PERC)
502 S. 19th Ave., Suite 211
Bozeman, MT 59718-6827
(406) 587-9591
fax: (406) 586-7555
e-mail: perc@perc.org
Internet: http://www.perc.org

PERC is a market-oriented think tank that focuses on environmental and natural resource issues. Its policy analysis research covers endangered species, forestry, fisheries, parks, public lands, property rights, the Superfund program, water rights, and environmental education. It publishes several research papers, including *Property Rights and Indian Economics.*

RAND
1700 Main St.
PO Box 2138
Santa Monica, CA 90407-2138
(310) 393-0411
fax: (310) 393-4818
Internet: http://www.rand.org

RAND is a public policy research organization dedicated to safeguarding and improving the public welfare and security of the United States through research and analysis. It publishes several books, including *Native American Affairs and the Department of Justice,* and maintains a website.

United States Commission on Civil Rights
624 Ninth St. NW
Washington, DC 20425
Library: (202) 376-8128
Hearing Impaired: (202) 376-8116

Index

203

Index